Russell,

I hope the summer has been a rewarding one for you. You did a great job volunteering in Lodz & representing the New York Jewish Community in Project Renewal.

All the best.

Tham Halp___

July 26, 1990

YONA COHEN / JERUSALEM UNDER SIEGE

JERUSALEM UNDER SIEGE

Pages from a 1948 Diary

by

YONA COHEN

Foreword by YITZHAK RABIN

RIDGEFIELD PUBLISHING COMPANY

Translated by Dorothea Shefer

Library of Congress Catalog Card Number: 81-5146
(AACR2)

ISBN—0-86628-017-0

Printed by Sivan Press Ltd., Jerusalem—Israel

Behold, I will make Jerusalem a cup of trembling unto all the people round about, when they shall be **in the siege** both against Judah and against Jerusalem.

And in that day will I make Jerusalem a burdensome stone for all people; all that burden themselves with it shall be cut in pieces.

(Zecharia, 12, 2)

Dedicated to the memory of my parents, Gershon and Aliza.

CONTENTS

Foreword by Yitzhak Rabin   9

Introduction   11

Jerusalem Confined By Curfew   15

Expectation, Revival and Anxiety   34

British 'Neutrality'   55

"And They Cast Lots Upon Jerusalem..."   82

Comradeship During The Siege   97

Announcement   108

A Struggle Fraught With Achievements And Failures . .   121

The Tortuous Ceasefires ·   153

Between Bombardments   185

We Willed It And It Is No Legend   216

APPENDICES   231

FOREWORD

All the heroic characteristics of a nation fighting for its existence, near and for its home, State and nation, in a battle which it knows to be just and moral, with a sense of mission and out of a firm faith in the future, were present during the war for Jerusalem in 1948.

The battle for Jerusalem was a focal point of the War of Independence for the nation and the State, and was conducted in every neighborhood, street and house as well as on the road to the city.

The battle for Jerusalem will not be forgotten. I was commander of the Palmah's Harel Brigade during the difficult days of the siege of Jerusalem. Like all the soldiers in Jerusalem, I experienced the sense of isolation of a besieged city, and like all the inhabitants and soldiers of Jerusalem, I believed with all my heart, even in the darkest days, that Jerusalem would remain in our hands as the capital of the Jewish State and a symbol of the fulfillment of the ancient Jewish vision of the nation's return to its land and its capital. This book does not describe the central role played by the Harel Brigade in the battle for Jerusalem, but it contains enough to make anyone who reads it realize what the battle for Jerusalem was like.

The veteran journalist and writer, Yona Cohen, has provided in this book, written in diary form, a faithful account of life in Jerusalem during the siege, under curfew and when rations were short. He has given a good description of the comradeship of the besieged inhabitants, the futile discussions about the internationalization of Jerusalem and the successes and failures in conducting the campaign.

9

This book is particularly important today, when here and there are those who doubt our military capacity. The nation and the younger generation should know how Jerusalem endured in extremely difficult conditions, during a period of foreign and hostile rule, whose forces often reaped the benefits of our victories. Everyone should know how Jerusalem survived when the enemy ruled large parts of the city and its immediate environs and the defenders of the city faced him with insufficent arms, food and water. The younger generation and the entire nation should read and learn about the daily courage of the residents of Jerusalem and the friendship of besieged civilians and soldiers during days and nights of suffering and hope.

Jerusalem was and remains the heart of the nation and the State, and its liberation and salvation were the foremost concern of the Government during its first days of activity. The fortitude of Jerusalem's fighters and inhabitants led to Israeli control of most of the city. Since the Six Day War it has once more been united and has started to develop at an Israeli pace. Only Israeli rule will guarantee the welfare and unity of Jerusalem. Only Israel has proved, since the complete liberation of Jerusalem, that there is free access to the holy places for everyone and freedom of worship to all religions. The future of Jerusalem will not be a subject for political bargaining; Jerusalem will always remain a united city and the capital of the independent State of Israel.

The State of Israel is now involved in the process of seeking a way to achieve peace. Jerusalem did not return to its sons and builders as the eternal capital of Israel on a silver salver. This has always been its nature, and so it will remain forever.

Yitzhak Rabin

Jerusalem,
March 1976

INTRODUCTION

This is the simple story of Jewish Jerusalem during the period of siege and battle in 1948, as it was written hastily and in trembling during the actual moments, in days and nights of suffering and heroism, when civilians and soldiers, front and rear, were one.

As soon as the U.N. decided in November 1949 on the partition of Palestine into two States, the British Government in effect abandoned Jerusalem, apart from guarding the lives of its soldiers. Under the noses of British policemen and soldiers, and sometimes with their cooperation and assistance, Arab bands attacked Jews in Jerusalem. After British rule in Palestine had ended and the inhabitants of the country were left on their own, the Jews began implementing the U.N. resolution whereas the Arabs intensified their attacks in order to bring about its annulment. They increased their fighting forces and augmented their weapons, both in quantity and in quality. They placed cannons aimed at the Jewish neighborhoods and their inhabitants on the hills around the city. Jerusalem was under siege.

Because the U.N. had decided to set up a Jewish State which did not include Jerusalem, the inhabitants of Jerusalem, whether openly or covertly, did not agree with the tendency evinced by certain leaders to comply with the bitter verdict, for lack of any alternative. The inhabitants of Jerusalem knew that every day that passed in acts of simple bravery, that every victim and every additional drop of suffering, formed another layer in the indestructible bridge between the State which was being built and its eternal capital. They knew full well that sooner or later the entire nation, and other nations too, would grasp the fact that the battle for Jerusalem was the battle for the whole State, and that the Jewish State could not be severed from Jerusalem.

11

The writer, Asher Barash, wrote on this subject in 'Jerusalem in Historic Texts', edited by Haim Toren:

"Jerusalem is the crown of Israel. Like the king who fought a terrible war with an enemy who was greater, stronger and richer than himself, and when his treasury was empty and he had nothing left except his crown, he pawned that in order to maintain his armies and save his country, so did we. We agreed to pawn Jerusalem, our beautiful crown, to the nations of the world, so that the body of our State would be saved. But even that sacrifice was not accepted and the abominable nations, the shameless, dishonorable ones, abandoned even the crown of crowns."

And so Jerusalem faced enemies which were stronger than it materially, though not spiritually.

Years later, after the Six Day War (1967), the Egyptian journalist, Hasnan Heikal, who was editor of the Cairo journal, Al-Ahram, for many years, admitted that Jerusalem was the bone of contention. Heikal discribed how an Egyptian statesman met the mayor, Teddy Kollek, and said to him: "I must tell you that the main problem between you and the Arabs is Jerusalem. Not Suez and not Sinai, not Sharm-a-Sheikh and not Abu-Rodeis, only Jerusalem." Kollek asked in amazement: "Is that the problem in Egypt too?" "Yes, it certainly is", the Egyptian replied.

It is symbolic that the War of Independence of the State and the nation was in Jerusalem, that the liberation of Jerusalem was the peak of our victory and that when Jerusalem and its inhabitants live in peace, all Israel and the countries around it will be at peace.

Knowing that their war and endurance bore a significance over and beyond the mere struggle for immediate survival, that victory in the struggle for Jerusalem carried with it a taste of eternity, its inhabitants of all ethnic communities and origins ignored the differences in customs and culture between them and formed a wall of fortifications for their city. They were inspired by a spirit of mutual help and forbearance, even when there was virtually no water, when food was rationed and allocated in minute portions and when the enemy bombarded the city with shells and bullets of death.

By the fellowship of those who were under siege and the heroism of its defenders, Jerusalem withstood and overcame the designs of the enemy. For nineteen years Jerusalem was bisected, wounded and split by barbed wire fences. The Old City was in the hands of the enemy. Every Saturday we ascended Mount Zion and looked longingly towards the Old City and the site of our Temple, standing in ruins. Because Mount Zion was in our hands we inhabitants of New Jerusalem celebrated the Festival of Purim (Lots) as if we were a walled city, on the fifteenth of Adar, because we were near old Jerusalem and could see the city, which had been surrounded by a wall ever since the time of Joshua the son of Nun. Our visits to Mount Zion only increased our yearning for Zion and the Old City. From Mount Zion we also exchanged glances with soldiers of the Arab Legion on the wall of the Old City. Sometimes we received an angry and hostile look in return, and sometimes the eyes that met ours were indifferent and cold.

In either case our eyes were full of jealousy and our hearts of sorrow. They, the Legionnaires, were there, inside the walls of our ancient city, while we were outside, with grief in our hearts.

Until the happy day when Jerusalem, the capital of Israel, was 'as a city that is compact together', that makes all Jews friends.

*

I was amazed when, in talks with youngsters from various groups, I learned how far away they were, particularly the non-religious ones, from any knowledge of the simple, basic events which led to the establishment of the State, and from our faith that we, the few and the just, would win. How far away they were from any acquaintance with the events which led to Jerusalem's inclusion in the State, as the jewel in the crown. The questions I was asked evinced incredible ignorance and painful lack of knowledge about the nation's firm resolve in a generation which renewed its day as of yore in the land of its fathers, fulfilling a religious and historic right. We knew perfectly well that we had neighbors, and hoped to achieve cooperation and understanding with them. For that reason we had accepted previous divisions of our country, including the establishment of the State of Jordan on the land of our fathers. We paid a heavy price of blood in paving the path to peace, and independence, but these facts were as a sealed book to many of the youngsters I met. I also heard and read things which cast doubts on these truths.

I came to the conclusion that impressions written at the time, describing life in Jerusalem during the siege and the war, should be printed in a book, to serve as a record for this generation and those to follow.

Because the book was written some time after the period it describes it was possible to include the impressions of other people involved in the battle, in different — sometimes contradictory — versions. In the appendices at the end of the book, therefore, I have included descriptions given by officers, politicians and journalists, Jews and non-Jews, who were active in Jerusalem at that time.

Naturally, here and there the material may be overly subjective, for it is merely the impressions of someone who worked as a journalist for Hatzofeh and Yedioth Aharonoth and was present at certain events in the life of Jerusalem during the siege. For this reason certain details may have been forgotten.

Finally, it is my pleasant duty to thank my colleagues who have given me sound advice, after reading the text, particularly, Dr. Yitzhak Raphael, Aviezer Golan, David Sitton, Prof. Mordekhai Eliav and Shlomo Gonen.

I would like to thank the Secretary-General of the Jewish Agency, Moshe Rivlin, the archives of Religious Zionism, the Zionist Archives in Jerusalem and the archives of photographs of the JNF (Keren Kayemet) and Keren Hayesod.

My grateful thanks to each and every one.

Yona Cohen

JERUSALEM CONFINED BY CURFEW

In December 1945 the Anglo-Jewish journalist, Jon Kimche, warned us that the British Mandate authorities might attempt to silence the central Jewish body, the Jewish Agency, which was recognised by them as the official representative of the Jews of Palestine. Kimche was considered by many to be in error, but few months later, in June 1946, British soldiers stormed the buildings of the National Institutions in Jerusalem and 'conquered' the offices of the Jewish Agency Executive. They confiscated thousands of files and documents and imprisoned the members of the Executive in Latrun camp (except for Ben-Gurion and M. Sneh, who were abroad), in accordance with the virulently anti-Semitic orders and policy of the British Foreign Minister, Ernest Bevin.

In practise, that Saturday, 29th June 1946, known since then as 'The Black Sabbath', marked the beginning of a stubborn, open and fierce struggle waged by the six hundred thousand inhabitants of the Yishuv* to open the gates of Palestine to the tens of thousands of Jews who had survived the hell of the Holocaust.

People in the know claimed that Britain had complicated the political problem of Palestine by deciding to 'involve' the Arab states in policy decisions on this question. By doing this they had, in effect, usurped the Arab inhabitants of Palestine and 'dictated' an extremist attitude in this sphere.

It would be distorting reality to conceal the fact that several people in

---

* The Jewish population of Mandatory Palestine.

15

Jerusalem, including Mr. Eliyahu Elyashar, one of the leaders of the Sephardic Jewish community, opposed embroiling the Arab states in decisions concerning Palestine (a detailed description can be found in his book, 'Living with Palestinians').

Rational politicans have noted that despite all the difficulties it would have been possible to reach an agreement with the Palestinian Arabs, but the involvement of the representatives of the Arab states in the discussions prevented this. Only because of their desire to avoid rejecting the proposals of the Mandate Administration, and after much hesitation, did the representatives of the Jewish Agency attend the conference held in London in 1938. This was the first time in the history of Palestine that the governments of Egypt, Iraq, Saudi-Arabia, Transjordan and Yemen were invited to the same conference in addition to the representatives of the local Arabs.

The Jews had been bitterly disappointed by British rule. A veteran inhabitant of Jerusalem, the lawyer, M.H. Jineo, wrote at the time: "England, the keeper of the keys, open the gates and let the remnant of our people enter. Do not claim falsely that my country cannot contain them all. It is like a merciful mother, from whom flow springs of salvation, bringing balm to their souls. England, bearer of the Mandate, do not ignore the nation which wishes to help its downtrodden sons".

During the eighteen months between June 1946 and the end of 1947 the Yishuv, as the 'State-on-the-way', conducted a political struggle, supplemented by military actions undertaken by the 'Haganah', the Irgun Zvai Leumi (Etzel) and Lohemei Herut Yisrael (Lehi). Each organization acted according to its own lights. In those months Jerusalem was a city of barbed wire fences and steel barriers, erected in the main streets by the British. Jerusalem, the city of peace whose inhabitants desired tranquillity, was trapped in armored claws and confined by curfew. Jewish Jerusalem experienced 108 days of curfew in 1946, namely, four months in which people were confined to their houses for ten hours each day. At sundown the Jewish population had to remain at home and anyone who tarried and was found outside was liable to be arrested, fined, imprisoned or even shot by a 'nervous' policeman or soldier.

The cultural life of Jerusalem was restricted, but did not come to a halt. The various events were confined by the 'Procrustean bed' of the hours in which there was no curfew. Thus, for example, the Palestine Philharmonic Orchestra had to adapt itself to the circumstances of the time, and hold its concerts during the day. One of these concerts, in the 'Edison' hall, was attended by His Excellency, the British High Commissioner, at whose command the streets of Jewish Jerusalem were deserted by the early evening and the Jewish inhabitants obliged to hasten and immure themselves in their houses.

The hall was full to capacity, despite the early hour. It was unusual, though interesting and encouraging, to see the denizens of Jerusalem, who usually hastened to complete their business and return to their homes before curfew, sitting quietly and peacefully in the hall. With half-closed eyes and contented faces they listened to the serene music of Brahms and Mendelsohn. They dreamed sweetly of a world cleansed of injustice, edicts and oppression.

The concert ended, and there was long and enthusiastic applause for the members of the orchestra and booing for the High Commissioner, a sharp shift from the kingdom of melody to that of melancholy. The doors were opened and the audience emerged into a world of tension, grief and pain. The untroubled audience became a crowd of individuals hastening to reach home before the curfew hour.

The British authorities adopted a policy which firmly opposed the immigration of Jews who had survived the horrors of the Holocaust, using force to send immigrant ships back to the countries of death and destruction. The Etzel and Lehi organizations, which were defined as 'dissidents' by the Yishuv's official institutions, adopted tactics of their own against the British, with the object of hastening their departure from Palestine.

In early February 1947 the Chief Secretary of the Palestine Government wrote to the National Council (Vaad Haleumi) requiring that it "...call on the Yishuv to cooperate with the (British) police and army by surrendering the members of the terrorist organizations to the authorities".

The Directorate of the National Council sent the following reply, signed by the chairman, David Remez:

I have the honour of replying to your letter of 3rd February. It was discussed in full at the plenary session of the National Council, which was held in Jerusalem two days later and was attended by the Chief Rabbis and deputies from the Jewish communities, municipalities and regional councils:

A. Throughout its existence, the Yishuv has invested all its resources in pioneering construction, in cooperation with the Mandate authorities, with the object of establishing the Jewish National Home. The 'White Paper' of 1939 took away from the Jews everything that had been promised them, regardless of justice or law, and destroyed the basis of the relationship between the Jewish nation, the Yishuv and the Mandate Government.

B. Upon the outbreak of war, the Yishuv called on its sons and daughters, irrespective of the White Paper policy, to volunteer for the Services. Tens of thousands answered this call. The sufferings they endured until their desire to fight as a Jewish force under their national flag was granted are well known. Their loyal actions during wartime are similarly well known.

C. It will be recorded in history that because of the White Paper we were prevented from saving our brethren from the gas chambers while this was still possible. We hoped that once the war was over justice would be restored and the sacred promises honored, but this hope has not yet been fulfilled. Despite the fact that in this war a disaster unprecedented in human history befell the Jewish people, and despite the recommendations of the Anglo-American Committe, the survivers of this catastrophe have not been enabled to immigrate to their country, and those who reach its shores are exiled.

D. These events affected a small group within the Yishuv in such a way as to drive it to madness and its members turned to acts of terror as a weapon in a political struggle, violating national discipline and neglecting the moral foundations which are the basis of our culture and our movement. The Yishuv's negative attitude to the shedding of innocent blood as a method of political warfare has been affirmed publicly by its elected institutions in repeated resolutions rejecting terror in the most unequivocal terms.

E. The National Council's recent resolutions call on the Yishuv to oppose by force the ascension of those who resort to terror. The Yishuv is prepared to use its own powers, to the best of its ability, to prevent the acts of terrorism it condemns. The Government now requires the National Council "...to call on the Yishuv to help the Government by cooperating with the police and army in revealing the hiding places of members of the terrorist organizations and handing them over to the forces of law". This request cannot be fulfilled by the Yishuv, which is subject to a cruel political siege and is fighting for its freedom.

*

In March 1947 Jerusalem experienced a grim 'military rule'. Curfew and military closure were imposed on an entire section of north-western Jerusalem, about 25,000 Jewish inhabitants were surrounded by barbed wire fences and barriers were placed between them and the rest of the city. The enclosed area was heavily guarded by British soldiers and telephone contact was severed. The area thus cut off included the Geula, Bucharim, Shearei Pina, Mea Shearim and Beth Yisrael quarters, whose inhabitants were suspected of aiding 'terrorists' and concealing arms. The British gave the code name 'Hippo' to this military operation. The inhabitants of Jerusalem, half in earnest, half in jest, said that the military closure would not succeed since it was directed against the residents of Geula and Beth Yisrael, names which symbolise a deep faith in the words of the minor prophets and exalt the streets which the British had surrounded with barbed wire. Knowing that it was the intention of the British to break their spirit, the inhabitants of these areas summoned their strength and refused to give in. The Jews of Jerusalem knew that the British would not achieve their end.

"Why have you sealed off these neighborhoods?" the Jerusalem newsmen asked Brigadier Davis, the commander of Operation 'Hippo'.

"We have to find several Jewish terrorists who, according to our information, are hiding in this area," was the reply.

"What is the justification for 'collective punishment' of this kind?" the reporters asked.

"No, no, this is not collective punishment, it is not our custom to penalize the public", the Brigadier said, somewhat affronted the question, and added: "All we have to do is catch the terrorists...".

"If that is the case, then why don't you let the workers leave the area and go to work, and allow the children to go to school?" the reporters persisted.

"That is impossible. Military rule has been imposed on the entire area," the commander replied.

Thus, the entire area was closed off and surrounded by barbed wire and heavily-armed soldiers. The residents of other areas, the relatives and friends of the people in the sealed off area, brought food parcels and gifts, which they threw over the barbed-wire fence along the road. The spirits of those under siege did not fall. A 'Committee of Residents of the Sealed off Area' was established, its members being Zeev Spiegel (chairman), D. Wigodski, M. Segal, A. Cahana and M. Albert, the leaders of the quarters affected by Operation 'Hippo'. The Committee organized the distribution of food and dealt with health and education problems.

The Jerusalem Communal Committee issued a declaration stating, amongst other things:

"Since Sunday a large proportion of the Jewish residents of Jerusalem have been placed under military rule. The pain and suffering of this section of the Yishuv is shared by the entire Jewish population of the city and the country.

"Let there be no panic. Merchants and tradesmen should charge the usual prices, let no one be able to accuse us of profiteering. Our suffering is great, but no power can undermine our desire to exist as a free nation in our homeland.

"Nevertheless, we beseech those whose deeds have led to this situation to end the acts of violence which dishonor our cause and may bring disaster upon us..".

*

"Come, O bride, Come, O bride, Sabbath, the queen.
"Peace be unto you, O angels of peace".

Sabbath descended upon the city while many of its inhabitants were confined to their houses by the curfew. There was a heavy silence all around. The trumpets announcing the start of the Sabbath were also mute. Heavily-armed British police and army units patrolled the streets of the closed-off area in Jerusalem. The sound of prayer could be heard from different sides.

The silence was broken by the threatening clatter of a British armored vehicle. The inhabitants of this area in particular were suspected of belonging to 'terrorist' organizations and aiding Jewish fighters. Every house seemed to the British authorities to be concealing illegal arms.

The garbage of a week had accumulated in the streets, but the houses and yards were clean. By Friday the besieged inhabitants had equipped themselves with candles, fruit and flowers, and were now sitting down like kings to eat.

A reporter who lived in the area was late in returning home. His family knew that his press card enabled him to move about the streets freely despite the curfew even in areas which had been closed off. Nevertheless, they were very worried. When he finally returned, he related that a British soldier and a policeman had 'detained' him, threatening to kill him. The British policeman had placed a revolver at his temple, cursing the entire Jewish people. With shaking hands the reporter had taken his press card out of his pocked and only then had he been set free, though not without hearing a few more muttered oaths.

From the street the sound of soldiers making a house-to-house search for 'youngsters suspected of belonging to Etzel' could be heard. In some houses they removed tiles from the floors, made holes in the walls and poked around in the cupboards, searching for arms.

The nights were full of dread. British soldiers and policemen would go wild, shooting in all directions indiscriminately. Sometimes they hit peaceful citizens, while sometimes they hit 'only' crockery, furniture or clothes in closets. On nights of frenzy like this the soldiers would stop passers-by and beat them. Late one night they detained a man walking along harmlessly in the Zichron Moshe quarter. Without saying anything, they struck his face, then ran away. Unfortunately for them, their victim was a foreign reporter, one of a group of British newsmen touring the Middle East. The man complained, both verbally and in writing, and ensured that his letter reached the High Commissioner and the Chief Secretary of the Mandate Government. The complaint was investigated and after that the number of 'hit and run' attacks declined.

An order issued to the British soldiers and containing virulently anti-Semitic remarks was signed by General Barker, the British military commander in Palestine. It said, amongst other things:

— Do not fraternize with the Jews;

— Do not buy anything from them;

— We must hit the Jews where it hurts them most, in their pockets...

A week later British soldiers entered Moshe Ba-Gad's drinks store in the 'Geula' quarter and ordered the customers to raise their hands. Their colleagues picked up crates of drinks, loaded them into their automobile and drove away.

Sometimes the violent and depressing atmosphere had its amusing side. One day a police car toured the streets of Jerusalem and an Arab supernumerary constable, who claimed to be an expert in Hebrew, issued police orders to the population over the loudspeaker:

"Forbear from stand in Mishorim Street". The people who heard his eventually realized that he meant that it was forbidden to stand in Meah Shearim Street.

The policeman continued: "Youngs to leave house, to identicalization". Somebody worked out that he meant that young men should leave their homes and go to the street for identification'.

It was more difficult to grasp the meaning of the next announcement: "Who dies, come to Spitzer for burning".

Not even the brightest among us could understand what was meant, until someone guessed that he meant that the relatives of someone who had died should go to the Spitzer hospital, where the committee which dealt with burials sat.

In mid-November 1947 there was another night of wild firing. Several bullets were fired at the house of Golda Meyerson, (Meir) the director of the Jewish Agency's Political Department, breaking windowpanes and glass dishes inside her home. Many bullets were fired at the apartment of Zerah Warhaftig, a member of the National Council's Directorate. Some of them were found near the bed of his young daughter. Dr. Warhaftig, who was an American citizen, lodged a complaint against the British with the American consul.

Ironically, that night of therror was preceded by the words of the radio announcer on 'Kol Yerushalayim' ('The Voice of Jerusalem'), who concluded the broadcast with the customary phrase, 'A peaceful night to you all'. The listeners heard and sighed, or smiled, but before they could say 'Amen', the 'concert' of firing had begun.

This phenomenon of firing at the Jewish neighborhoods at night even influenced the way people talked at home.

A husband and wife were quarreling, as was their custom. The husband said: "Be quiet, you talk like a British machine-gun". The wife said: "And you're like a mine in the house".

The exchange continued. Then the woman went outside, despite the strict curfew. She went up to the military patrol and said: "There's a 'bomb' in my house. A mine. Get it out".

The soldiers ran to the house. A detachment went in carefully, began looking for the bomb but found nothing. "Where's the bomb you were talking about?" they asked the woman. "There, in front of you", she replied, pointing to her husband. The soldiers shouted angrily "Are you playing jokes on us?" "Who's playing jokes?" the woman answered, "Don't you know him? He's worse than a bomb or any mine. Take him away".

The soldiers understood what was going on, smiled and said: "No. We won't interfere, that's your private affair".

*

In August 1946 about ten thousand Jews were assembled in the 'Hapoel' sports ground, near the Sanhedria quarter of Jerusalem, for identification. The officer in charge of the operation, the brigadier of the 'Royal Yorkshire' Battalion, allowed me to observe the proceedings and to be present while the detainees were identified by the British soldiers.

The 'Hapoel' sports ground looked like huge 'concentration camp' divided into four and surrounded by a barbed wire fence. Large army and police units patrolled the perimeter in armored cars, equipped with walkie-talkies, mobile canteens, etc.

Thousands of men aged 17 and over had been gathered there, from the Kerem Avraham, Geula, Meah Shearim, Shearei Pina, Bathei Warsaw, Bathei Ungarin and Beth Yisrael quarters. Some had been brought by truck, others on foot, some were only half-dressed, while others had managed to put on their work clothes. Hundreds of yeshiva students stood in groups of ten behind the fence, reciting the afternoon prayer followed by psalms. In another part of the camp a group of youngsters were singing and dancing: 'David, King of Israel, lives and endures".

There was also a bridegroom there, one of Rabbi Dushinski's students. He had been wed the day before and was borne aloft on the shoulders of his friends. They were joined by many other youngsters, who covered their heads and danced, singing: "The right hand of Lord exalts, the right hand of the Lord succeeds greatly".

The examination of the detainees' identity began only in the afternoon. The old men were the first to be released and sent to their homes. The youngsters, who were checked carefully by the Hebrew-speaking English detectives, were transferred to a special camp for suspects. Two hours later the camps were empty. About one hundred youngsters were kept overnight, only to be released two or three days later. The people the British had hoped to find still eluded them.

What bothered us most were the barbed-wire fences which the British erected in the heart of our city and along our streets, separating our houses from those inhabited by the British. Later on the barbed-wire also divided Arab quarters from those of the Jews.

Prior to the days of 'chaos' which the British wished to bestow on Jerusalem, the Jewish part of the city was characterized by the grim expression: "Ye shall build, and others shall inhabit. At one of the press conferences the Director of the Press Section, Richard Stubbs, announced curtly: "The Mandate Government considers it necessary to establish a fortified area in the center of the city, where the Government and military offices will be situated".

The order was executed and seven large blocks of buildings, including the Apac building, the new Post Office, the Generali building and the Russian Compound, were appropriated by the Mandate Government. All the tenants and owners of stores and offices in these buildings were given notice to quit. That was just the beginning. Two weeks later another two thousand Jewish families were ordered to leave their homes "within forty-eight hours". The 'Mizrahi' organization had just finished building an office block for its world directorate, named 'Beth Meir' for Rabbi Meir Berlin, near the buildings of the National Institutions. Before they could be inaugurated they were confiscated and British soldiers were their first 'tenants'. Thousands of Jewish families became refugees in their own city.

A woman came to the offices of the newspaper, weeping bitterly: "For seven years", she said, "I and my family have been on the move. First we were expelled from our home by the Polish authorities. Polish anti-Semites persecuted us, moved into our apartment and threw us out. Then the filthy Nazis came and shifted us from one camp to another. All our friends and relatives perished in the concentration camps, we are the only survivors of a large family. The remnant of our nation was gathered and sent here as refugees, us among them. We sailed in a shaky boat and reached here by some miracle. We hoped that at last we had found a haven, but again we are being evicted and forced to wander. Can it be possible? Write about it in the paper, shock the world!"

Regrettably, there were also negative aspects, and some of the Jewish inhabitants tried to 'exploit the situation' by profiteering at the public's expense. The Communal Committee established public courts to deal with cases in which the Yishuv was being harmed economically, edicts issued by the authorities were disobeyed or profiteering was attempted. The courts were manned by volunteers who were not necessarily knowledgeable in legal or procedural matters. However, the trials were conducted on a common sense basis, and this also served to determine the punishment, whether it was to be a warning, rebuke, fine, cessation of supplies for a certain period, etc. The positive aspects were in the majority, however. An 'Accommodation Committee' functioned alongside the Communal Committee, dealing with people evicted by the British army and police from 'closed' areas. The Committee asked the inhabitants of the city for help and the response was considerable. Dozens of Jewish families who had been turned out of their homes in 'Security Areas' were put up in the homes of neighbors within a relatively short time.

The terrorist organizations 'decorated' the walls and notice boards with handbills directed against the Mandate authorities:

"Get out! You are no longer fit for your task! The Yishuv demands free immigration and a Jewish state!"

Many Jews read the notices and shrugged their shoulders, not believing that the idea was practicable. In private conversations in synagogues, markets, street corners, workshops and offices the subject would be raised over and over again: Will the day ever come when the British leave us and the Arabs alone?

*

The report of the U.N. Special Committee on Palestine that the British Mandate be abolished and that Palestine be granted independence, after a brief interim period, was published in August 1947. A majority within the Committee maintained that Palestine should be divided into two states, one Arab and one Jewish, and that Jerusalem should be placed under international rule. The Committee also stated that the two countries should be linked in an economic union.

The leaders of the Jewish Agency announced that they accepted partition in principle, while the Arab leaders proclaimed their rejection of the proposal.

The British Government declared its readiness to leave Palestine, though without aiding the implementation of partition. Discussions were held among the Great Powers about the borders of the two countries. Because they wanted to help the British, who were eager to have the Negev in order to establish a military base there, the Americans suggested that the Negev should not be included within the Jewish state, but would be part of the Arab one, being in effect under British influence. A vigorous campaign conducted by Professor Weizmann and directed at the American president. Harry Truman, changed this, and the Negev was included within the borders of the Jewish state (the details can be found in Chaim Weizmann's book, 'Trial and Error').

On 29th November 1947, in addition to the partition resolution, it was determined that until 1. August 1947 the British would allocate the Jews a free port, through which Jews would immigrate to Palestine unrestricted. The British authorities disregarded this decision, and no such port was provided.

In January 1948 the U.N. organized an 'Implementation Committee', which was to be sent to Palestine in order to undertake the partitioning of Palestine. The U.N. also instructed the Mandate authorities to transfer government gradually to the Committee. The British disregarded this too.

A prepatory section of the Implementation Committee arrived in Jerusalem, headed by Dr. Pablo Ascarate of Spain and including a Norweigan officer, who served as the military adviser, a Greek lawyer and an Indian economist. The chairman of the Committee defined the group as 'isolated pilgrims'. No representative of the Mandate government bothered to meet the group on its arrival at Atarot (Kalandia) airport, and the members made their own way to the King David Hotel, where they were accommodated in a basement room. The Committee asked for an 'international force' which would help in implementing partition, but no such force was forthcoming.

The refusal of the British to help in implementing partition led the Americans to change their minds about the resolution. The members of the Committee also witnessed the Arabs' preparations for attacking the little Jewish state once it was established.

On 20th March 1948 the American representative to the Security Council, Senator Austin, announced that the U.S. was withdrawing its support from the partition resolution, in the light of the difficulty of implementing it. The Americans also proposed that a special session of the General Assembly be convened in order to discuss a new resolution.

The attempt of the British and the Americans to 'put the clock back' and cancel the partition resolution failed. The majority, led by the U.S.S.R. and Australia, demanded that the resolution be left as it stood, and the General Assembly had to be content with appointing a mediator on its behalf.

The British remained adamant, and continued to prepare 'chaos'.

Between December 1947 and April 1948, when the convoys to

Jerusalem were fired at mercilessly and passengers were left undefended, the British arrested Jewish guards and confiscated their arms. The British continued to claim that they were responsible for law and order, but did nothing to protect any Jewish village or neighborhood.

The one thing they were ready and willing to do was to aid any Jewish resident of Jerusalem to leave town, and any Jewish inhabitant of the Old City who was prepared to leave the area. British officers suggested this to the inhabitants of various quarters in both the New and the Old Cities, but the Jews rejected this with disdain.

Both the Jews and the Arabs began to doubt the genuineness of the British government's willingness to leave Palestine, despite the fact that just a month previously the British High Commissioner, Sir Alan Cunningham, had threatened the Jews and the Arabs that if they did not stop quarreling the British would abandon the country, leaving it in a state of ohaos.

In the final event, on 12th May 1948, the journalists received an announcement through the Government Press Office from the Secretariat of the Mandate Government, which was situated in the King David Hotel, stating: "The British Mandate for Palestine will end legally immediately after midnight on the night between 14 and 15 May 1948. His Excellency, the High Commissioner, will leave Jerusalem for Haifa on 14th May, and will depart from Haifa in H.M.S. 'Orialos', at midnight. The army will also start leaving Jerusalem and the rest of Palestine on 14th May".

On 14th May 1948 the British High Commissioner boarded the ship, saluted and sailed away, to the strains of the British National Anthem. Only at the end of June did the last British soldier leave Palestine, bringing thirty years of British Mandate to an end. The inhabitants of the country, including Jerusalem, were now masters of their own fate.

*

The partition 'Implementation Committee' left Palestine empty-handed. Meanwhile, the Security Council appointed a Consular Committee to settle the ceasefire between the sides. It comprised the U.S. Consul, Thomas Vason, who was killed by an Arab sniper and was replaced by John Mac-Donald; Ian Neuhaus, the Belgian Consul-General, and René Nobil, the French Consul-General. All three attempted to make Jerusalem an international, namely Christian, city, and worked to achieve this end.

A serious competitor of the Consulary Commission was another body, the international Red Cross Organization headed by Jaques de-Reynier, who worked vigorously to bring all of Jerusalem under its wing.

Declaring his intention of "safeguarding the welfare of Jerusalem and its inhabitants", de-Reynier announced that he would consent to extend his patronage gradually to the entire city. When asked to protect the scientific equipment and installations of the Hebrew University, the National Library and 'Hadassah' Hospital on Mount Scopus, he made his assent conditional on the removal from Mount Scopus of every young Jew capable of bearing arms.

De-Reynier intended to exploit the fact that a Jewish delegation from Jerusalem, including Daniel Oster, Vice-Mayor of Jerusalem during the Mandate and later on the Mayor, and Mordechai Eliash, the Legal Advisor to the Jewish Agency and later Israeli ambassador to London, was participating in discussions held in New York to formulate a constitution for international Jerusalem.

The attacks by the Arabs on the inhabitants of Jewish Jerusalem, both in the old and the new parts of the city, the murder of citizens and the destruction of synagogues and cultural institutions, as well as their attempts to wrest the city from the Jews put an end to the plans for internationalization and foreign rule in Jerusalem.

De-Reynier decided upon three areas where the flag of the Red Cross was to fly: The King David Hotel and the Y.M.C.A., the Terra Sancta building and Government House (Armon Hanatziv) on 'The Hill of Evil Counsel'.

As if this was not enough, rumors reached Jerusalem of the appointment of Harold Evans of Philadelphia as U.N. 'Commissioner' for Jerusalem. Someone apparently wanted to revive the plans for internationalizing the city, but one day later, on 14th May, the (Transjordanian) Arab Legion invaded the Old City of Jerusalem. The Etzion Bloc settlements went up in flames and battles raged in Jerusalem. The 'Commissioner' came to Jerusalem, stayed there a few hours, and then went back again.

The Jewish inhabitants of Jerusalem, both young and old, men and women trusting in the Rock of Israel, their Redeemer, defended their city valiantly.

*

Even before the U.N. resolution approving the establishment of a Jewish (and Arab) state was passed, discussions had been held about the name of the future Jewish state.

In December 1947 Dr. M. Abner published an article in 'Haaretz' suggesting that the state be called Judah or Judea rather than 'Palestine'.

About a month later Rabbi M.D. Gross published a reply to Dr. M. Abner, proposing the name 'Eretz-Yisrael', and rejecting the names 'Hebrew' or 'Land of the Hebrews'. He explained that this term is mentioned only once in the Bible, when Joseph appears before Pharoah, and refers solely to the area around Hebron. He also emphasized the fact that assimilationist Jews in Austria, and in Germany too to some extent, had preferred to be called 'Israelites' rather than 'Jews'.

On the day the U.N. convened for its first discussion on Palestine's political future (28.4.1947), the National Council issued the following call to the 'United Nations':

"Today you begin your special session to discuss the Palestine question, and our good wishes are sent to you from Jerusalem.

"Even if we had not suffered the holocaust of Hitler's destruction in this war you, the United Nations, would have had to keep your promise to us based on historic truth and ultimate justice.

"Even if the Jewish minorities dwelt in peace, beloved and desired by all peoples on earth, the world could not have condemned them to remain a minority nation, without a homeland of its own, forever.

"We cannot imagine that the right of the Jewish people to liberty and a state is inferior in your eyes to that of any other nation.

"By pioneering labor we sustain the vision of our suffering and persecuted generations. We are imbued with love as the faithful redeemers of the desolate land of our forefathers, and enter it with dedication. We extend the hand of peace and goodwill to our Arab neighbors, both near and far, who rule large, uninhabited, independent states.

"Discuss wisely! Strengthen the faith in the heart of an ancient people that the soul of the world was not burned in the Nazi ovens!"

When the resolution was passed regarding the partition of Palestine and the establishment of a Jewish and an Arab state, the National Conncil issued the following announcement:

"Our endeavors, steadfastness and justice were victorious last night at the United Nations. Opposed by one third, which included the six Arab states which already sit round the table at Lake Success, the plan for establishing a Jewish State won an honorable majority of more than two thirds, headed by the two world powers, the U.S.A. and the U.S.S.R. This great deed, at all three of its stages – the majority opinion of the Investigatory Commission, the ratification of this opinion by the plenum of the Palestine Committee and the enduring resolution of the National Assembly – will be a source of pride to all those who supported, it and a lasting disgrace to those who opposed it. Every political deed, whether moral or not, is considered in terms of its worthwhileness. Whereas in bad deeds it is the petty account, the benefit of the moment, which is decisive, in good acts it is the overall concept of justice which prevails.

"The United Nations' just decision places interesting and responsible burdens on the nation and the Yishuv. If we have made good use of our right to independence, we must implement it in practical terms. We must create an improved State, whose democratic and social quality will elevate it beyond its restricted territory, and whose difficult conditions of growth will bring it to a perfect level of sovereignty, placing it at the table of the nations with equal rights and of commensurate worth.

"By virtue of our genuine aim for peace, our courage in self-defense and our economic and scientific efforts, we will gather into our State our scattered and persecuted brethren from Europe and Africa, and all Jews who desire redemption, wherever they may be.

"Arise, O nation, arise, O Yishuv, to practical acts which will express our deep yearning for redemption".

Jerusalem, Saturday night, 29.11.1947

EXPECTATION, REVIVAL AND ANXIETY

11.11.1947

Wherever I turn there is anxious speculation. Everyone is asking: when the U.N. meets to discuss Palestine's political future, will two-thirds of the U.N.'s members support the proposal for the partition of Palestine?

No one asks any more whether the resolution is good or not. Even those who spoke or wrote vehemently against the partition plan seem to have shelved their opposition and joined the great camp of those who wait, hoping secretly that the necessary majority will be found and a new chapter in our history will begin.

The head of the Jewish Agency's Department of State, Mrs. Golda Meyerson (Meir), held a press conference "Before the U.N. Debate". It was the first time that Arab journalists from Syria and Lebanon, as well as a great many foreign reporters and Jewish and Arab newsmen from Old and New Jerusalem, participated in a press conference of this kind.

Mrs. Meyerson began by saying that she would prefer to answer the journalists' questions. The first one was asked by several foreign reporters, both Arab and English, each one in his own language and style: Were the Jews of Palestine prepared to establish institutions of government if and when the partition plan was approved by the majority in the U.N. and if so to what extent.

Calmly and thoughtfully, choosing her words with care, Mrs. Meyerson replied. There would be no shortage of potential members of a Jewish government, she said with a faint smile. Presumably, at the

34

first stage temporary institutions would be established under a provisional government. Elections would be held for the institutions of the new State, and then a permanent government would be formed. Young people were already now preparing to work in government posts in the spheres of education, the postal services, labor, health, transport, etc.

The foreign reportes continued to ask: would the Arabs who remained within the borders of the Jewish State be accorded civil rights?

Of course, the head of the Department of State replied. In the Jewish state all inhabitants, regardless of religion, nationality and origin, would have full and equal rights. Arabs would be able to vote, and also to be members of parliament. Women would have the vote. Arabic would be recognized as the second official language. Jewish youngsters would learn more Arabic and Arab pupils would probably want to learn Hebrew too.

At this point an Arab journalist from Beirut asked: "And what will you do if, for example, all the inhabitants of Nablus will want to move to Tel Aviv? Will you prevent them from doing this?"

After a moment's thought Mrs. Meyerson said: "And what will happen if the residents of Tel Aviv wish to move to Nablus? There will not be special laws for a certain section of the population".

Another Arab reporter asked "What will you do if Arabs who oppose the Jewish State refuse to cultivate their land, go on strike and upset the life of the State? Won't you pass laws against them?

"No", Mrs. Meyerson said, "The laws will apply to all citizens, without differentiating between them. According to the proposal now being brought before the General Assembly, about thirty Jewish settlements will remain within the borders of the Arab State, and Arab areas will also exist within the Jewish State. We would like to hope that the Jews in the Arab State will feel at ease in it, just as the Arabs who remain in the Jewish State will".

A representative of 'A-Difa', a paper published in the Old City, asked: "Are you expecting bloodshed in the wake of the U.N. resolution to establish a Jewish State?".

Mrs. Meyerson: "We never expect bloodshed, but we are prepared for it".

Another Arab newsman asked: "How are you preparing for it?"

A. A body representing all the parties has been founded and is responsible for recruiting members for a 'Civil Guard' etc. The moment we need to defend lives and property we will do so, without having to ask others to do the job for us.

Q. In other words, there is a Jewish force which is prepared to undertake military tasks?

A. I did not say that. I said that when the time came and the need arose for defense, everything would be done so that we would be able to fulfill this task adequately. We are capable of defending our State, and when we are told, "Here is your State, look after it", we will do so.

Q. And if the Arabs begin rioting?

A. I do not think that that is serious. When the times comes the Arabs will also grasp the value of a State. Obviously, however, this is eventuality taken into account amongst the various difficulties of obtaining an independent State.

Q. What will be the legal status of the Jewish Agency once the British Mandate is ended?

A. The situation is not like it is in India, where all the Indians are concentrated in their country. Our nation is scattered throughout the world and it will be necessary to maintain constant contact between it and the Jewish State. This contact can be organized only by the body known today as the 'Jewish Agency'. But then it will have a different name. The Jewish institutions of today will be reorganized and there will be a Zionist movement in the diaspora which will be interested in what goes on in the State, even from afar. There might even be non-Zionists who will ask the Jewish government in Palestine for help. I can imagine that Jews in the diaspora will want to learn more about Jewish history, the Hebrew language, etc.

Q. What will the State be called, Palestine?

A. I don't know yet. There are several suggestions.

Q. Where will the capital be?

A. That will become clear after the U.N. resolution has been passed. The members of the Executive (of the Agency) have several views. Jerusalem has not been ruled out, but the question has not yet been brought up for discussion officially.

Q. What will you do if there is not a two-thirds majority in the U.N. for partition? Is the Jewish Agency preparing an alternative proposal?

A. No. There is no alternative to the simple and just claim to independence of the Jews in their own country. We hope and believe that the resolution will be passed. It is too early to think about what will happen if it is not.

Q. I plucked up my courage and asked: "How will religious affairs, such as observing the Sabbath, be arranged in the independent State?"

A. Naturally the Sabbath, which has been our rest day since time immemorial, will be an official day of rest in the Jewish State. It is also clear that the Arabs or the Christians will be entitled to keep their day of rest. We will try to arrange matters in the State as is done in every democratic country, making them conform with the basic requirements of the Jewish religion, without harming the religious sensitivities of citizens belonging to other faiths.

27.11.1947

There are only three days until the General Assembly meets. The fateful vote will be held on 29th November. Hardly anyone defines the subject for debate as the 'partition proposal'. Most people call it simply the decision to establish a Jewish state.

It is Thursday today, a regular day. Nothing special about it. The area in front of the Western Wall is full of people praying, far more so than usual. Old people are fasting all day. The wise men of the North African communities have been fasting for the last three days. They have taken a vow not to utter a word and are deep in study of parts of the 'Zohar'. In stores and offices people are betting for money, and have even reached sums of IL 50. Will there be a two-thirds majority or not?

30.11.1947

My hand is shaking with excitement. Tears of joy filled our eyes. Our efforts have been rewarded. The resolution to establish the Jewish State was approved. More than two thirds of the countries voted in favor. The representatives of 33 States answered: yes. The representatives of 13 States were against and one abstained (Siam). Praise be to the Creator of the world. Now we will have to wait and see what kind of State it is.

The heads of our institutions have already expressed their satisfaction with the decision. It is a good thing that they did not forget to say that their agreement to the partition of Palestine into two States does not mean that they relinquish our rights to the entire country. We accept this part on its own hoping and believing that henceforth there will be peace in the holy city of peace.

The ink has barely dried on the decision, and already jokers among us are asking: What will our Ministers be called? In general, when will the State be 'established'? What does it mean, 'established'? Meanwhile, many people quote the brief sentence Weizmann said in Yiddish: 'Klein ober mein' (small but mine).

Our joy knows no bounds. Since 3.a.m., as soon as the results of the vote were known, masses of people poured into the streets, like a mighty river. Blinds were opened and lights switched on. Many people went out onto the balconies, the courtyards and the streets. Excitedly they called to one another 'Congratulations'! (Mazal Tov!).

A full moon hung in the sky, casting a delicate light over Jerusalem. Some people did not even get dressed, going out into the street in their pajamas. The barbed-wire fences, which surround important parts of the center of Jerusalem, seemed no longer to be so menacing and piercing. Everything was so tranquil and friendly. A halo of light and mercy was spread over the city and its inhabitants.

Before dawn broke, the drivers of the urban bus company, 'Hamekasher', took the buses out of the depot. Hooting their horns, they took people into the center of town gratis. One of the drivers got the members of the Blind School band out of their beds and brought them to the Jewish Agency compound, where they sat and played.

Thousands of people streamed spontaneously towards the Jewish Agency compound, like Hassidic disciples on their way to the rabbi, singing and dancing. Young and old, members of every ethnic group, all congregated there. The Zionist flag was hoisted as the crowd sang 'Hatikvah' in amighty roar emanating from the hearts and throats of the thousands gathered there. Many people wiped the tears from their cheeks.

Golda Meyerson appeared on the balcony, flanked by public leaders and journalists, their faces shining with happiness. Mrs. Meyerson spoke briefly and to the point: "We are happy and ready for what lies ahead. Our hands are extended in peace to our neighbors. Both States can live in peace with one another and cooperate for the welfare of their inhabitants. Long live the people of Israel!"

People joined hands and formed dancing circles. The Rishon Letzion, the Sephardi Chief Rabbi, Ben-Zion Hai Uziel, also arrived. Everyone fell quiet. Rabbi Uziel called upon the inhabitants of Jerusalem to reject the decision that the Holy City should be outside the boundary of the Jewish State. Sooner or later Jerusalem would return to the State, and the State to Jerusalem, he said. The crowd roared in reply: "If I forget thee, O Jerusalem, let my right hand forget its cunning"!

People stood and wept. As daylight appeared the torrent of people in the streets swelled. Children were given a vacation from school and people continued to flow to the Jewish Agency courtyard. At nine Moshe Haim Shapira, a member of the Jewish Agency Executive and jointly responsible for the Aliyah Department, arrived. The local reporters and foreign journalists surrounded him, asking him to say something.

40

"Thank God. The third kingdom of Israel has been established", he said.

People danced, singing "David, the King of Israel, lives and endures".

When David Ben-Gurion arrived from Tel-Aviv he was carried on the shoulders of the throng to his office in the Jewish Agency building. When he appeared on the balcony he cried out excitedly: "Let us be worthy of this moment of our becoming an independent nation"!

Additional speeches were made, and after each one the 'Hatikvah' was sung enthusiastically.

The settlements in the Judean Hills passed on the message to one another by lighting beacons on the hill-tops, just as in ancient times, during the period of the Second Temple, similar fires had been lit to signal the new month. In Kfar Etzion the policeman rang the bell and the members of the settlement gathered in the dining room. They pronounced the traditional blessing of thanksgiving ("shehehiyanu"), And lit a beacon to inform their colleagues in the other settlements of the Bloc, who replied by lighting beacons of their own. They all danced around the fires until morning.

As dawn broke, the congregants in the synagogues recited parts of the special prayer for festivals and high holy days (Hallel) spontaneously and from the depths of their hearts. The members of the 'Shaarei Hesed' congregation informed their associates that Rabbi Jacob Moses Harlap had recited the prayer in full. Newspapers were much in demand. Every word was devoured avidly. British armored vehicles driving along the streets of Jerusalem were 'conquered' by children who climbed up on them. The British soldiers did not push them off or stop them. Jewish refugees who had survived the holocaust decorated the balconies of their homes with flags, tears of joys streaming from their eyes. Vendors of drinks presented their wares free to passers-by. In the law court the Justice of the Peace, Benjamin Halevi, merely admonished defendants, whether Arabs or Jews, and did not impose any penalty in honor of the event.

The resolution determined that there were to be two States, which were to be economically united. For some reason the Jewish State was to pay IL4,000,000 per year to the Arab one, in order to maintain its social services.

When the resolution was approved there were 165 thousand inhabitants in Jerusalem, 100,000 of whom were Jews, 40,000 Arabs and 25,000 Christians. In the Old City there were 1,700 Jews, 24,000 Moslems and 5,000 Christians.

Suddenly we heard that Jewish passengers in an 'Egged' bus on its way from Natanya to Jerusalem had been attacked in the Ramle area and that five of them had been killed. There was concern on everyone's faces. Our hearts were filled with anxiety for what lay ahead.

3.12.1947

The apprehension felt by many of us that 'things would not be settled so easily' has been cruelly verified. The Arabs, encouraged overtly or covertly by the British, have declared a three-day strike to protest against the U.N. resolution, hoping to lead to its annulment.

An Arab mob broke into the Jewish commercial area, 'Shema', on the way to the Jaffa Gate. At first they hesitated, trying to get past the policement in the way. The British policement did not move a muscle. This encouraged the rabble to increase their anti-Jewish cries. The number of demonstrators grew every minute. They carried an Arab flag enfolded in black cloth and marched from Mamilla Street to Princess Mary Street, making for Zion Square. As they walked they cried enthusiastically 'Atbah al Yahud'! (Death to the Jews!). A young Jewish man fired two shots in the air and the Arabs retreated in alarm, scattering to all sides.

A small Ford made its way down Princess Mary Street. Inside was the Jerusalem correspondednt of 'Haaretz', Asher Lazar, who had come to cover events at first hand. Beside him sat one of the paper's managers, Moshe Shamir. They suddenly came across a group of Arab youngsters, shouting at the tops of their voices and brandishing sticks and knives. Lazar tried to turn the car round, but could not, and it stopped in the middle of the road. Shamir managed to open the door and get away. Lazar tried to escape, but one of the Arabs came up behind him, stabbed him and fled. For many weeks Lazar lay in hospital, but eventually he recovered and returned to his job as a journalist.

That morning an Arab youth shot and wounded Martin Rosenberg, aged 40, who worked in Rosenstoch's store in Princess Mary Street. It seemed that a new, difficult and interesting period was beginning for us Jerusalem reporters. We ran towards the commercial center. An Arab mob was looting Jewish shops, watched by British and Arab policemen. A British police unit took up positions across Jaffa Road, next to the Municipality building, blocking the way to Jewish youngsters who wanted to help the Jewish store-owners there.

Next day Mrs. Meyerson sent the First Secretary of the Mandate government photographs showing a British police officer standing in the Jewish commercial center and smiling with pleasure at the sight of a gang of Arabs ransacking and burning Jewish stores. She demanded an investigation, with appropriate measures, etc. The British promised 'to look into the matter'.

The British army and police officers who accompanied the High Commissioner on his tour of the scorched and pillaged commercial center observed Arab trucks loaded with commodities from the Jewish stores. Urgent calls reached the police from Jewish public figures as well as from the Acting Mayor, Mr. Graves. They reported in alarm that there had been acts of violence, arson and robbery, and demanded that steps be taken to stop them. The officer replied with Olympian calm: "We know. The matter is being dealt with"[1].

---

[1]   In his memoirs, Mr. Graves wrote that the Regional Governor, Mr. Pollock, told several people who asked him to end the rioting: "We"ll give them a day or two to work it out of their systems."

At the same time British policemen began arresting Jewish youngsters in the streets and suburbs of Jerusalem, confiscating their defense weapons. Anyone found possessing arms was tried. Several Jewish soldiers, together with members of the 'Haganah' who were also wearing khaki uniforms, managed to reach the commercial center, enter the Angel, Berman and Weismann Jewish bakeries and save about 110 tons of flour. Under a hail of Arab bullets they loaded the sacks of flour onto trucks and within a few hours had transferred them to a safe place. The owners of the bakeries sent a gift of IL 115 to the five policemen and 'Haganah' youngsters, who transferred the money to the 'Defense Fund'. A letter of thanks was sent to the British officer, Park, who helped them reach Mamilla Road and saved them from the Arab rioters.

Jewish youngsters, wishing to take revenge on the Arabs for burning the Jewish commercial center, set fire to the Arab cinema, Rex, in Princess Mary Street. The initial estimate made by the journalists was that fifty Jewish stores had been burnt down. A great deal of Jewish property was lost. The British director of the Jerusalem Electricity Company, Mr. Gresham, photographed the damage caused to Jewish stores and the slogans scrawled in English at their entrances, cursing all Jews. Mr. Gresham told the reporters openly "I am ashamed at what my fellow Englishmen have done".

Jewish buses were also attacked. A bus making its way from Natanya to Jerusalem was attacked on the Lydda-Ramle road, four passengers were killed and another four wounded. Another attack was directed against a bus going from Hadera to Jerusalem, and a woman was killed. These items of news were bitter drops in the cup of happiness of those days and a bad omen for the future.

On the second day of the strike the Arabs attacked the Yemin Moshe quarter. Yitzhak Ben-Zvi, the Head of the National Committee, and the lawyer, Mordechai Eliash, requested that the First Secretary of State increase the guard on the neighborhood.

7.12.1947

The National Council of the Jews of Palestine (Vaad Leumi) has published the following leaflet in Arabic calling on the Arabs to live in peace with the Jews, and it has been distributed to the Arab population:

"Arabs! The National Conncil of the Jews of Palestine greets you in peace and calls upon you to refrain from following those who preach violence and bloodshed. We do not address you from a position of weakness, for if the plunder and murder are not stopped by the Government, the Jews will take the necessary steps, and we are well able to defend ourselves. But it is friendship, not strife, that we desire. The Jews intend to build their State within the borders allotted them by the U.N. resolution. Remove the agitators and accept the hand extended to you in peace".

Regrettably it seems that the Arabs interpret this appeal as a sign of weakness. They continue to attack Jewish traffic in the city. Buses go to and from the coastal plain via Rehovot, by-passing Ramle, where stones are thrown at every Jewish vehicle that passed and sometimes shots are fired too. There are rumors that every bus will carry a guard with concealed weapons, despite the danger and the heavy penalties imposed by the British on anyone found possessing 'illegal' arms.

The burned-out Jewish coinmercial center is still under curfew, to the joy of the Arabs and despair of the Jews. Every application to the British authorities to enable the store-owners to repair their shops and return to their businesses is rejected. This is done by typical British bureaucratic delays. The applications of the Jewish shop-keepers are submitted to the offices of Mr. Pollock, the Regional Governor. He transfers them to the First Secretary of the Mandate Government, in the King David Hotel building. The Government asks the police for their 'opinion'. The police reply that in this case they must consult the army. The army announces that it is undertaking a 'security check'. Meanwhile, the check continues, as do the curfew and the disruption.

*

After all kinds of delays, the authorities gave the Jerusalem 'Burial Society' permission to take several corpses in a convoy for burial on the Mount of Olives. The army provided a guard of two soldiers. When the convoy reached the bend in the road by the A-Tur quarter on the Mount of Olives the Arabs opened fire. The members of the 'Burial Society' abandoned the car with the bodies and took cover in a ditch at the side of the road. The soldiers repelled the assailants by firing at them. As a result, the police have issued an order that henceforth funerals will be held only twice a week, before 6 a.m.

This morning I met an Arab journalist from the Old City, with whom I have had contact from time to time. We talked about 'the situation'. He told me simply "Our attacks till now have been child's play. We are waiting for instructions and aid from the Arab countries. Our leaders are about to meet in Egypt. Soldiers from Syria, Lebanon, Jordan and Iraq will aid us. There will be a great war, you'll see".

I passed on what he had said to the appropriate quarters and was amazed by their lack of surprise at the news.

The Chief Rabbis, Herzog and Uziel, issued a call to Moslem religious leaders in Palestine and all the Arab countries, saying:

"Brothers, at the time when the Jewish people has returned to its land and country, in accordance with the word of the Lord and those of his servants, the prophets, in his sacred books, and in accordance with the U.N. resolution, we call upon you for peace and amity.

"Remember the peaceful and friendly relations between our two peoples in the Arab and Moslem countries during the Golden Age, when the foundations of wisdom and science were laid for the entire world; and remember the words of the prophet, Malachi:

'Have we not all one father? Hath not one God Created us? Why do we deal treacherously every man against his brother'?"

(See Appendix 1 for an account of the weapons possessed by the 'Haganah' prior to the War of Independence).

10.12.1947

Today there were long lines at the entrances to stores. There were
lines for sugar, flour, fish and fresh vegetables. There is talk of an
increasing shortage of food in the near future if transport from Tel Aviv
to Jerusalem encounters difficulties. In some places there were fights of
a minor kind, while in others women joined hands, making sure that
people kept their places.

*

Yesterday David Ben-Gurion moved to Tel-Aviv. Reporters were
told that the Jewish Agency Excutive is to be split up. Part of it,
including the Head of the State Department, Mrs. Meyerson, will
remain in Jerusalem, and part will move to Tel-Aviv, to deal with
'preparing the State'. Moshe Shertok (Sharett) is in the U.S.,
representing our interests at the institutions of the U.N.

*

"The nation needs you, stand up and be counted"! This call has
appeared on the front pages of newspapers and on billboards in
Jerusalem. Youngsters have began presenting themselves at the
recruiting offices and are given jobs.

11.12.1947

Ten members of Kfar Etzion, Massuot Yitzhak, Ein Tzurim and
supernumerary constables accompanying them were cruelly murdered
on the road from Jerusalem to the Etzion Bloc. They were bringing
supplies to the settlements of the Bloc and when they reached the
fifteenth kilometer, not far from Bethlehem, came under fire. The
vehicles stopped and the assailants killed their occupants, mutilating the
bodies.

A few hours beforehand I had seen them, talked with them and bidden them farewell, as they loaded the supplies in Hasollel Street. They had also been photographed there before setting off. I had cheerfully said goodbye to a friend and fellow youth counsellor in the 'Bnei Akiva' movement, Shalom Karniel (Treller), one of the leaders of 'Hashomer Hadati' in Poland, and an hour or so later he was among the fallen.

An uncomfortable thought creeps into my mind: is it possible that the Etzion Bloc settlers will be unable to hold out against a sea of Arab inhabitants from the neighboring villages?

15.12.1947

The nights of the Festival of Lights (Hannuka) are difficult ones. The strains of 'O Fortress, Rock of my salvation', (Maoz Tzur) are accompanied by shots and explosions. Members of Etzel (Irgun Zvai Leumi) are retaliating against the Arabs. Every day someone is killed, and at 'best', only wounded, whether Arab or Jew. A cycle of bloodshed has begun, who can tell where it will end? Jewish prisoners have been transferred from Acre gaol to the central prison in Jerusalem to protect them from being harmed. The offices of several newspapers have received letters from Jewish youngsters imprisoned in Kenya by the British authorities. They write: "Do everything to convince those with influence to have us brought home".

The Arab attacks on urban and interurban traffic are increasing. They have advanced from throwing stones at buses to firing at them. Transport to the Talpiot and Mekor Haim quarters in the south is conducted only in convoys. It is nothing short of a miracle that people have been only slightly wounded or not harmed at all.

At the same time, the British are intensifying their searches for defensive weapons in Jewish urban and interurban buses. Mrs. Golda Meyerson told reporters that the Jewish Agency had asked the British to guarantee the urban and interurban traffic and to show some concern for the welfare of the passengers. The British were told that if they did not do this, they should not prevent Jewish organizations from assuring their safety.

The British continue with their false 'neutrality'. A search for defensive arms was conducted the following morning in Jewish neighborhoods which had served as the target for a barrage of firing from Arab aggressors for a whole night. After examining the clothing of passersby, the British began searching in apartments and courtyards. This began by placing all inhabitants under 'house arrest'. The lengthy harassment of those who had been under attack was annoying and painful, but the Jewish inhabitants had to bear their suffering and anger in silence.

On rare occasions British soldiers or policemen show understanding and consideration for Jewish defenders. A British officer once entered a 'Haganah' position. Since he came unexpectedly, the boys did not manage to conceal their arms. The officer anounced that he would return to conduct a search, and left. The defenders took the hint, and on his return, about half an hour later, he found no weapons.

The desertions by Arab supernumerary constables with their arms also continues. Twenty Arab supernumerary constables from the police unit at the Railway Station and the Government Press Ofice deserted with their guns, as did eleven from the Broadcasting Service unit. The timing of the desertion is known in advance, the day after their salaries have been paid. The officer in charge, Kennedy, was advised not to give the constables arms, only batons, during the period before they received their pay. He replied that he knew what was going on but had received no orders to prevent them from obtaining arms.

The road to Mount Scopus which passes through the Arab village of Sheikh Jarrah, has also become more dangerous. Veteran residents of this quarter, who have been friends of the Jews of the Nahlat Shimon Hatzadik neighborhood for many years, have been evicted from their houses, which are now occupied by members of Arab terrorist gangs.

The 'Standing Committee' of the Communal Council attends to problems of transport, food supplies and claims for damages incurred at the 'Shema' commercial center. The major bakeries in town have given their assurance that they will not raise the price of broad, and that a loaf will not cost more than four mills.

The Housing Committee appointed by the Standing Committee asked the inhabitants of Jerusalem to inform them of empty rooms or store-rooms, so that they could be used as accommodation by the Jewish families evicted from their homes. The response went beyond all expectations. The Standing Committee regards it as an achievement that the Governor has agreed to station some Jewish supernumerary constables in Jewish areas, and has allowed others to accompany convoys making the journey between Jerusalem and Tel-Aviv.

18.12.1947

Reporters continue to meet the 'spokesman' of the Press Office, Richard Stubbs, in the offices of the Government Press Office in David Building, at the end of King George Street. Jewish, Arab and foreign newsmen participate in these meetings. The First Secretary of the Mandate Government is very proud of the existence of this 'institution', which he defines as 'the most democratic in the world'.

As usual, Stubbs emphasized the fact that, despite the difficulties, the Mandate Government has maintained its policy of 'neutrality' in the Jewish-Arab conflict. The Jewish journalists among us smiled bitterly on hearing this.

Through the window in the 'spokesman's' room, on the fifth floor of the building, we witnessed British 'neutrality'. Arabs emerged from behind the walls surrounding the Old City, took up positions on Mount Zion and fired at the Yemin Moshe quarter. We could see the aggressors clearly and pointed them out to the British 'spokesman'. As we were looking we saw a unit of British soldiers surround Yemin Moshe and conduct a search there.

At last week's press conference my fellow-reporters pointed out certain facts. It had happened that a bullet fired by Jewish defenders had hit an Arab child. The Government Press Office had rapidly published a communiqué emphasizing the details, to prove how cruel the Jews were. On that very day a Jewish child had been killed while travelling with his mother on a bus. The Government communiqué had said: 'A Jewish passenger was killed'. Another instance was the constant firing at Jews from the houses of Sheikh Jarrah. Once shots were fired at Arabs from a house in the shimon Hatzadik quarter. The next day British soldiers seized the house and evicted the Jewish occupants.

The Mandate Government's spokesmen stated that all this was 'pure coincidence'.

When the Jewish journalists remarked that Arab attacks were continuing on Jewish transport between Jerusalem and Tel-Aviv, the 'spokesman' read out the following announcement: "The Government has decided to preserve law and order and maintain safe transport between Jerusalem and Tel-Aviv at all costs". We knew that the object of this was to prevent any independent Jewish defense being organized to protect transport.

The spokesman also asked the reporters to refrain from publishing reports about acts of retaliation, so as not to encourage them, he said. He added an open threat: "If you ignore this request, the Government will have to wield its powers of censorship".

25.12.1947

The Jewish Quarter in the Old City is still cut off from the rest of the city and comes under fire from the murderers' weapons. Arab snipers, including deserters from the police and other paramilitary units, have taken up positions on the roofs of houses in order to 'hunt' passersby and use them as live targets. The rabble has also prepared ladders and sharpened its knives, waiting for the right moment to go up on the roofs and make its way to the Jewish Quarter across the roof-tops. A week ago they reached Habad Street and set fire to one of the houses. At the same time they fired from a medium machine-gun situated in the courtyard of a mosque, and from rifles and machine-guns on the roofs of houses in the largely deserted Armenian Quarter. The Arabs thought that the 'conquest' was at hand, until they over-hastily informed the foreign press of this by phone.

All would have been lost had it not been for the brave defenders, mothers and fathers, teachers, clerks and laborers, young boys and girls, still in the spring of their lives, who faced them. They arose courageously, scorning the dangers, to protect their homes and families. The waves of attackers surged forward, and were repulsed. It was during this defense that Yitzhak Solomon from Rosh Pina fell, at the age of 18.

I was taken to see these defenders. I went down to observe and taste the bitterness of the battlefront. For a day and a night I remained with the young fighters who had come from the New City to help the veteran inhabitants in their heroic stand. Old people who lived in the 'Bathei Mahseh' houses blessed the courageous young 'Zionists'.

When we left the new city we tooked like a group of hikers off to breathe some country air. We left a city bathed in light, with lines of people at the entrances to movie-houses, and made our way to the Old City. We did not have far to go from Jaffa Road, via the 'Kishle' (the police station near David's Tower) and the winding Street of the Armenians to the Jewish Quarter, accompajied by our fears of danger at every step. We travelled in a bus with wire mesh on its windows, followed by three supplies vehicles, and were escorted both in front and behind by armored cars of the British police.

About a dozen defenders were waitinig for us in the Jewish Quarter, near the 'Parness' matza factory and the Talmud-Torah building. Gradually night fell. Supplies were distributed by candle-light. Faint lights shone through the windows. A mother sang her child to sleep with a soft lullaby. The sound of men learning the Torah could be heard from the 'Bathei Mahseh'. On the roofs nearby we could see figures. The authorities had posted 'neutral' guards there to 'protect' the 'border' between Arabs and Jews. For some reason their rifles were pointing towards the Jewish side, I was told.

Our guide said the password and the door of one of the houses was opened. In a large room we found a group of young defenders. Both we and they were surprised by the unexpected encounter. Many of them were known to us. It was astonishing to find that they had left everything and come to do this job. They were youngsters from religious and secular youth movements. A young doctor lay on a camp bed nearby. We all shook hands. There were two young commanders, who had left warm homes and families in the New City and had volunteered for this task. The 'privates' were in a good mood. At the sight of one of their 'raw recruits', who had just returned after a brief leave in town, they joked. "Hey, you, you missed a bit of shooting", someone said. "Yes, it was just like carnival night. They fired and we fired", someone else added. "Come over here and get acquainted with our trigger-happy friend", said a third.

A youngster with a girlish face and an apron tied round his waist was the group's cook. His comrades accepted his concoctions in a spirit of understanding, ignoring his 'errors'.

They were waiting to do their stint of guard duty. In the meantime some of them were learning a tractate of the Mishnah and others were playing checkers in another corner. When the signal came, they would get up and repulse the enemy.

We set out on a brief tour of the darkened alleys. We passed charitable institutions which had been established many hundreds of years previously and synagogues and houses of learning which had produced famous rabbis. We were in the Street of the Jews. We entered the courtyard of the 'Hurva' ('Ruin') Synagogue, where the Etz Haim Yeshiva had been situated until 1936, when it had moved to the New City. It had been from this synagogue that rays of national hope had emanated when Herbert Samuel, the first British High Commissioner (whom the Jews proudly called, 'The First Commissioner of Judah') had read the portion of the prophets, 'Comfort ye, comfort ye, my people', in 1920, and returned on foot, in order to avoid desecrating the Sabbath, to his residence on Mount Scopus (The Augusta Victoria Hospital today). The rabbis of Israel and the Yishuv had assembled here to sound the alarm and pray when the terrible news of the holocaust in Europe had reached them (in 1944). We walked up the parallel road, Habad Street. Further up there was a steep alley which exhausted all those who climbed it and was called 'The Alley of Hannah and her Seven Sons', and contained the 'Or Haim' synagogue of Rabbi Haim ben Atar. This was where Rabbi Shmuel David Kahane, the rabbi of the Old City (formerly the rabbi of Warsaw), had lived till recently, when he had moved to the New City. Nearby was the home of A. Weingarten, the leader ('Mukhtar') of the Jews of the Old City and the chairman of their committee. The courtyard of Rabbi Yeshayahu Bardaki's 'Sukkat Shalom' was also situated here.

A little further on we came to 'Beth El', the center of the kabbalists in Jerusalem. On the wall we found the 'coded messages' which the twelve members of the 'Ahavat Shalom' group had agreed on in 1757, the first signatory being Rabbi Shalom Sharabi (Harashash'). A few paces away stood the synagogue of Rabbi Yohanan ben Zakai. For many generations this had been the public and spiritual center of Sephardic Jewry, which constituted the majority of the Jewish inhabitants in both the Old and the New City. It was here that the Sephardic Chief Rabbi was crowned and given the noble title, 'Rishon Letzion'. The building comprised four rooms, each one of which was a synagogue. And there was the Istambul synagogue of the Jews from Constantinople, containing the 'genizah' of sacred scrolls and parchments from all over Jerusalem. In the corner stood the synagogue of Elijah the Prophet, which was built in 1586 on older foundations. From there we walked to the 'Bathei Mahseh', buildings erected in 1861 by German Jews, also known as 'Deutscher Platz'. Rabbi Haim Zvi Shneorson was sent to Australia to raise funds for their construction. Nearby stood the 'Misgav Ladach' Hospital, which was built in 1854 by Abraham Cohen, using the funds of Baron Rothschild of Paris. In one of its rooms was the large and important library of sacred books belonging to Rabbi Haim Hezkiah Medini. We went down some steps and reached the Porat Yosef yeshivah of Spanish Jewry, which was built in 1919 with funds donated by Yosef Shalom of Baghdad, and had a glorious history. Hundreds of rabbis learned there and became teachers throughout Palestine and the diaspora.

Until late at night we walked around the Old City. Fear lurked at every corner. A short whistle from the officer accompanying us was answered by another, reassuring us that all was well. It grieved us to see the deserted road leading to the Western Wall, all that remained of our Temple. The officer whispered a few words in conclusion "We have to fight the Arabs, and also contend with the threat posed by the 'neutral' British, who seize our defensive arms. Every British military vehicle that brings us supplies may take away deserters. But, thank God, very few have chosen to take that step. We encourage the residents in their decision to stay put and not to abandon the City of David".

As dawn broke the following day we took our places in the armored vehicle and returned to the New City.

BRITISH 'NEUTRALITY'

28.12.1947

A convoy consisting of three Egged buses, a truck and ten small automobiles, left Tel-Aviv at noon on Friday, two days ago. Mrs. Golda Meyerson and Yitzhak Greenbaum, members of the Jewish Agency Executive, were among the passengers. When the convoy reached Bab-al-Wad (Shaar Hagai), it came under fire, and bullets pierced the tires of some of the automobiles. The passengers, including Mrs. Meyerson, were transferred to other vehicles and continued on their way to Jerusalem. After passing Kiryat Anavim a police car came towards them and stopped them. The British policemen searched for arms in the vehicles, found nothing and allowed them to continue.

Near the Arza convalescent home in Motza the convoy was attacked again, this time by a hail of bullets coming from both sides of the road. Hans Beit, the head of Youth Aliyah, was killed on the spot. Abraham Sher, Menahem Oren (Sosnovski) and Aharon Silman were seriously wounded and died later of their injuries.

The buses reached Jerusalem full of holes. No military or police vehicle was to be seen on the road, except for the one whose passengers had searched for arms.

There were heavy attacks on Jewish transport on Friday. In one case a bus going from Jerusalem to Har Tuv came under fire and three Jewish supernumerary constables were killed, and in another a lorry carrying phosphates from the Dead Sea was ambushed. The Jewish Agency spokesman in Jerusalem called a press conference, where he accused the British authorities of abandoning Jewish traffic to its fate. He vigorously denied the British spokesman's statement that the Jewish supernumerary constables had opened fire on the Arabs, 'leading to a battle'.

*

Sixteen national service recruitment offices have been opened in various parts of Jerusalem. Notices and illuminated flags mark their position. During a press tour we found that the response was good and that many people were offering their services. This applied both to the offices in the central neighborhoods, such as the Menorah Club, the Tahkemoni and Lemel schools, and to far-flung quarters, where young men and women came to join up. The entire city has been flooded with posters calling on people to join. The recruitment office directors told us that many of the volunteers are not required to serve for a variety of reasons, such as age, health, etc., but insist on being allowed to participate in the national effort. Included in this category are high school pupils, most of whom falsify their age in order to be accepted. Their requests are studied by a special committee.

A group of blind people turned up at one of the offices, asking to be recruited. When asked what they could do to help, they replied that their acute hearing could help on guard duty at nights. Some of them said they could help casualties by giving massages. Sermons about the obligation to help at this hour of national need were given in dozens of synagogues on Saturday. Chief Rabbi Herzog spoke in the Yeshurun synagogue, and Chief Rabbi Uziel spoke in the Nahlat Shiva synagogue.

5.1.1948

The inhabitants of Jerusalem must learn to beware of a new method of slaughter used by the Arabs, sniping. A man may be walking along the road harmlessly when an Arab sniper fires at him from the roof or window of a house, putting an end to his life or wounding him seriously. Several casualties have been caused by snipers in the last few days.

*

The Semiramis Hotel in Katamon, which served as the center for Arab terrorist attacks and the location of the activities of the Arab youth organizations, Nejada and Patwa, was blown up by the Haganah. About twenty people, including the Spanish consul, were killed. Large quantities of arms and ammunitions were found in the hotel.

*

Most of the neighborhoods of Jewish Jerusalem are plunged into darkness as a result of frequent and extended 'breakdowns' in the electricity supply.

7.1.1948

In a courageous operation, Etzel members destroyed the 'Arab National Guard' position at Jaffa Gate this morning. This position barred the way for supplies conveys making their way to the Jewish Quarter in the Old City. The Etzel men threw a bomb from an armored vehicle, killing fourteen Arabs and wounding forty. The vehicle had been 'appropriated' from policemen the previous day. The engine gave out during the retreat and the boys had to abandon it and get away on foot. The British policemen fired from the roof of the Generali Building, killing three of them, Ephraim Levi, Shimon Levi and Nissim ben Haim.

At a press conference, the Mandate Government spokesman said that his Government recognized the Arab defense organization and acknowledged its right to set up road blocks and even to conduct searches. On the other hand, he condemned the Haganah's action in blowing up the Semiramis Hotel in Katamon, although he admitted that "some of the guests in the hotel had connections with the Arab Gangs".

We asked the spokesman how he could explain the fact that a sub-machine-gun taken away from a Haganah member by a British policeman was found in the possession of an Arab rioter the next day. The spokesman asked for the number of the gun so that he could request an investigation.

16.1.1948

The Mandate Government continues to be consistent in its policy of obstructing the implementation of the U. N. resolution. The British police and army appear to be acting in accordance with the distum:'The worse the situation is (for the Jews), the better it is (for the British)'.

There is a great deal of resentment against the British, who disregard the continuing attacks on Jewish transport. Their only 'interference' is to seize arms from Jewish defenders. The actions of the representatives of the authorities indicate how great is their desire to prevent the implemention of the U. N. decision to establish a State. Perhaps they are deluding themselves with the idea that somehow the nations will ask the British to postpone or cancel their departure from Palestine. (Appendix 2)

The following announcement was issued yesterday by the Mandate Government:

"In view of complaints by both the Arabs and the Jews that Government security forces protect one side to the detriment of the other, His Excellency, the High Commissioner, wishes to make it clear that as long as the Mandate is in force it will be the task of the security forces to prevent, without discrimination, any attack whatsoever by either side.

"The intervention of the security forces has always been undertaken in order to protect life and property, without investigating which side is involved. This has been the Government's policy ever since the disturbances began, and this point is emphasized again as a result of the misunderstandings among the public".

18.1.1948

Grief and sorrow surround us. Thirty—five youngsters who were on their way tohelp the beleaguered Etzion Bloc were trapped on their way from Har Tuv and were all killed after a long and bitter battle with hundreds of Arabs from the surrounding villages. Their names are on everyone's lips. I knew some of them well. They were led by the valiant young commander from Jerusalem, Danny Mass. These reinforcements were the hope of the defenders of the Etzion Bloc, who have been attacked every night for the past two weeks by thousands of Arabs. The assailants have suffered heavy losses, but the defenders of the Bloc are growing weaker daily. Two nights ago a platoon set out from Jerusalem on its way to the Etzion Bloc, but returned because it had lost its way. Last night the same platoon set off again, apparently from Har Tuv, and had to make its way across thirty kilometers to reach Massuot Yitzhak in the Etzion Bloc before dawn. They were all killed in battle. (Appendix 3)

24.1.1948

Today the telephine link between Jerusalem and Tel-Aviv and the rest of the country was cut off. Till now there were very few lines which functioned properly. It seems that from now on only those with a radio-telephone will be able to maintain contact. A special radio has been prepared by the owner of a store for radios and loudspeakers (Elbinger) so that I can contact the office of 'Yediot Aharonot' in Tel-Aviv and give in my reports of what is happening in Jerusalem. Our signal is: Ni-Na-No. This morning's experiment was very successful, although there was interference for some minutes. I managed to broadcast to Dov Yudovski at the paper's office in Tel Aviv and report on events in Jerusalem for the Jerusalem edition of the paper.

25.1.1948

A Palmah unit exchanged fire with an Arab gang in the Castel region, which is in Arab hands and threatens Jewish traffic between Jerusalem and Tel-Aviv. When the battle began to go in our favor and the Arabs were retreating, the British army intervened as a so-called 'ceasefire force'. The British soldiers, however, directed their fire only at our men. Ten Palmah fighters were killed and the Castel remains in Arab hands.

*

While death lurks on the roads, menacing traffic between the cities, Jews and Arabs gathered together recently at Government House for an official ceremony. The occasion was the Mandatory Government's awards given to 35 outstanding officers and civilians, including several Jews. Amongst the recipients was Joseph Sapir, who had served as mayor of Petach-Tikvah for many years and who did not attend the ceremony. The others were Kalman Cohen, Assistant Police Inspector, Menashe Bar Dayan, Tova Brilovski, Arieh Shamir and Yitzhak Shvili. A royal award was granted to Dan ben Dor, Elsa Gabriel, A. Corngold, A. Matar, S. Samburski, Sister R. Berger, R. Guttman, Mrs. Davidovitch and Mattityahu Epstein.

Service medals were also awarded to two Jewish sergeants who served in the British Sappers Brigade, Arieh Katz and Haim Rabinowitz, who both fought the Nazis.

A hint was given to both Jews and Arabs from 'above', through the British police, that there should be absolute quiet in Jerusalem and its environs on that day. Jewish journalists and guests passed through Arab streets and reached Government House unharmed. At the Governor's residence there was a veritable idyll. Jewish and Arab dignitaries ate, drank and shook hands as if the tension and the strife were in some distant land. The hosts were British, the servants and waiters Arabs and the musicians Jewish. The Jewish recipients of awards who were from outside Jerusalem were brought into the city in

British military vehicles and were returned in similar fashion. At that time a bitter battle for the control of the Castel was initiated by Abd al Kadr Al-Husseini's men.

*

As compared with some two hundred trucks that used to bring supplies to Jerusalem every day, these days only about fifteen reach the town, travelling in a convoy. We asked the 'Standing Committee' if and when additional trucks would be arriving. The reply was pessimistic: "Let's hope things don't get worse". The Standing Committee is trying to deal with two problems, preventing the hoarding of food and arranging the equitable distribution of foodstuffs brought into the city.

26.1.1948

At a press conference Mrs. Golda Meyerson said that the Jews are defending the U.N. resolution on the fate of Palestine. We are maintaining the U.N's honor and sovereignty, she said, and it is our right to demand not to be abandoned.

One of the correspondents asked: Can partition be implemented if the U.N. does not send an international force here?

G. Meyerson: It cannot be said that it is impossible to establish a Jewish State for any reason, but it is in the interests of all concerned that an international force be sent or some other way be found of proving to the Arab rioters that partition will be implemented despite acts of violence.

In answer to other questions, the Head of the Jewish Agency's Department of State said that the British had failed to eliminate Arab aggression, had been to hasty in imposing curfews, often unjustifiably, in Jewish neighborhoods and had gone too far in arms searches in Jewish houses. We were all amazed by this false 'neutrality' of the British. In concluding she said that the Jewish institutions had drawn up

62 JERUSALEM UNDER SIEGE

plans for providing housing and employment for the thirty thousand illegal immigrants still detained in the Cyprus camps.

*

The Government spokesman, Stubbs, told reporters today that the Old City will be peaceful only when the members of the Haganah and Etzel leave it. He claimed that the one hundred British soldiers placed in the Old City to preserve law and order were sufficient. This subject was also raised in the meeting between Chief Rabbi Herzog and the First Secretary of the Mandate Government, Henry Garney.

The spokesman confirmed that several foreign consulates in Jerusalem have been permitted to bring in a certain number of soldiers to guard their buildings. The Syrian and Saudi consulates immediately brought ten soldiers each. Twenty guards will soon be posted at the Lebanese consulate. The Iraqi and Transjordanian consulates will be guarded by the Arab Legion.

The correspondent of the Arab newspaper, 'Palestine', which appears in the Old City, asked why the British have sold 21 planes to the Jewish 'Aviron' company. The spokesman replied that a tender had been published for the sale of the planes, that about twelve Jewish firms had participated and that the 'Aviron' Company had won by offering the highest price.

28.1.1948

Yitzhak Ben-Zvi, the Head of the National Council, has declared that we will not do as the Mandate Government wishes, and will not act on its 'advice' to remove the members of the Haganah, Etzel and Lehi from the Old City, leaving only old people and children there. "We are imbued with the firm belief that Jerusalem has been and will be the heart of the nation and its capital. When and how? God knows. For hundreds of years Jews have always lived in Jerusalem. The Divine Presence (Shehina) has not left the Western Wall and the Jews have not left Jerusalem".

The Jewish Agency spokesman said that the Jewish National Institutions hed sent a declaration to international institutions and Governments refuting the statement made by the British Government spokesman and circulated at the U.N., that "The blockade of the Jewish Quarter in the Old City began only after the Jews bombed the gates of the Old City". The Agency spokesman stressed that many Jews had been killed between the 1st and the 13th of December, and that the Jews had bombed the Damascus Gate after the Arabs had attacked and killed Jews in the streets of both the Old and the New City. He said that the Jewish Agency opposed the system of throwing bombs, but that the British Government should publish the facts, and not a distortion of the truth.

The spokesman also denied the Mandate Government's assertion that 'freedom of exit and entry had been assured for the Jews of the Old City'. Even a small number of doctors and teachers had been permitted to enter the Jewish Quarter only after repeated requests, and it was impossible to speak of 'freedom of movement'.

*

The New Year for Trees (Tu Bishvat) was felt more inside the walls of the Old City than anywhere else, it seems. There were parties all day, children planted saplings in pots and everyone sang and danced. Members of kibbutz 'Beth Ha'arava' sent the inhabitants of the Jewish Quarter crates full of fresh vegetables and 50 kilos of carp.

The distribution of passes for travel outside Jerusalem has not yet been organized. The Standing Committee is trying to arrange a 'just allocation'. About 500 people are already on the list and only 30 or 40 passes can be issued each day. Of course there are urgent cases, such as people with sick relatives, people from outside Jerusalem who have been 'stuck' in the city and people with tickets to go abroad. An additional problem is the fact that several air and shipping companies charge an extra fee for obtaining an 'exit pass' in Egged's armored vehicles. The Transport Committee attached to the Standing Committee will bring charges against these companies. Now the public is complaining that recommendations for exit passes are usually given unjustly, for people with 'pull'.

*

Thirty judges, including lawyers, merchants and public figures, sit on the special courts set up by the Communal Council. In urgent cases Magistrate Dr. A. Perlmutter sits alone. Eight decisions have recently been handed down and goods whose prices were raised unreasonably, which were hoarded illegally or were hidden without being distributed as required, were confiscated.

During the proceedings the judges are not bound by any fixed procedure, conducting the trial on the basis of their understanding and conscience. The prosecutor is appointed by the Public Prosecutor. Forms have been issued for submitting claims and complaints. Various kinds of punishment have been instituted, including reprimand and warning, suspended sentence, cessation of supplies for a defined time, cessation of transport, forced sale, confiscation, closure of business, fines and publication of sentence.

In some instances, as soon as the matter was brought before the Supervisory Committee of the Supplies Committee, the accused paid a voluntary fine even before the matter was brought to court.

29.1.1948

The poet Uri Zvi Greenberg has been awarded the 'Bialik Prize' for 1948. He has donated the prize money, IL100, to the children in the Old City. In a letter to Yitzhak Ben-Zvi, the President of the National Council, the poet wrote:

"On the night of the ceremony when I was awarded the 'Bialik Prize' for 1948 I sat and thought to myself: If the Temple still stood I would go up to Jerusalem and offer a sacrifice at the altar. But since our glory is departed from the mount, I will go to Jerusalem and present the money I was given, one hundred pounds, to the Jewish children in the Old City. Because of the dangers on the roads and the siege imposed by our enemies I am unable to do as I wish. My heart leaped with joy today when I read in the paper of your statement, President of the National Council, that the National Institutions are firmly resolved 'not to evacuate Jewish Jerusalem inside the walls' etc. My heart rejoiced and I hereby send you, through the Jerusalem branch of 'Haaretz', my 'Bialik Prize' for the benefit of the precious Jewish children in the Old City of Jerusalem, the crown of the Jewish nation, to which all our eyes are turned.

I know that the sum is far smaller than the need, but this is all I have. Accept this gift from my heart, a gift of love, which does not yet have a kingdom of its own, neither currency of its own, just the currency of dreams. Let others arise and do as I have done, each man according to the dictates of his heart, and let this be a public affirmation of the National Institutions' firm resolve to preserve the heart of the nation, which lies within the sacred walls, for our life is no life without Jerusalem.

With greetings to the guardians of the wall in Jerusalem and the precious Jewish children within it, for the freedom of our Jerusalem.

Uri Zvi Greenberg"

30.1.1948

At a press conference Dr. Bernard Joseph (later Dov Yosef), chairman of the Jerusalem Committee, denied a statement made to reporters by the Mandate Government spokesman to the effect that the British "allow Jews to enter or leave the Old City freely". As an example Dr. Joseph cited the case of Rabbi Yitzhak Ornstein, the Chief Rabbinate's supervisor at the Western Wall, who has been in the New City for several weeks, and is unable to return to his home and work in the Old City.

The British police, for reasons of their own, have helped to empty the Old City of its Jewish inhabitants. The journalists have been summoned on various occasions and asked to write in their papers that the police wish to help those Jews who are ready to leave the Old City, which is in danger, and move to the New City. There were a few who submitted to the temptation and informed the authorities that they were leaving their homes, thinking to return once the troubles were over. But most of the residents of the Old City paid no heed to the 'advice' of the British, informing them: we are staying.

About thirty shells fired partly by British soldiers fell on the Jewish Quarter of the Old City during the last two days, destroying several houses and wounding a number of people. By a miracle no one was killed.

The Jews are angry because a day before the bombardment the High Commissioner called on 'Jews and Arabs' to keep the peace in the Holy Land. Everyone regards this as part of a British-Arab plot to force the Jews to leave the Old City.

                                                                        2.2.1948

This time the enemy directed his wrath at the heart of Jerusalem. It is symbolic that the building against which they acted was that of the English-language Jewish paper, the Palestine Post. Last night at eleven, Jerusalem was rocked by the sound of a huge explosion as a car loaded with explosives blew up in Hasollel Street, between the 'Post' building and Glick's paper warehouse. Fire broke out in the cellar and quickly spread to other buildings. Chief Rabbi Uziel lives in the next building.

It has since become apparent that this happened only because the members of the 'People's Guard' (Mishmar Ha'am) have strict instructions not to search British cars going through the barriers. Only because of the freedom enjoyed by the British 'guardians of the law' could British collaborators with the Arabs go through with their automobiles, taking with them a truck full of explosives. That is how a truck went through the barrier next to the Regional Governor's house and entered Hasollel Street without anyone attempting to stop it. This street is regarded as the 'Fleet Street' of Jerusalem, as the offices of 'Haaretz' are situated there and the agent of 'Yediot Aharonot' is on the ground floor of the same building. The offices of 'Hamashkif', 'Al Hamishmar', the U.O. and S.T.A. press agencies and the British Government censor are also in the same building.

The position of the workers in the basement where the Palestine Post is printed was difficult and dangerous. Their colleagues and members of the 'People's Guard' as well as several journalists and passersby who rushed to the spot, brought them out and saved them from the flames. Several employees of the newspapers and the various agencies escaped because the stairs did not collapse. A printer, Haim Farber, and a woman were killed instantly. Sixteen of the compositors were wounded. The explosion blew off the roof of the adjacent building, which housed the 'Ahva' Press, where the Histadrut's journal, 'Haolam' (The World) was printed.

Serious damage and incalculable loss was incurred by the auther and journalist, Abraham Almaliah. His immense archive of important manuscripts on North African Jewry and personalities, documents on the history of the Jews of Jerusalem and its resettlement as well as a large quantity of material concerning the activities of the 'Alliance' in Israel was all burned.

Many windows were shattered in the nearby buildings. Cars parked in the street were overturned, iron shutters were bent and trees uprooted. Ambulances of Magen David Adom (the Jewish Red Cross), whose center was in Hasollel Street, were seriously damaged. Among the wounded was the landlord, Mr. Amnon White, and his wife, Sarah.

Journalists and all the residents of Jerusalem were happy to hear that soon after the explosion the 'Post' editorial board moved to the 'Hamadpis Lipschitz' Press and continued printing the paper. The Palestine Post appeared the following day at its usual time, though in a smaller edition. This proved that what David Courtney wrote in an editorial, that 'the truth will defeat the explosives', was not just an empty phrase. Many people purchased a copy of the reduced edition of that historic paper so as to keep it as a souvenir.

Most of the Tel-Aviv morning papers carried articles praising the employees of the Palestine Post, commending its regular appearance and vigorously condemning the perpetrators of the explosion. The Palestine Journalists' Association sent a congratulatory cable to the editors of the 'Post' today, saying, amongst other things: "We are sure that this attack will not shift you from your courageous position or deter you from continuing your activities". In the second part of the cable the National Association of Journalists expressed "anger and dismay at the dastardly attack", sending the paper and its employees its condolensces at the loss of life and property.

The Jewish daily, 'Hayom', appearing in Jerusalem wrote an editorial headed, 'Bloodied but Unbowed', containing the following passage:

"The family of Hebrew journalism heard with pride and gratification that the employees of the Palestine Post went straight after the tragedy to print their paper at another press, having been forced to flee their flame-enveloped home. Despite the despicable crime which destroyed the Palestine Post building, and despite the fact that most of today's paper had already been set in print when the explosion occurred, the Palestine Post will nevertheless appear today. Its reduced format will be regarded as a mark of honor and distinction".

The other Jewish journalists who were in or near the building at the time of the explosion did the same as the employees of the Palestine Post. They did their jobs and contacted their editorial offices. The Jewish reporter, who continued doing his work under fire, identified with the other defenders of the Yishuv in the battle, for 'we are chips of the same block'.

*

The inhabitants of Israel argue at great length about the name of the Jewish State which is soon to be established. First of all, we will abandon the initials, EI, and the brackets in which this term has been enclosed since the British conquest of our land. Henceforth we will be able to write clearly on every publication, Eretz Yisrael (the Land of Israel). It seems that this will be the name of the new State, why not? It is, after all, its oldest name, a Biblical name, Eretz Yisrael. Perhaps in brackets we'll write (Jewish State). Another suggestion is Judah or 'State of Judah'. The name, the Jewish State in Eretz Yisrael, was proposed in one newspaper. Another suggestion was, State of Eber, its inhabitants to be called 'Hebrews', derived from the verse, 'For indeed I was stolen away out of the land of the Hebrews', which is what Joseph said to Pharoah's butler. For the moment the name of the new State is a great unknown. The main thing is that there should be no delays in its establishment.

*

4.2.1948

The day after the explosion at the Palestine Post we went to the home of the 'Rishon Letzion', Chief Rabbi Ben-Zion Hai Uziel, and found him and his household calm and smiling. They were extremely joyful and grateful to the Lord that they had been spared in the explosion in Hasolled Street, where their house is.

The Communal Conucil blessed the rabbi and his family with the Benediction on Deliverance. The rabbi reminded us of the verse in the Book of Zechariah: 'Jerusalem shall be inhabited as towns without walls for the multitude of men and cattle therein. For I, saith the Lord, will be unto her a wall of fire round about, and will be the glory in the midst of her'. (Zechariah 2, 4-5).

These blows, the Chief Rabbi said, are like scratches to us. As he spoke he showed us additional verses: 'As the mountains are round about Jerusalem, so the Lord is round about his people from henceforth even for ever'. (Psalm 125, 2)

The Chief Rabbi pointed to other verses with evident joy: 'Jerusalem is builded as a city that is compact together'. (Psalm 122, 3) 'A city that makes all Jews friends'. (Jerusalem Talmud, Tractate Hagigah, 3).

Thus the Rabbi went from one verse to another, encouraging himself and his audience, both Jews and non-Jews, to face the difficult days with stout hearts and firm faith.

*

The explosion at the Palestine Post building and the other houses in Hasollel Street brought a fresh stream of people in need of attention to the Communal Council. Representatives of the community went to the damaged houses and determined what should be done.

The Communal Council asked the Economic Council in Tel-Aviv to consider Jerusalem's financil needs in planning supplies for Tel-Aviv. The feeling is that now more than ever Jerusalem needs the financial assistance of others.

*

The British Acting Mayor of Jerusalem, R. Graves, informed the institutions that the British Government intended appointing six hundred policemen, half of them Jews and half Arabs. They would constitute a 'municipal police force' and each unit would receive a hundred rifles. A British officer would be in charge. Despite the fear that the weapons would be transferred to the Arab gangs, and despite the fact that the cost would be borne primarily by the Jews, who consititute the majority of the city's inhabitants and will have to pay IL 75,000 for the arms, the Jewish National Institutions agreed to this plan.

The position of Jewish clerks in Government offices is particularly difficult. After weeks of danger, shooting and attacks, the Jewish Clerks informed the heads of the Government offices that they would go to work only if they were protected. This week the English heads said to them: "We will not provide any protection. If you think it is dangerous, don't come".

*

The shortage of fuel is becoming more and more acute. The possibility that the Arabs will prevent oil supplies from reaching the U.S. has also been mentioned. The press has reported that James Forrestal, the American Minister of Defense, has said that the loss of Arab oil could endanger the continuation of the Marshall Plan, the vast aid plan for Europe.

It has been said that the U.S. government will buy the private oil companies so as to assure a supply of oil for itself and its allies.

Offices have been opened in townissuing tickets with which to buy oil twice a week. Each head of a family will receive three quarters of a can (about 15 liters). Single people will receive a quarter can (about 5 liters). The Supplies Committee has announced that the payments demanded by some of the neighborhood committees in return for 'ration cards' for the distribution of foodstuffs are illegal, and no such payment should be made.

*

Meanwhile, the various spheres of Mandatory government are collapsing. The main post office and most of the branches in town have been closed. Letters have accumulated in the mail boxes.

There are rumors that Arab mail clerks destroy letters from Jews to friends and relatives in the U.S. The situation regarding telephones is worse. They are particularly obstreperous to anyone requesting a 'trunk' call out of town. Sometimes one has to wait seven or eight hours for a call. The Post Office chief promised journalists that calls to their editorial offices in Tel-Aviv would be put through quickly, but this promise has not been kept.

*

"Jerusalem is crumbling", one of my Arab colleagues, Farah, a reporter for 'A-Difa' which appears in the Old City, said to me. "No mail, no newspapers, no food and no Government services. How long can the Jews take it?" he asked me.

"We have a God in heaven", I replied", our leaders have taken everything into account. The Arabs may yet regret what they are doing. It's a pity as we could have been good neighbors, and maybe we still will be".

Farah shrugged his shoulders and hurried to the offices of his paper in the Old City, while I went to my branch office. We each filed our copy to our papers, each one in his own way, concerning the events of the day.

6.2.1948

The Jewish Agency spokesman, Walter Eitan, at his daily press conference, praised the dedication of the employees of the Palestine Post in continuing to work as usual, making sure that the paper appeared regularly. He also thanked the foreign correspondents who had taken an active part in salvaging what could be saved.

At another conference, the Jewish Agency spokesman issued the following statement to home and foreign correspondents concerning the perpetrators of the crime:

'A careful investigation is being conducted as to those responsible for the explosion. At present there is no evidence as to who did it. The B.B.C. hastened to announce that it was the work of 'Arab or Jewish terrorists', but there is as yet no proof that it was done by 'Arab terrorists'. The Jewish Agency has sent a vigorous protest to the Government regarding the circumstances of the explosion, particularly in view of the fact that the People's Guard is not allowed to stop and search military vehicles. The explosives were brought last night in a Dodge truck'.

A journalist asked: Was it a military truck?

The spokesman replied: Apparently. Its registration number is known.

Question: Have the authorities promised to cooperate with the Jewish Agency in the investigation?

Answer: The authorities have noted the Jewish Agency's demand. If there are clear results, the Agency will publish them.

The foreign correspondents in Jerusalem informed their papers that reliable information has reached the authorities that British policemen were involved in the explosion at the Post building. The men involved got away in a Humber, one of the automobiles used by the British police in Palestine, with the registration number M 746.

In answer to other questions put by reporters, the Jewish Agency spokesman said that events which had occurred at the police station in Meah Shearim near the time of the attack aroused serious suspicions. A British sergeant had left the station suddenly, contrary to regulations and in an unusual manner. A few minutes later two other British sergeants had left the station. One of them used a Humber car with the registration number M 746. The explosion occurred half an hour later.

About ten minutes after the explosion the three men returned to the station and went up to their rooms on the second floor, breathing heavily. They did not record their departure and return in the station log book.

A few days later someone phoned the Post's operator and asked her if she understood English. When she said 'yes', he said: 'The Post building was blown up by British policemen, including me', and rang off.

The next day, when the British police inspector came to continue investigating the crime, the telephonist told him of the call. The police officer said to her: "You've got no sense of humor".

What the Mandate Government 'did not know' is common knowledge throughout the Yishuv. The underground broadcast of the 'Voice of the Jewish Defender' (Kol Hamagen HaIvri) has revealed that it has been proved beyond all shadow of a doubt that British policemen blew up the 'Post' building in Jerusalem. Their names and the numbers of the vehicles they used in reaching and leaving the scene of the crime are known. The Jewish Agency has transferred all the evidence it has gathered on this subject to the authorities[1].

8.2.1948

The Rabbi of the Western Wall, Rabbi Ornstein, is still cut off from the Jewish Quarter and the Western Wall in the Old City. The Communal Council is trying to get permission from the British for him to return to his home there. There are mothers in the New City who are unable to return to their small children.

The convoy of food for the Jewish Quarter is also being held up and the authorities delay providing guards to protect it.

*

Internal publications of the Haganah state that important secret documents have come into their hands. They reveal that the Arab High Council spies on the actions of King Abdullah and his court.

This spy ring is headed by Emil Guri, one of the leaders of the Arab High Council and a resident of the Baka neighborhood of Jerusalem. He goes to Ramallah every day, accompanied by a heavy complement of Arab guards. The Haganah has brought its information about his deeds to the knowledge of the Transjordanian Government.

11.2.1948

The authorities and the public are preoccupied with problems arising from the weight and price of bread. The price of a standard loaf of

---

[1]   Details on the background of British anti-Semitism to the explosion at the 'Post' building were published by Haviv Canaan in his book, *The War of the Press*, pp. 258-262.

bread is 34 mills. The bakers were recently given permission to add four mills onto the price of a loaf, but they added six. The Communal Council opposes this and has appointed a committee to examine the question. In the meantime an increase of four mills only is in force.

*

In heavy rain the convoy has reached the Old City, enabling residents who have been cut off from their homes and families to return there at last. The British checked the list of passengers very carefully, lest an extra Jew should enter the besieged Jewish Quarter, God forbid. Shoes were sent in addition to the usual items of food.

The 'Misgav Ladah' hospital in the besieged Jewish Quarter has informed us that the first boy to be born during the blockade has been delivered and that they are waiting for the authorities' permission to send in someone to perform the ritual circumcision.

*

The Communal Council has decided to impose a temporary room tax, in addition to the community tax, of between 100 and 250 Palestine mills per room per month.

*

The Communal Council has received a letter from the Jewish prisoners in the Gilgil camp in Kenya. Amongst other things, they write:

"The last few weeks have increased our fears that developments in Palestine will serve as an obstacle to our return. Do whatever you can to make the appropriate authorities bring us back. The mood in the camp is very tense as a result of the grim news from home".

The leaders of the community immediately transferred the message to the District Commissioner, who passed it on to the central authorities.

*

Transport problems in the city are growing. People are afraid and worried about what will happen, but there is no panic or dismay.

13.2.1948

The British commit one disgraceful act after another. British policemen entered a house in the Old Beth Yisrael quarter, and arrested four youngsters, members of the Haganah, on the grounds that they were 'suspects' who had to be taken for questioning. The four were Eliyahu Kessler, Naftali Scholl, Leon Shalom and Shimon Nisni, all of them aged nineteen or twenty. They were taken away in a tender. About two hours later the police were informed that the bodies of four young Jews had been found near the New (Lion) Gate, on the road to Jericho.

A British sergeant-major admitted that he had 'released' the youngsters on the way to the Old City, near the Damascus Gate. It transpired that the British had in fact taken them to the Damascus Gate, where they had handed them over to the Arab mob in return for a few bottles of beer.

This foul deed, which made our blood boil, served as a turning point. The commander of the Jerusalem region, David Shealtiel, has ordered Jews to resist searches made by British policemen who are not accompanied by Jewish policemen. Abraham Arest, one of the Haganah leaders, framed the following announcement, which was broadcast several times by the Haganah station, Kol Hamagen HaIvri ('The Voice of the Jewish Defender in Jerusalem'):

'Last night four Jews were murdered in cold blood by British troops. Four defenders were arrested on the pretext that a search was being conducted. They did not resist, thinking that they were under the protection of the British army. They were found dead in an Arab area an hour later.

'Consequently I command:

'Henceforth all Haganah members in Jerusalem should forcefully resist any search for arms or arrest by British forces who are not accompanied by Jewish policemen'.

The President of the National Council, Y. Ben-Zvi, demanded that the High Commissioner and the commander of the British forces appoint a committee to investigate the crime and try those responsible. The British, as usual, replied: 'An investigation has been opened'.

The Jewish Agency spokesman told reporters that there is a connection between the hostility to Jewish prevalent among the heads of the British Government in Palestine and the acts of British soldiers of lower rank. This explained their participation in appalling acts such as these.

That day did indeed serve as a turning-point. Jewish defenders no longer submitted to arrest by soldiers or policemen who were not accompanied by Jewish policemen. The British authorities apparently realized that this time they had gone too far. British soldiers or policemen were no longer permitted to enter Jewish areas unless escorted by Jewish policemen.

Then, as if by magic, the cases of Jewish children wounded by mines which British soldiers had 'forgotten' here and there in the fields near Jewish houses, ceased.

The Communal Council sent the following letter to the Jerusalem District Commissioner:

'The Jewish inhabitants of Jerusalem were shocked by the coldblooded and calculated murder of four members of the Haganah, whose bodies were found last Thursday near the New Gate in Jerusalem. Those four men were arrested, disarmed and taken away by the army in a military vehicle. They were not tried or taken to a police-station or gaol, nor were they returned to their homes. Their bodies were found in an Arab district where Jews have been killed in the past. The only possible conclusion is that they were handed over by the soldiers who arrested them to their murderers or that they were murdered in cold blood by the soldiers and their bodies placed near the New Gate, where they were found.

'Since the beginning of the disturbances we have witnessed the indifference of the security forces to the Jewish population of the city.

Jewish property has been burned and pillaged while soldiers and policemen stood by without lifting a finger to prevent it. Jews have been killed before the eyes of the policemen and soldiers, whose only reaction was to disarm the Jews. The vile deed of last Thursday was, however, the peak of the acts of provocation perpetrated by the security forces in Palestine.

'The Jewish population of Jerusalem will not be silent or calm until the perpetrators of this heinous crime are brought to trial and punished with all the gravity of the law, so that this may serve as an example to others'.

20.2.1948

The Mandate Government's spokesman, Stubbs, told reporters that an agreement for the disarmament of the Old City of Jerusalem will soon be signed. He maintained that the security situation there is 'improving' and that the number of armed Arabs infiltrating into Palestine from the Arab countries 'is also growing smaller'. The spokesman did not, however, have an explanation as to how the Arabs had managed to transfer the badly-wounded attackers of Tirat Zvi from Beisan to hospital in Damascus.

The Jewish Agency spokesman has refuted every claim made by the Mandate Government spokesman, citing several facts to prove how false is the neutrality to which the British adhere. British weapons are sold to Arab states in the knowledge that they will reach Palestine. Jews in the Old City live in a state of siege and the authorities do not lift a finger to raise it. The Arab Legion, whose officers and arms are British, is still stationed within Palestine, even though it is known that its soldiers are involved in Arab attacks on Jewish villages, and so on.

*

Jewish residents of the Old City who have immigrated from Morocco, Tunisia and Algeria in North Africa have applied to the

French Consul (since these countries are French colonies) and asked him to come and see how difficult their plight is. They have also requested that the French Consul, through his government, appeal to the British authorities to change their inhuman behavior.

*

Today an Arab mob set fire to a lovely little synagogue of the Yemenite community in the Nahlat Shimon quarter. We often prayed there, joining the congregants in sitting on the carpets spread on the floor. The authorities made no attempt to find out who had destroyed a place of worship in the Holy City.

22.2.1948

The enemy continues to sow death and destruction in Jewish Jerusalem. Trucks loaded with explosives blew up at six this morning in Ben-Yehuda Street, at the heart of Jewish Jerusalem. More than fifty men, women and children were killed when three large buildings collapsed, burying their occupants beneath the ruins. It is reported that an armored police vehicle led the convoy of trucks. A British policeman sitting inside the armored truck indicated to the Haganah man at the barrier to the Romema Quarter that 'it's alright', and they were allowed to pass.

The trucks stopped in Ben-Yehuda Street, their drivers set the explosive devices and went away.[2] The buildings which were completely destroyed included the Atlantic Hotel, the Wilenczok building and many stores. Ben-Yehuda Street, an important center of Jerusalem, has become a pile of rubble (see Appendix 4).

---

[2] It was later learned that an Arab. Azmi Jaouni, was sitting next to the policeman, and that the truck drivers were Britons who had deserted from their units and joined the gangs of Arab murderers. Two of them, Eddie Brown, who had been an officer in the British police, and Peter Marsden, had also both participated in blowing up the Palestine Post building in Hasollel Street.

After collecting evidence about the crime and dealing with the most pressing needs of the survivors, the Communal Council issued the following announcement, 'To Jewish Jerusalem':

'At the sight of the loss and destruction suffered at the heart of Jerusalem, as the smoke still rises from the ruins and the efforts to locate and save any survivors continue, the Communal Council calls on the inhabitants of Jewish Jerusalem:

— To maintain order and discipline, and to unite in suffering;

— To make renewed efforts to rebuild what has been laid waste and re-establish the town center;

— To extend a helping hand to accommodate those who are homeless;

— To show readiness on the part of artisans to mend and repair the damage.

'The Communal Council requests that every worker, craftsman and trader in suitable materials will prefer to repair the homes of those affected by the blast than to erect new buildings.

'The Communal Council prohibits all price-rises and every exploitation of the situation by builders, carpenters, glaziers, painters and members of allied trades.

'The Communal Council asks owners of large apartments to allocate part of their homes for the homeless.

'Out of a sense of unity and friendship in suffering, we will march over the piles of rubble to construct and be victorious'.

25.2.1948

The heads of the Jerusalem Burial Society, Supreme Court Judge Gad Frumkin, Rabbi A. H. Zwebner and Israel Bardaki, the President of the National Council, Yitzhak Ben-Zvi, and the Regional Officer, Abraham Bergmann, have decided on the area of the Government's experimental agricultural station in the Sanhedria Quarter as a new cemetery.

This is the first time that one Burial Society, that of the Community, deals with burial. The Mount of Olives is divided into separate plots for the various communities and Burial Societies. A special part of Sanhedria has been set aside for the 'conditional' burial of people who have already purchased burial plots on Mount Scopus.

The first bodies to be buried in the new site were the fifty casualties of the explosion in Ben-Yehuda Street. Heads of institutions attended the funerals and the Chief Rabbis 'inaugurated' the area with a special prayer.

"AND THEY CAST LOTS UPON JERUSALEM..."

27.2.1948

The National Council for the Jews of Palestine has issued an announcement expressing its anxiety and concern at the discussions of the Council of Trustees concerning the legislation about the internationalization of Jerusalem. They fear that the Jews of Jerusalem will be a permanent minority in the Jerusalem Legislative Council which is about to be established there.

Robert Graves, the mayor of Jerusalem appointed by the Mandate Government, has threatened that from 1st April the municipality will cease to supply services since the inhabitants do not pay their rates.

Daniel Oster has noted that the Municipal Committee headed by Mr. Graves was appointed three years ago as a 'temporary' body to remain in existence for a few weeks only.

The Jews are not represented on this Committee. The solution proposed by Mr. Oster is to divide the city into Jewish and Arab areas, each section conducting the affairs of its citizens separately. Yitzhak Ben-Zvi, Head of the National Council, has come out against this suggestion, stressing the fact that the Jews have formed the majority of the population of Jerusalem for the last 75 years, and that institutions for running the city should take this fact into account.

28.2.1948

One hundred and eighty Jews served in the Transjordanian Border Force between 1940 and 1946. This force was established in 1922 by

82

the British and was funded and controlled by the Palestine Government. Its task was to guard the Transjordanian Emirate (before Abdullah became king he was the Emir of Transjordan) and later the borders of the Kingdom of Jordan.

The National Council of the Jews of Palestine opposed the establishment of this force initially, regarding it as the start of an Arab army. The British allowed Jews to serve in its ranks, though restricted their numbers severely. Between 1941 and 1943 the Border Force was deployed on the Syrian-Turkish border, and its men fought against Germany and the Axis forces. Jewish soldiers in this force in Syria helped the Jews of Aram-Tzuba (Haleb or Aleppo, in North Syria), bringing books or letters from Palestine to emissaries who operated in the underground there (including the author) or teaching Hebrew to the Jewish children of Aleppo and Damascus. Some of them helped to bring illegal immigrants from Syria into Palestine overland.

On the eve of the War of Independence the Transjordanian Border Force, under British command, declared its support for the Arabs. The Jews began to fear that this force would serve as a strike force against the young Jewish State, and their apprehensions were verified (Appendix 5).

In order to reinforce the impression of being 'neutral' in the Jewish-Arab conflict, Britain announced that it was disbanding the Border Force. In practice, this was done in order to enable the force to operate in a different guise, that of the 'Arab Legion', and to give it military freedom of action.

On the day the Border Force was disbanded, which was in effect the day the 'Legion' was established, the Haganah issued the following statement:

"It has officially been proclaimed that the Border Force is to be disbanded.

"The Minister for the Colonies, the High Commissioner and the Commander of the Army in Palestine have sent letters of thanks to this force, citing its efficient and loyal service and discipline for the 22 years

84 JERUSALEM UNDER SIEGE

of its existence. They have also expressed their regret at its disbanding.

"The Jewish population has a special account to settle with this force. The Border Force was established when the Palestine Supernumerary Police Force was disbanded. That force contained many Jews, some of them veterans of 'Hashomer' who regarded their membership in its ranks as the duty of a loyal Jew. In establishing the Border Force the authorities wished in effect to establish a force that would be 'free of Jews'. The Jewish institutions voiced their vehement opposition to its establishment. Most of the soldiers in the Border Force were Arabs and Cherkassians from both sides of the Jordan River. This Arab force, which was commanded by Arab and British officers, was unable to manage without the services of Jews as experts in radio operation, mechanics, etc. At one point there were 200 Jews in the Border Force, but their conditions of service were such that their number dropped to ten, in a force of 3,000 men.

"The Border Force began its existence as a camel-mounted border unit and developed into a fighting formation and military unit of cavalry and motorized battalions, stationed initially on the borders between Palestine and Transjordan and later moving to the eastern part of Transjordan. At times almost the entire force was stationed in Western Palestine.

"We have very clear memories of the time when the Border Force was stationed in Palestine. Its soldiers often attacked the inhabitants of Jewish villages near which it was situated, raping women, stealing our possessions and attacking our men. This Force was particularly cruel in preventing illegal immigration by Jews along Palestine's northern border. We have not forgotten the bloodshed at Kfar Giladi, when soldiers of the Border Force murdered Jews at the command of their officers. This force has made its contribution to the slaughter of Jews during the last few months too.

"The British Minister for the Colonies, the High Commissioner and the Commander of the Army in Palestine have all expressed their 'gratitude to the Border Force for the discipline it has maintained throughout'. Does this refer to the soldiers, whose number exceeds one thousand, who deserted during the last few years?

"And when the British Ministers in Palestine thank the Border Force for its loyal service throughout the years of its existence, do they mean the service the Border Force gave the British Army during the World War? Let us remind them, then, that when the Nazi revolt of Rashid Ali Al-Kilani broke out in Iraq and a squadron of the Border Force was despatched to defend the oil pipe-line, the soldiers refused to fight against the pro-Nazi rebels. Berlin radio broadcast a message of thanks to Shukri Amura, the Palestinian Arab who commanded the Border Force detachment which refused to participate in suppressing the Nazi revolt in Iraq. Berlin radio noted then that thanks to Shukri Amura the Border Force had not helped subdue the rebellion, and under his command might even join the forces of Rashid Ali.

"With the dissolution of the Border Force, most of its soldiers and officers will probably join the armies currently infiltrating into the country to take an active part in the British-Arab assault on the Jewish population and the United Nations. It was not for nothing that the Commander of the British army in Palestine wished all the officers and men of the Border Force every success in the future. It is hard for us to join in these wishes. The Commander of the Army in Palestine was undoubtedly correct in stating, further on in his letter, that the disbanding of the Border Force would be regretted primarily by those who had served in it.

"The question to be asked is: to whom will the considerable quantities of arms and equipment of the Border Force be given? Will this also find its way to the gangs?

"We have demanded that the violent Border Force be removed from Palestine. The official disbanding of this force as the attack on our enterprise is about to be intensified requires additional vigilance and readiness on our part".

1.3.1948

The expanded Standing Committee (The Communal Council plus the members of the Select Committee) has discussed the matter of permits for travelling outside Jerusalem. A committee has been appointed to deal with it in coordination with the security institutions. On the committee are M. Baram, Feivel Meltzer, Zvi Schwartz and H. Gerling. Permission to leave the city will be granted only for urgent medical reasons or an important public mission.

The Religious Council of the Jerusalem community has issued the following statement: "Malicious tongues have proclaimed falsely that the permission granted to supply provisions to Jerusalem on the Sabbath was given by the Secretary alone. The truth is that the permission was granted by the Rabbi of Jerusalem, The Gaon R. Z. P. Frank, in the presence of the Secretary of the Religious Council, Rabbi Zaslanski, and Rabbi P. Nathan of the National Council. On the same Sabbath morning the matter was brought before the Chief Rabbi, Rabbi Herzog, and he also agreed that the permission should be given. The rabbis asked only that the thing be done, as far as possible, without undue publicity and in a spirit of gravity, as befits a deed which involves saving Jewish lives".

2.3.1948

The question of the status and political future of Jerusalem occupies its inhabitants, the heads of its institutions and the media, despite the fact that we are all in a state of siege. There are those who approve or disapprove of the internationalization of the city, though the opponents are increasing in number. The demand that it should be attached to the State of Israel is swelling.

In the negotiations preceding the U. N. decision of November 1947, the representatives of the Jewish Agency agreed to the partition of Palestine, the establishment of a Jewish State in narrow borders and the international rule of Jerusalem. A year previously the leaders of the

Yishuv's institutions had agreed to even less, the entry into Palestine of 100,000 survivors of the holocaust and an annual quota of immigrants instead of an independent State. It was the British Mandate rulers and the Arabs in particular who caused our leaders to be less pliant, as the same thing happened to them as had happened to their forefathers: "And the Lord hardened the heart of Pharaoh..."

When the leaders of the Jewish Agency and the National Council, as a result of the circumstances of the time and the stubborness of Ernest Bevin (British Foreign secretary) as well as of the Arabs' refusal to 'have anything to do with the Jews', dared to mention the name of the 'Jewish State', they did not venture to demand that the Christian world recognize the right of the Jewish people to rule the Holy City.

The agreement to the internationalization of Jerusalem was given, of course, because there was no alternative, nor was there any hope of any other possibility. No one thought then how things would turn out. It was hoped that the City of Peace would not be included in the political or military arena and that Jerusalem, which was so dear to the hearts of all beliefs and faiths, would not be harmed. The leaders of the Jewish population made no attempt to conceal the assumption that the true meaning of the U.N. decision to internationalize Jerusalem was that Jerusalem would come under Christian rule. In view of the war between the Arabs and the Jews, the Christian countries decided to take the crown of Jerusalem and place it on the head of the Christian world.

The most amazing thing in all this is that still today representatives of the Yishuv participate in working out the details connected with the 'constitution' of the 'State of Jerusalem'. Messrs. Shertok (Sharett) and Oster as well as Dr. M. Eliash sat on the committee appointed by the U.N. to prepare the constitution, where they discussed borders, elections to 'State' institutions, the rights of its citizens, etc.

The committee has recommended that "International Jerusalem shall extend as far as Bethlehem in the south, Ein Karem in the west and Shuafat in the north". Our representatives' demand that the borders of the international city should be extended to include King Solomon's

88 JERUSALEM UNDER SIEGE

Pools in the south and Atarot with its airfield in the north was not accepted.

The committee has also recommended that "Jerusalem shall be declared an open city and no military force shall be stationed there. The Council of Trustees shall appoint a governor for the city who is neither Jew nor Arab, neither a member of the Palestinian State nor a resident of Jerusalem". In this way the job of governor was defined in such a way that only a Christian could fill it. This committee also changed the way in which the Legislative Council of the 'State of Jerusalem' was to be elected. Instead of proportional elections, the committee decided, contrary to the stand adopted by the Jewish representatives, that the Council was to consist of one third Jews, one third Arabs and one third Christians.

The Supreme Judge, it was laid down in the committee's recommendations, should be neither a resident of Jerusalem, nor an Arab nor a Jew.

The other paragraphs of the recommendations stipulated that, apart from a local police force, there should be an 'international police force' in the 'State of Jerusalem' numbering about 1,500 men, whose main function would be to guard the holy places and supervise events there. Hebrew and Arabic were to be the official languages, though English and French would be used in dealing with international institutions. Education would be supported by the 'State' and every group would be entitled to establish a separate educational network.

The arrangement, it was stated in a special paragraph, was to remain in force for ten years only. At the end of this time discussions regarding the relations between the two States and future arrangements would be renewed.

With heavy hearts the leaders of the Jewish National Institutions give their agreement to the partition resolution and the decision to internationalize Jerusalem, like the real mother in the judgment of Solomon, who cries out in agony: "Give her the living child, and in no wise slay it". On the other hand, because of the murderous attacks on

Jerusalem, the opposition to the internationalization of the city is growing.

The fact that Rabbi Meir Berlin, the leader of 'Mizrahi', supports the decision to internationalize Jerusalem has aroused much surprise. At a meeting with reporters in his house in Jerusalem the rabbi explained this in the following way

"The international rule of Jerusalem is by no means ideal. It is false", he said angrily, referring to statements made by certain circles, "to say that I have arranged meetings to disseminate this idea. On the contrary, may I live to see Jerusalem the capital of the Jewish State, for Jerusalem is our capital and will remain such for ever. It is the capital of the Jewish people and its country. But for the moment", he continued sighing, "we have no choice but to announce that we support the U.N. decision of 29th November which declared that Jerusalem was to be ruled by an international body, and we must uphold that decision".

"But why should we"? the journalists asked again.

Rabbi Berlin elaborated his theory, which was designed to prevent the division of Jerusalem into two cities, saying:

"If Jerusalem is not internationalized it will be split into two parts, one Arab and one Jewish. The Old City with all the holy places and the relics of our glorious days of yore will be in their part and then the Emir Abdullah (King Hussein's grandfather) will be King of Jerusalem, because the Old City is Jerusalem. That would be the greatest disaster in our entire history".

Some newsmen suggested that a 'referendum' be held on the subject of Jerusalem's political future. Others proposed that the decision be postponed for several years. Meanwhile some residents of Jerusalem referred to Tel Aviv in their letters as "the temporary capital of the State of Israel".

It is interesting to note that in a nationalist newspaper like 'Haboker' a reporter, Shalom Shwartz, expresses the fear that international Jerusalem will be surrounded by Arab villages. After taking it for granted that Jerusalem will be international he notes that any Jew who wishes to reach the City of David from outside will have to go through the Arab State. Further on in his article, however, Schwartz rejects the suggestion that several Arab villages in the less immediate vicinity be incorporated within Jerusalem, since this would artificially make the Arabs a majority within the city.

During the course of the deliberations on the future of Jerusalem, the British have attempted to minimise the number of Jews in the city. The Jewish Institutions cited a figure of 97,000 Jewish denizens of Jerusalem, 2,000 of them in the Old City. Something happened and the Zionist leader, Dr. Abba Hillel Silver, by a slip of the tongue, said that he represented the 75,000 Jews of Jerusalem when he addressed the Special Palestine Committee at Lake Success.

The newspapers, 'Hatzofeh' and 'Davar', supported the American proposal in order to claim that Jerusalem should be included in the Jewish State. Two weeks ago the Americans suggested that Jaffa should be included within the Arab State even though it would not be territorially contiguous with it. They spoke of creating a special 'enclave'. Articles in these papers demanded that our representatives adopt the American proposal regarding Jaffa and use it to include Jerusalem in the Jewish State.

Articles have appeared in various newspapers criticizing the Yishuv representatives, who are in too much of a hurry to take part in the discussion on the political future and international government of Jerusalem (Appendices 6, 7, 8).

*

4.3.1948

Another day of grief and mourning. Sixteen youngsters have been killed together with their commanding officer, Noam. They were returning by daylight from an action against Arab traffic on the Ramallah Road. Hundreds of Arabs surrounded them and they were killed after a long and heroic battle.

5.3.1948

The departure of Jews from Jerusalem, each on a different pretext, is worrying. It is thought that of some 100,000 Jews living in Jerusalem before the partition resolution, about 70,000 or less are left.

Many leave by virtue of their positions in government and public institiutions, for the State is being 'prepared' there. Numbers of people go because they are afraid of a siege or because they wish to live in a Jewish State and not an international city.

Public figures in Jerusalem note with pain that everything is being transferred to Tel-Aviv, the offices, the workshops, the factories and the industries. All the meetings of Jewish organizations, people and institutions and of the new bodies currently being established are held there, in Tel-Aviv. Jerusalem bleeds and looks enviously and anxiously towards Tel-Aviv, which is developing and growing both qualitatively and quantitatively. Lip service is paid to Jerusalem and every article and speech abounds with high-flown phrases about 'the heart of the nation' and 'the eternal capital', but Tel-Aviv is the capital in practise.

*

The residents of the Nahlat Shimon, Nahlat Yitzhak and neighboring quarters were forced to leave their homes this week and move to the center of town. They were accommodated in an underground hall belonging to the 'Alliance' School in Aggripas Street. Because time was short and firing could be heard in the vicinity of these neighborhoods, the inhabitants abandoned most of their possessions, taking whatever came to hand with them. Most thought they would be able to return after a while.

7.3.1948

The British have arrested Abraham Halpern, the commander of the Haganah, who is officially considered to be 'the representative of the community' of the Old City. He worked devotedly to ease the life of those cut off within the city walls and was the moving spirit behind the educational and social undertakings there. The British promise that they will send him back to the Old City, but it is doubtful whether they will do so.

The heads of the Institutions praised him, telling reporters that Halpern hed ensured that there was work for everyone' in the besieged Jewish Quarter. He got the old people to read psalms, the men to build fortifications and the youngsters to mount guard and form defense units. (Appendices 9-12)

8.3.1948

The disruption of communications between Jerusalem and the coastal plain is increasing. It takes hours to send a cable from Jerusalem to Tel-Aviv. The most disturbing point is the fact that Jerusalem is left without electricity. The paper, 'Hayom' for example, printed the following announcement this week "The supply of electricty to most of the Jewish areas of Jerusalem was interrupted yesterday, and as a result it was impossible to work the printing press. The newspaper is obliged, therefore, to appear in an edition reduced to half". The paper was in fact limited to two pages, was set by hand and had double spaces between the lines.

*

I have returned from a quick visit to the Jewish Quarter in the Old City. Anyone who lives outside the walls imagines life in the Jewish Quarter to consist of empty streets, closed stores, people staying home and no one going out unless on urgent business. In other words, a 'dead' neighborhood. But this is not so.

The true picture is very different. People walk about the streets, buy and sell, laugh and shout, study and pray, and the sound of prayer ascends from the synagogues and houses of study. Of course, the Jewish Quarter is under siege, but precisely for that reason it is encouraging to see how the inhabitants overcome the situation and continue with their lives, making an effort to adapt to siege conditions.

The most encouraging fact is that the number of Jews returning to their homes in the Old City is larger than the number leaving. The Public Committee there ensures that there is work for everyone. The old people study the Bible by day and by night. About 360 pupils attend the two schools, spending their free time at the club. There I also found the smiling face of Eliyahu Hacarmeli (Lolo), who has volunteered to work in the Jewish Quarter.

Children are the same wherever they are. Those in the Jewish Quarter are very well-acquinted with military terms. One hears them talking about 'Stens', 'Brens', 'Toffees' and 'Parabellums'. The schoolchildren are hard at work filling the windows with sandbags as protection against bullets and shrapnel.

A 'Young Defender ('Hamagen Hatzair') club has recently been opened in the Jewish Quarter for children in the 7th and 8th grades. The youngsters who have completed elementary school are organized in a unit of 'runners'. The people in the besieged quarter have nothing but praise for these youngsters, relating how they skip from one alleyway to another on various risky missions, 'under the noses' of the Arabs, and no one notices.

10.3.1948

The British Government Information Office issued an official announcement today stating that, "Three British policemen who deserted from the force were captured at the battle for Neveh-Yaakov when the Jerusalem Guard pursued an armored police vehicle without a number, and arrested it. The names of the British policemen are Stevenson, Ross and Ekhurst".

We have known for some time that British policemen and soldiers are ridden with anti-Semitism and aid and abet the Arabs in their attacks on our villages, and especially on Jerusalem.

Yesterday the Jewish village of Neveh-Yaakov served as the target of the murderers' assault. Four armored vehicles of the Arab Legion and one of the British police, in which the three policemen were found, took part. The armored vehicle and the policemen were captured by the defenders of Neveh-Yaakov and the policemen who helped them withstand the attack. The battle began at 2.p.m., when about two hundred rioters began advancing from two directions. For two hours they fired at the village, trying to draw nearer with the armored vehicles. Only afterwards, when the assailants had begun to retreat, did British policemen and a few soldiers arrive. In the meantime the British armored car with the three deserters had been taken. Stevenson and Ross had participated in bombing Ben-Yehuda Street. They are also accused of having murdered two Jews near Givat Brenner at the beginning of February. Ekhurst is also accused of murdering Jews.

Atarot was also attacked last night, and its defenders managed to repel the invaders.

*

The Communal Council has received a letter from the Railway employees, containing the following passages:

"We, the undersigned, laborers and clerks at Jerusalem Station, have ceased going to work because of the mortal danger involved. The Station is in the hands of Arab policemen who are liable to attack Jews at any moment which seems appropriate to them. As Jews who wish with all their hearts not to desert this position which is so important for the Jewish public, and because we are aware of the railway's importance in bringing supplies for the Jewish population, we are prepared, even at the risk of our lives, to attend our work in order to fulfill a function we believe to be essential for our nation.

"We have read that the authorities have decided to recruit six hundred supernumerary constables, half of them Jews, and we request that six Jewish constables be posted with arms to accompany the Jewish employees from the town to the station and to guard the railway station, the warehouses and the customs during working hours".

*

The Mandate Government's spokesman announced today that, "As a result of the theft of six mail vans by the Etzel, mail deliveries to the Jewish neighborhoods of Jerusalem will be stopped until the vehicles are returned".

When Jewish journalists asked the spokesman if mail deliveries had been stopped in the Arab neighborhoods as a result of the theft of two mail vans the previous week he replied that those had been vehicles of a different kind.

11.3.1948

Once again there has been a malicious attack at the heart of Jerusalem. The Arab chauffeur of the American Consulate, Anton Daud, using the fact that he was known to the guards, drove into the courtyard of the National Institutions, parked the Consulate's automobile, with its pennant, at the entrance to the Jewish Agency, and walked away.

The guard decided that the vehicle obstructed traffic where it was parked and looked for the chauffeur. When he could not find him, he himself drove the car to the entrance of the JNF (Keren Hayesod) building.

Soon afterwards the automobile, which was loaded with explosives, blew up, completely destroying a wing of the JNF building. Thirteen men and women were killed, including Dr. Leb Yaffe, one of the founders of the JNF. One hundred others were wounded[1].

---

[1] Abdullah El-Tal wrote as follows in his memoirs about the blowing up of the National Institutions buildings: "On the morning of 11th March 1948 the brave 'fedayun', Anton Daud, succeeded in driving his automobile loaded with explosives into the Jewish Agency building in Jerusalem, bearing the American flag. The vehicle blew up with a mighty explosion which rocked all Jerusalem. Many important people were killed, including Yaffe, the founder of the JNF, Ben Zvi, Shmuel Dov and other leaders of the Jewish Agency".

Thus El-Tal 'killed' leaders who continued to live on for many years after the establishment of the State, even though he had every opportunity of verifying the accuracy of his statement before he committed it to print.

The Jewish Communal Council issued the following announcement:

"Jewish Jerusalem was not shocked to its soul yesterday by the sound of the explosion, which was heard throughout the city, and which struck this time at the heart of the Jewish National Institutions. Together with our concern for the welfare of those who labor on behalf of the community, which brought thousands to the site of the explosion within minutes out of a desire to extend whatever help they could, it was possible to see on the faces of every inhabitant of Jerusalem: we shall not be intimidated, nor shall we be discouraged.

"The community of Jerusalem expresses its condolences to the National Institutions on the death of Leb Yaffe, one of the first to establish the legend and convert it into reality".

COMRADESHIP DURING THE SIEGE

12.3.1948

The dearth of basic foodstuffs is increasing. It is encouraging to note that women help one another. I saw women offering to exchange an item they had for one possesed by their neighbor. In this way flour was traded for sugar, oil for matches and a can of sardines for a can of fruit.

The Standing Committee deals with the problems of supplies for man and beast and also tries to prevent hoarding and ensure the equitable distribution of rations. The Committee issued an announcement that: "There is no fear of a shortage of kerosene or foodstuffs". People smile when they read it. Rumor has it that the residents of Jerusalem have stopped taking baths as all the bath-tubs are full of kerosene.

*

Some dispute appears to be inevitable in Jerusalem. While the Institutions and the population are looking for ways to solve the problem of supplies, a quarrel has blown up between the Communal Council and 'Agudath Yisrael' about the area of the new cemetery in Sanhedria. 'Yedioth Hakehilla' writes that Agudath Yisrael's claim that it has a separate cemetery is unfounded. The community news-sheet contained the following statement:

"It is obvious that just as the number of live members of Agudath Yisrael is minimal, obtaining representation on the various committees only by pressure and threats of resignation, the number of their dead is also small. Just as most of the living belong to the general congregation, so do most of the dead".

97

An additional controversy with Agudath Yisrael centers round the name of and authority for the 'People's Guard' ('Mishmar Ha'am'). Agudath Yisrael has protested that the People's Guard is subject to the Communal Council, on which it is not represented. They have proposed that the People's Guard be called: 'The People's Guard of Agudath Yisrael and the Communal Council'.

*

This year, 1948, the day following the end of Passover falls on a Saturday, meaning that we will have to eat matzoth (unleavened bread) for eight days this year. As it is we have barely enough flour for baking matzoth for the seven days of Passover.

*

The Jerusalem bus company, 'Hamekasher', has again requested permission to raise fares on all lines in the city. The Communal Council has permitted a certain increase: on regular routes the fare will be raised by 5 mills to 15 mills, including one mill 'Settlement Tax' and one mill for fuel. An increase of another fifteen percent has been approved for journeys within the city after eight at night. No decision has yet been made regarding the fares for travelling in armored vehicles to Talpiot, Mekor Haim and Mount Scopus.

16.3.1948

'The Messiah', a Jewish sage from Iran, Emmanuel Nissan, wanders around the streets of Jerusalem. He is a tall Bible scholar with blazing eyes and cannot remain silent when he sees the Sabbath violated. He lives a hermit's life in one of the caves of the Sanhedrin at Sanhedria. In order to fulfill the injunction, "thou shalt surely admonish", he places a chair at the entrance to the laborers' restaurant in the Histadruth building in King George Street, stands up on it and speaks of the obligation to preserve the Sabbath and the dietary laws (Kashrut).He also states that the victory of Jewish Jerusalem is assured, quoting verses from the Bible and the writings of the sages to prove his words.

*

There are rumors in the city that the Arabs have placed huge barriers "which cannot be removed" at Bab-al-Wad (Shaar Hagai). From Shaar Hagai to the village of saris stone walls have been erected, and God alone knows how and when our people will be able to remove these obstacles, enabling the convoys of food and ammunition to reach the city.

17.3.1948

Today the buildings of the Shneller orphanage passed into our hands, and the news gave rise to widespread rejoicing. For many weeks it has been feared that the Arabs would capture this camp, which was a thorn in the flesh of the denizens of the nearby neighborhoods, Geula, Meah Shearim, the Bucharan Quarter, etc. (Appendix 13).

19.3.1948

While we are still struggling to survive, gathering strength to withstand our attackers and anticipating the day when we will begin to be masters of our political and military fate, the American representative at the U.N., Austin, has proposed postponing partition and establishing a 'Trusteeship' in Palestine. Observers claim that the new proposal derives from the Americans' reluctance to send their army to the area. The papers write that the Americans fear the disruption of oil supplies to Europe and that they are no longer convinced that the Jews of Palestine are able to survive the attacks on interurban traffic.

24.3.1948

A food convoy has entered the Old City. Because of the limited number of vehicles available to the community, not all the parcels and goods prepared for this convoy were sent. A social worker, baby nurse and kindergarten teacher as well as some private individuals were also included in the convoy. About one hundred and fifty people have requested permission from the Communal Council to enter. The list was submitted to the Governor, together with an explanation of the damage and suffering caused to these people, who are cut off from their families in the Old City. The problem of the teachers who wish to return is particularly difficult. The British allow in only a few at a time, and there are very many who are separated from their homes.

The British apparently still hope that they will be able to cause as many Jews as possible to leave the Jewish Quarter, emptying the Old City of its Jewish inhabitants. The people living in the Jewish Quarter have said that anyone wishing to leave does not have to repeat his request. A brief declaration is sufficient for the British authorities to transfer him without delay to the New City.

It should be noted that to date not a single Jewish resident of the Quarter has made such a request. On the contrary, the Governor's office is flooded with applications to return to the besieged Jewish Quarter.

*

Several times a convoy was about to leave for Tel-Aviv but was delayed. It is said that mines were laid in the area around Neveh Ilan and that Haganah sappers went out to remove them. At last the convoy set off. Heaven knows when another one will leave for Tel-Aviv.

*

In the Romema Quarter I saw the sign 'This store is Jewish' displayed in several windows, so that our people do not blow it up. Here and there I saw the ruins of Arab stores and houses which had served as vantage points from which to fire at our traffic.

*

There are long lines for kerosene. Each can costs fifteen grush now. There are also lines for obtaining rations of sugar, coffee and a little rice. Water is distributed four or five times a week, each person being allocated ten liters per day.

*

Anyone wishing to go to Talpiot has to travel by armored vehicle. Yemin Moshe can hardly be reached. There are very few pedestrians in Talbieh, for fear of snipers on the walls. People run half-bent, or hug the walls of the houses.

1.4.1948

It is a pleasant feeling to participate in festivities and celebrations during these days of siege. The desire to survive and the feeling of 'Nevertheless and despite everything' prevail. Sorrow and joy, grief and happiness are intertwined in our lives, and in the life of a people which exists despite everything. The special circumstances of life in Jerusalem are also reflected in the nature of the celebrations. Thus, for example, a couple who recently got married received as wedding-gifts a chit for an extra can of water, a large quantity of spring onions, a sack of rice and an oil lamp. The newspaper report of this continued: 'These gifts were given to the happy couple instead of flowers, which are difficult to obtain in Jerusalem just now'.

*

The notice-boards in town are full of posters and announcements put out by the various organizations. In the 'Hamaas' posters Lehi calls on the Jews of Jerusalem not to leave the city. They demand that the

National Institutions bring ten thousand defenders from all over the country to Jerusalem in order to ensure that the city and its environs remain in Jewish hands, and that they should 'stop establishing the kingdom of Israel in Tel-Aviv'. The members of Lehi are particularly critical of the Institutions, which agreed to abandon the Nahlat Shimon and Nahlat Yitzhak quarters instead of populating them with defenders and fighters. In another broadsheet they welcome the emptying of the Lifta, Romema, Sheikh-Badr and Dir Yassin areas of their Arab occupants. They have warm words of praise for the Yeshiva boys, who organized themselves to defend Jerusalem and went out to dig trenches in remote neighborhoods even on Friday nights (when such work is forbidden).

In an indictment published by the Neturei Karta sect, we read:

"If the nations decide to give the Zionists a State in part of Palestine, we must state a loud 'no' and utilize every opportunity of declaring that the Bible opposes a Jewish State on the current basis, which means destroying the Jewish religion in the Holy Land. If, Heaven forfend, Ben-Gurion and his colleagues gain power, the orthodox community will disappear, education in secular schools will become compulsory and those members of the orthodox community who attempt to protest will be severely punished as dissidents. In the Jewish State we will be obliged to deny the Law of Moses. All the spiritual leaders of Israel reject the Jewish State".

*

The director of the Mandate Government Press Office has told reporters that the Government is unable to control the borders. There are 'infiltrators' and the situation is like 'a state of war'. The British spokesman condemned the despatch of the food convoy to the Etzion Bloc without giving the authorities prior notice. He said that the army can maintain law and order if it is given advance information about movements on roads.

The Jewish Agency spokesman rejected these claims, dismissing the Government Press Office spokesman's words as 'ridiculous'.

2.4.1948

Kol Hamagen HaIvri broadcast the following announcement: "The synagogue of Rabbi Judah the Hasid was damaged last night by shells fired by the British army".

British soldiers did in fact open fire on the Jewish Quarter of the Old City last night. The Government Press Office stated that Jews fired at an army position in the Old City and that the soldiers returned the fire with machine gune. Continuing his 'story', the British spokesman said that Jews used guns fitted with silencers, to which the soldiers replied with 'Fiat' anti-tank shells and heavy cannon. Yesterday was the first of April, and this was apparently a British 'April Fools Joke', since their imagination supplied us with a weapon we do not possess, a rifle with a silencer.

What really happened was that the army opened fire last night on our positions in the Old City, illuminated the Jewish Quarter with flares that were seen throughout the city and fired cannon and mortar shells. Our people did not return fire and there were no casualties. The 'Fiat' shells caused serious damage to the splendid Old City synagogue of Rabbi Judah the Hasid, however. The central chandelier fell and broke. The British are 'very apprehensive' as to the fate of the holy places, and now they have shown why.

The Chief Rabbinate sent urgent cables to the U.N., the British Prime Minister, Clement Attlee, and the Commander of the British Forces in Palestine, protesting the shelling of the Old City by the army. The cable, which remained unanswered, read: "The Chief Rabbinate in the Holy Land calls upon you to give your fullest attention to the regrettable fact that shells fired from the army barracks in the Old City on Thursday damaged the holy synagogue known as 'The Ruin'. The bombing broke the roof, causing the central chandelier to fall to the ground. This sacred

and historic building was damaged again yesterday by shots fired by
British soldiers. We vehemently protest this shameful desecration of a
holy place. We beseech you to take steps to prevent a repetition of the
damage caused to this and other synagogues".

In a cable sent to the High Commissioner, Rabbi Zvi Pessah Frank
wrote:

"We are shocked to the depths of our souls at the terrible desecration
by force of arms of the great and sacred synagogue in the Old City of
Jerusalem. Although because of the political situation the Jewish
community does not have access to the holy places, the fact that this
ancient and glorious synagogue was a target for enemy fire is a stain on
the record of the British Government, which has extended its protection
to the synagogue ever since it was restored and prayers were said in it
for the welfare of the kingdom, at the King's request.

Signed: The President of the Great Synagogue of Rabbi Judah the
Hasid, Zvi Pessah Frank, Chief Rabbi of Jerusalem".

Rabbi Frank also sent the following cable to the Association of
Rabbis of America:

"Raise the voice of protest, make the world resound at the malicious
damage caused by enemy forces to the holy place, the great synagogue
of Rabbi Judah the Hasid".

*

At an off-the-record press conference a doleful picture was painted of
Jerusalem's present position. The city is effectively cut off from the rest
of the country, apart from radio contact and occasional sorties by a
'primus' (small, two-seater plane). Essential supplies are almost
completely depleted. The communal leaders of Jerusalem and the
security forces have decided to break the siege. A plan known as
'Operation Nahshon', involving large numbers of soldiers, has been
drawn up. The objective is to gain control of the hills and villages along
the road between Jerusalem and Tel-Aviv, rid the hills around Shaar
Hagai of enemy forces and bring a large supply convoy into Jerusalem.

4.4.1948

The streets of Jerusalem resound to the 'unfinished symphony' of shots fired by rifles and machine guns. Mothers lull their children to sleep with the sounds of this 'music'. Our belief in the justice of our cause and in our future has not diminished and we feel that our victory is assured, whatever happens. We are confused and disturbed, asking questions to which there is no answer, except the phrase we have all adopted: 'Never mind, things will work out'. That is the reply spoken with a smile, in a spirit of acceptance and friendliness: things will work out, my friend.

With these words on our lips we set off to dig trenches and repel assailants, Strange, but in a cramped army position, under a hail of bullets, while death hovered overhead, I dreamt of green lawns, a pool of sky blue water, sunshine by day and electric light by night. I saw friends and acquaintances walking side by side, enjoying God's glorious world. Oh, when will those days come? Will we ever see them? With God's help we will. The clatter of machine gun fire brought me back to a world of killing, destruction and blood. How long? God knows.

5.4.1948

Who ever imagined that the road from Tel Aviv to Jerusalem would go via the Dead Sea? Today we discovered that this is the case. A group of inportant people who had to reach Jerusalem came that way. They included Bernard Joseph, Yitzhak Ben-Zvi and Yaakov Tzernovicz (Tzur), who was responsible for recruiting people to the defense of Jerusalem. They flew to the Dead Sea coast in a small plane from an improvised airfield near Tel-Aviv, landing near the 'Kalia' Hotel. They hoped to join the convoy taking phosphates to Jerusalem, which was accompanied by British soldiers. This time, however, they were in for a disappointment. The British declared that the inclusion of Jewish civilians in a convoy of phosphates would "annoy the Arabs", and they would not permit it any longer. And so the group returned to Tel-Aviv. (Appendix 14)

10.4.1948

I think that this is the first time in the history of Jerusalem that the city has been subjected to a cannon bombardment. For several hours we were shelled on Friday night and Saturday. At first we thought that no building would be left standing, the noise was deafening. We feared a large number of casualties, and the suspicion that we would not be able to hold out crept into our hearts.

But Jerusalemites become accustomed to cannon too. They sought shelter in cellars and the corridors of the houses. When night fell darkness enveloped the city, the 'contribution' of the British-Jerusalem Electricity Company.

The 'symphony' of shots fired from the Sheikh Jarrah area, where the British army holds sway, also ceased towards evening. The denizens of Jerusalem have learned, nevertheless, to walk at the sides of the roads, as close as possible to the walls, as a protection against snipers or indiscriminate firing. Automobiles speed past. Youngsters in the spring of their life sing as they go on their way, sweeping passers-by along with them and imbuing them with faith and confidence. Every vehicle stops at the barrier for a routine check. The man from the 'People's Guard' drags his legs and goes to check the occupants, yawning. Suddenly a joyful and surprised voice calls out from one of the cars: 'Father! Hallo, Father'.

Father and son meet here. The son is in the vehicle with the fighters and the father is on guard at the barrier.

The father disrobes himself of his official position and assumes the role of father, asking: 'Coming back or going out'?

And the son, without elaborating, answers: 'Going out'.

The barrier is raised and the vehicles speed through.

The father murmurs softly: 'God bless you'. His companion on guard responds: 'Amen, so be it'.

The inhabitants are full of praise for the drivers of the convoys bringing food from the coastal plain to Jerusalem. Groups of adults, including elderly people, set off to dig trenches, on the Sabbath and on

weekdays. The city is harnessed to the defensive effort and the War of
Independence.

*

As when Sennacherib, king of Assyria, besieged Jerusalem, today,
too, men like Shebna and his group have arisen. Saboteurs within the
camp are plotting to stab the nation in the back as it fights for its
freedom. 'Neturei Karta' ('The Guardians of the City') is their name,
although the public regards them as the destroyers of the city. They
distribute broadsheets decrying the war of the inhabitants of Jerusalem.

The heads of the Yeshivoth are moderate and fair-minded. Their
concern is that the holy law should continue to be studied in the
besieged city. They desire that there should not be a single day or hour
in which the Torah is not studied. The Institutions have released the
Yeshiva students from the obligation of participating in the battle.
Nevertheless, many of them help in digging trenches and some even join
the fighting forces. The Yeshiva students have been concentrated in one
battalion, 'The Benei Tuvia Battalion'. They justifiably regard the battle
for Jerusalem as a holy cause, and have also given their lives for it.

'Neturei Karta', on the other hand, has dissembled and deceived the
public by publishing a statement supposedly made by Rabbi Yitzhak
Hacohen Kook against participating in the war. His son, Rabbi Zvi
Yehudah, uncovered this base forgery, since Rabbi Avraham Yitzhak
Kook wrote this in 1917, thirty years ago, during England's war against
Germany.

11.4.1948

During the last two days we journalists have been summoned to
several press conferences concerning one subject, the conquest of the
Arab village of Dir Yassin by Etzel and Lehi forces. During the first few
hours after the news that the village was in our hands reached us we
were very happy. An Etzel officer handed out the following
communiqué:

ANNOUNCEMENT

"This morning fighting units of Etzel and Lehi attacked and conquered the Arab village of Dir Yassin, west of Jerusalem.

"Dir Yassin harbored a strong gang which terrorised the inhabitants of the Jewish neighborhoods in the west of the city with its sniping. We received information that special reinforcements of Iraqi and Syrian soldiers had arrived in order to conquer these neighborhoods.

"At 2.a.m. our soldiers set out in four groups for Dir Yassin. At 4.30 a.m., after the units had reached their destinations, the signal was given for the attack to begin. Despite the heavy fire directed at our forces by the enemy, which was in fortified positions, our units advanced in military order and stormed the enemy's positions. After the women and children had been evacuated the fortifications were blown up and dozens of enemy soldiers were buried beneath them. During the attack orders were given over the loudspeaker for women and children to leave the area immediately and take cover on the hillside. Most of them obeyed the instructions and were saved.

"Two of our armored vehicles advanced into the village, encountered a trench one and a half feet deep and remained stuck there. A unit of sappers managed, after strenuous efforts for more than an hour, to fill in the trench, despite incessant enemy fire.

"In hand-to-hand combat in the village our soldiers succeeded in conquering one house after another, gaining control of the village. The remnants of the gangs fled in panic and managed to entrench themselves in a house some distance from the village, on the way to the Castel. Meanwhile large Arab reinforcements arrived. An Arab gang came from Ein Karem, took up positions on the ridge of the hill facing Yefe Nof and opened fire with heavy machine-guns.

"Throughout the battle contact was maintained between the base and the units at the front. Reinforcements of men, equipment and food were sent in.

"Our losses so far include two dead, three badly wounded and several lightly wounded. Enemy losses are dozens of dead, at a conservative estimate. Our soldiers took prisoners of war, who were brought back to our base. A Jewish Red Cross armored vehicle came under fire as it evacuated the casualties.

"HaIrgun Hatzavai Haleumi, in Palestine, Jerusalem Headquarters. Lohamei Herut Yisrael, in Palestine, Jerusalem Headquarters".

*

A Haganah commander assembled the journalists this evening and expressed his reservations concerning the action. He mentioned the cruelty of the Etzel fighters to the Arab villagers, who 'had hardly fought at all', and rejected the statement made by an Etzel commander that the Haganah had known about the action in advance and had purportedly offered help too.

At a press conference organized by Lehi the claim that the Haganah had known about the action was reiterated and the Haganah officer's condemnation was censured.

The following day 1 received an 8-page document entitled 'The Lesson of the Dissidents' Action at Dir Yassin'. It was directed at Haganah soldiers and was published by the Intelligence Officer, Operations Branch.

The leaflet began:

"Instead of analysing the action of the two breakaway organizations at Dir Yassin on the morning of 9.4.1948, sections from three reports will be quoted below.

"1. The report by the Intelligence Officer, Abraham, to the Commander of the Jerusalem Region. Top Secret. This contains a description of the 'total disorder' which Abraham found among the members of Lehi whose commander had invited him to Dir Yassin on Friday 9.4.1948. At another point in the short report the officer writes: "All the members of the breakaway groups walked about the village stained with blood, boasting of the number of people they had killed. There was an evident lack of education and intelligence in them, in contrast to our soldiers".

"2.   The report by the Battalion Intelligence Officer to the District Commander. Top Secret. This report also contains a description of the slaughter of the villagers, the disarray among the soldiers and the ignorance of field training, etc. The following passage served as an 'appendix' to this report: 'It should be noted that the entire action was undertaken without the agreement of our forces. After the dissidents' liaison officer was informed of zero hour etc. Our positions were given the appropriate instructions regarding aid during the retreat, medical assistance, etc. Because the operation was militarily inadequate, it was decided to give supporting fire in the morning. This help was expressed in two ways: A. The road was blocked to the Arab reinforcements from Malha and Ein Karem; B. Fire was opened on the Arabs who had entrenched themselves on the western ridge of the village from the rear'.

"3.   The report of the commander of D Unit, Fourth Division of the Palmah to the Commander of the Jerusalem Region. Secret. At 6.30 were informed of the attack mounted by Lehi and Etzel on the village of Dir Yassin and of their desperate situation, being unable to evacuate their casualties. I asked the regional commander for permission and the reply was: 'You are to go to the ridge and provide cover for the removal of casualties only'. I advanced within the bloc to locate enclaves of Arabs and reached the center of the village. (A description of the disorder among the men of these two organizations, the absence of a commander on the spot to give orders, etc. follows). I went past a few more houses in order to check that the house previously noted was the one against which I had to act. The information appeared to me to be correct and I returned to my unit. I gave the order for three shells to be fired at the northern wing of the building, after which the firing stopped.

"At Givat Shaul I met the Lehi and Etzel commanders, who were very interested to hear what was happening at the village. I told them that my presence was unnecessary as the snipers had stopped firing and all that was needed now was to organize the brave fighters and take control of the entire village. I reported this to the Regional Commander and the orders I received were: 'You must be ready to provide cover for the removal of casualties or retreat when necessary, but do not intervene in any other combat activity. As an officer you are entitled to give them advice, should they request it'."

*

People from various groups in Jerusalem have expressed their pain and sorrow at the inner divisions among us even at this fateful and difficult time. The Second Temple was destroyed, they said, because the enemy besieging Jerusalem found its inhabitants divided among themselves. Today, too, we fight separately, with the Haganah in one camp and Lehi and Etzel in another. (Appendices 15-19).

12.4.1948

Jerusalem is dependent on other cities. Its bread is brought from afar. Its water is brought in from outside. If there is rain there will be water. Jerusalem is experienced in suffering and siege.

For 13 days no convoy has reached Jewish Jerusalem. Here and there we have been racked by doubts and illuminated by a ray of hope. We were truly glad when we heard that the defenders of Jerusalem had conquered the village of Castel and entrenched themselves round about it. And one fine day a long convoy of Jewish trucks wound its way up the road to Jerusalem. In the streets people spoke enthusiastically of the defense forces which had broken the blockade, removed the barriers and brought in the convoy. The soldiers took themselves off to their bases without saying a word, cracking jokes about the spring weather in the Jerusalem hills, as if what they had done was a mere trifle.

*

The men of the 'People's Guard' are at their positions in the streets of Jerusalem, beside the barriers, in the markets and in the thoroghfares. Housewives move from one line to another, from the one for kerosene to the one for vegetables, eggs and milk, And, praise be to the Lord, if one stands in line one can get almost everything. The sound of firing echoes through the outlying neighborhoods, as usual. There are 'experts' who can already distinguish between 'our' firing and 'theirs'. And apart from a few of little faith who are inveterate hoarders, thus encouraging price-rises and confusion, everyone helps his neighbor.

*

Here and there classes of schoolchildren can be seen with hoes in their hands, making their way to the fields to the west of Jerusalem to gather wild plants for food and flowers for decoration.

Our soldiers walk around the city. It is only because they are accustomed to nights of fear because of foreign soldiers that most inhabitants of Jerusalem remain at home from the early evening. But they are gradually getting rid of the habit. They are starting to organize meetings and lectures in the evenings, as well as evening clases for pupils and workers, dancing and musical performances. Mention has also been made of the intention to renew the 'Journalists' Newspaper' on Friday nights.

*

As 'departure day' for His Majesty's forces draws nearer, their hatred for our undertaking of revival becomes more obvious. Now they do not even bother to make any pretence of 'neutrality', leaving this to their 'spokesmen' and commanders. The rank and file and their officers openly support the Arabs. Mount Zion, the site of King David's tomb, who is also venerated by the Moslems, swarms with rioters under the noses of the forces in the King David Hotel and the Government Press Office building. From this building the Director of the Press Office and his associates watch rioters attack the Yemin Moshe neighborhood, and then compose pronouncements about 'exchanges of fire between Jews in Yemin Moshe and Arabs on Mount Zion'. And if the defenders manage to inflct a few casualties on the enemy, the army hastens to shell the Jewish neighborhood with cannon.

British army officers and police often visit the Sheikh Jarrah quarter, training the rioters in methods of destruction. With the aid of army floodlights in the Italian Hospital, the rioters destroyed several Jewish houses in the Nahlat Shimon and Nahlat Yitzhak quarters. The same applies to all the outlying quarters of Jerusalem. Under the auspices of the British army, which ensures that the Jewish defenders do not retaliate against the rioters, Arabs kill Jews every day.

*

This week the details of a Arab-British plot against the Jews of the Old City came to light. A plan of provocation had been planned in every detail, and in order to implement it the army had mobilized a scientific set-up headed by the Government Archaeologist, Mr. Jones Brashaw. The London 'Daily Express' published a horror story a week ago on its front page under the headline: 'Jews Digging Beneath the Old City, Plan to Blow Up the Church of the Holy Sepulchre'.

According to Lord Beaverbrook's Jerusalem correspondent, the Haganah is digging one tunnel towards the Christian holy place and another towards the Al Aksa mosque.

Information has reached the Haganah and was broadcast on Kol Hamagen HaIvri, that the Arab-British plot was to blow up the Christian and Moslem holy places and put the blame on the Jews. Now it transpires that the British press was also involved in this provocation.

Apparently the army has been laying its satanic plans for over a week, and the visit by British journalists on 4th April was intended to point out what had been achieved to date. All kinds of cock and bull stories about mined underground passages and rifles fitted with silencers have been taken out of the stores of the army and its civilian advisers in order to inspire fear of the Haganah in the Old City throughout the word.

Jerusalem Radio has also been roped in, and on 5th april it did its bit by broadcasting an item about a mysterious explosion in the Old City the previous night, which of course never occurred.

It is said that the British army even gave the grandiose plan the code-name 'Reichstag 1948'.

14.4.1948

A cruel and base massacre was perpetrated yesterday by the Arabs on the convoy travelling from town to the Hebrew University and 'Hadassah' on Mount Scopus. Seventy-eight doctors, scientists, nurses and workers were killed or burned by the Arabs in the blood-stained neighborhood of Sheikh Jarrah. The Arabs boast of their deeds, adding 'Dir Yassin' (namely, revenge). And again it is annoying to note that the massacre was undertaken 'under the noses' of the British, who even prevented help from reaching those under attac. (Appendix 20).

15.4.1948

Exciting rumors have reached the press corps and those in public positions. 'Foreign news sources' behind enemy lines have let it be known that Jewish leaders have met with Abdullah, the King of Transjordan. The Jewish Agency is at pains to deny these rumors, but the news continues to reach us from new and different quarters. I have not managed to get to the bottom of the rumor and to ascertain to what extent it is true. (Appendices 21-24).

*

We Jerusalemites are pierced as if by arrows when we see that instructions issued by our Institutions, the 'State on the way', originate from Tel Aviv. Will Tel Aviv really be the capital of our State? Today, for instance, we read the following statement, signed by the Jewish Agency for Palestine and the National Council:

"Until further notice, all Jewish government employees are required to continue working in their present offices, so that no harm is caused to public services when the Mandate Government leaves".

A group of Jerusalem reporters and foreign correspondents toured the Tel-Aviv — Jerusalem road. The Haganah officers told us of the conquest of observation points along the route and of the chances of keeping the road open to traffic.

A British journalist asked whether the Haganah intended to hold on to this road. The officer replied briefly: 'We received an order to open the road, and we did so'. Another foreign correspondent asked: 'What is the Haganah's policy of conquest?' The young Officer smiled and said: 'Any place which interferes with our patrols is taken'. Another foreign correspondent wanted to know who was now in control of the positions at Shaar Hagai. The officer evaded giving an answer, summing up the situation again briefly: 'Three weeks ago the Arabs declared that Jewish Jerusalem was under siege. We made up our minds to break the blockade. Positions which were held by the Arabs were attacked and the road from Jerusalem to the coastal plain is open'.

The officer took an envelope out of a package of documents and photographs, saying that they had all been found in positions taken from the Arabs. We saw a picture of Abd al-Kadr Al-Husseini, the commander of the Castel, passports and documents belonging to British sergeants who had deserted and joined the Arab gangs, pamphlets attacking the Jews printed in Arabic and English, etc.

16.4.1948

The siege of Jerusalem has been raised, but for how long? Some people regard this as a turning-point in the battle for Jerusalem. The peak of the Castel has finally been captured from the Arabs. This hill has passed from one side to another several times. Like the Jews, the Arabs know that whoever controls the peak controls the entire area. From their positions on the Castel the Arabs disrupted traffic and prevented the convoys from getting through to Jerusalem.

This was part of a bold military operation known as 'Nahshon', which was mounted a few days ago with the object of opening the road to Jerusalem. About 1,500 soldiers from all over the country took part in it. The first step was the conquest of Arab Hulda and Dir Muhsein. Abd al-Kadr Al-Husseini commanded the Arab gangs on the Castel[1].

On 7th April the mountain was captured by Palmah soldiers of the Harel Brigade. The next day the Arabs launched a counter-attack, in the course of which their commander, Al-Husseini, was killed. They advanced furiously nonetheless, spreading the rumor that 'the commander has been captured by the Jews', and our men retreated. The following day our forces recaptured the hill and the road to Jerusalem was opened. This operation enabled a large convoy bringing food and ammunition to reach Jerusalem[2]. (Appendix 25)

Suddenly, the British police were given a hint from 'on high' and left the police quarters near Mahaneh Yehudah (near the Central Hotel today). The journalists were summoned to observe the entry of the Jewish police to the building which had served the snipers who had cast their shadow over all the neighbourhoods in the center of Jerusalem. With tears of joy in their eyes, the residents watched as the Jewish flag

---

[1] We learned later that the Arabs had planned to 'destroy the Jewish State before it could be established', through attacks by Arab forces in Samaria, led by Fauzi Al-Kaukji, and in the center of the country, led by Abd al-Kadr Al-Husseini, making for Jerusalem, which they would starve, destroy with cannon-fire and conquer. All this was to occur before the British left in mid-May. The death of Al-Husseini put and end to this scheme.

[2] Several years later Ben-Gurion said at a 'Givati' Brigade anniversary: 'Had that operation not succeeded I do not know if we would have been able to proclaim the establishment of the State.'

was raised above the building which had been a source of fear for many months. Many Sabbaths had been spoiled and several celebrations interrupted because of the 'inhabitants' of this building. Numbers of people pronounced the blessing of Deliverance ('HaGomel') on having been saved from the guns of the policemen.

The reporters on the spot noticed that the British policemen appeared to have fled in haste. They had managed to take only some of their possessions with them, the rest remained torn or destroyed. Tables and chairs were broken and doors had been smashed in anger. Amongst the pamphlets found was 'An English Guide to the Hebrew Language'. On the roof there were gun emplacements aimed towards the Jewish neighborhoods.

Jewish policemen arrived, wearing armbands with the words: 'Jerusalem Municipal Police', in Hebrew. The residents were filled with joy at the departure of the British, who had supposedly been stationed there in order 'to keep law and order and protect the lives of the citizens'. Everyone said: 'Good riddance to them'.

*

Today I experienced a different kind of siege. Jerusalem seems to have shrunk in size. One can no longer 'jump' to Mount Scopus, the Old City, Rachel's Tomb and its environs. We have to take care when we walk between the 'Generali' Building in Jaffa Street and the Mahaneh Yehuda or Rommema quarters or Beth Yisrael and the Sanhedria neighborhoods.

From a hill in old Beth Yisrael I looked toward the empty lot that separates me from my neighborhood, Nahlat Shimon, In the distance I could see the wild flowers, but I could not go over to them. I said to myself and jotted down in my notebook: the flowers are also under siege.

19.4.1948

Jerusalem reporters are included in the category of 'individuals engaged in heavy physical labor' who are eligible for extra rations of food. There are some, however, who oppose this and decline to accept their extra ration.

The report of the local Journalists' Committee notes the boost given our work with the arrival in Palestine of the U.N. Commission. Reporters have been assured free access to the members of the Commission and participation in its tours of the country. The Journalists' Committee sent a cable to the U.N. Secretary-General, Trygve Lie, protesting at the attempt made by the Lebanese Government to prevent the entry of Jewish journalists accompanying the U.N. Commission into Lebanon. No reply was ever received, but the Lebanese consulate in Jerusalem withdrew its objections and issued entry-permits to several Jewish reporters.

*

The representative of the 'International Red Cross' in Palestine, Dr. Paul de-Rainier, proposed to the directorate of Hadassah that the hospital on Mount Scopus be placed under his wing. He has demanded that every armed man be removed from Mount Scopus as a precondition for this, leaving only a few doctors, nurses and auxilary workers.

The Jewish Agency spokesman rejected the Red Cross proposal. He stated that negotiations are still continuing with the Commander of the British army for protection for the convoys of Hadassah personnel travelling from the town to Mount Scopus following the dastardly slaughter of members of the medical and scientific convoy on its way to Hadassah. It was stressed that the Red Cross had avoided condemning this attack.

We are very concerned to hear that the British Army has handed the El-Alamein Camp, between Baka and Talpiot, to the Arab Legion. The presence of Arab soldiers in this camp could endanger the Jewish neighborhoods of Talpiot, Mekor Haim and kibbutz Ramat Rachel, and disrupt the connection between them and the New City.

20.4.1948

The road to Jerusalem was cut off again, after the biggest convoy reached the city. The convoy was ambushed by large numbers of Arabs and there was heavy fighting before it managed to get away. Several vehicles had to be abandoned.

22.4.1948

The Jewish Agency for Palestine has appointed a special committee to act as a Central Public Emergency Committee. It will deal with all the problems of the inhabitants of Jerusalem, which is in effect cut off from the rest of the country. The Committee has seven members, three lawyers, Bernard Joseph (who appears to be the chairman), David Abulafiya and Daniel Oster, as well as Haim Salomon, Isaac Werfel, Charles Pasman (from the Joint Organization) and Reuben Schreibman. An Agudat Yisrael representative, Moshe Porush, will also be attached to the Committee, we are informed.

The members of the Committee were given letters of appointment, signed by David Ben-Gurion, which read as follows:

"The Jewish Agency Executive has discussed the situation in Jerusalem and had decided to appoint a Jerusalem Committee of seven members whose function will be to ensure the supply of food, water, fuel and raw materials to the Jewish residents of Jerusalem (namely, their acquisition, storage and distribution), to guarantee transport within the city and between it and its surroundings as well as between Jerusalem and Tel-Aviv and the rest of the country, to recruit manpower for Jerusalem's security and commercial needs, to prevent profiteering, to accommodate refugees and take care of those injured in the disturbances, and to deal with and supervise the National Guard and the Jewish Police (internal security which is not within the jurisdiction of the security forces). This Committee will not be concerned with the services provided by the National Council — education, health, etc. — or with the matters customarily attended to by the Communal Council.

"The Committee shall make one of its members responsible for submitting interim reports of its activities to the National Council and the Jewish Agency Executive.

"It is advisable that the Committee should meet today in order to organize its activities.

"The Jewish Agency Executive will give as much aid as possible to enable the Committee to implement its tasks". (See Appendix 26)

A STRUGGLE FRAUGHT WITH ACHIEVEMENTS
AND FAILURES

3.5.1948

Passover (Pessah) this year finds Jerusalem in the pincers of its British and Arab enemies. We appear to be confronting an unclear and threatening future. All Jerusalem's neighborhoods are on the front line. Every day fresh victims are accompanied to their final resting place. The 'Iraqi' and 'local' gangs have gained a foothold in Katamon, which is near Kiryat Shmuel and Rehavia, in Musrara, which is near Meah Shearim, in the 'Palace' building in Mamilla Street and on the surrounding hills. The noose of the siege is drawing tighter and the area free of snipers' bullets has become much smaller.

The Almighty has been generous with the spring this year. There is an abundance of flowers, in all colors and shades. One does not tire of looking at them, bathed in dew. But the spring seems to be under siege too. The fields are open to enemy fire.

There are increasing signs of the blockade. In many houses there is not a drop of kerosene. Before Passover the electricity supply was reduced to a few hours each day. The supply of candles, matches and other simple articles which one needs for every day life has run out. The stores are quite empty. Storekeepers sell bundles of twigs and pieces of wood for heating and cooking. At kiosks they sell water mixed with a little wine, at thirty mills a glass. Here and there one hears of sons who have given up some of their meager rations for their parents, and parents who have done the same for their children. In the fields to the west of Jerusalem, which are relatively safer than the other suburbs, people gather edible grasses and herbs. The wives of residents of prosperous neighborhhods like Rehavia have asked women from Oriental communities to advise them as to which plants are the wide-leaved mallow plant and what dishes can be made from them. The mallow ('Khubeisa') soon found pride of place on the tables of Jerusalem's 'European' inhabitants too. 'The Voice of Jerusalem' also broadcasts instructions on how to cook 'Khubeisa'.

Three large convoys, one every few days, broke through the renewed cordon and reached Jerusalem from the coastal plain before the Passover festival. The convoys were received with bouquets of flowers, with excitement and rejoicing, and with cold water, which is the most precious commodity these days. The third convoy came under heavy fire in Shaar-Hagai, five defenders were killed and many were wounded. Several vehicles had to be abandoned, but their cargo was saved.

That convoy was also the last before we were totally cut off for so long, so cruelly. Hundreds of drivers from the coastal plain have been obliged to remain in Jerusalem. The Chairman of the Jewish Agency Executive, David Ben Gurion, also reached Jerusalem in that convoy and is to spend the Passover holiday here.

There is a sense of relief in the city. Once again there are lines of people in the stores waiting for their rations of rice, sugar, eggs and vegetables. No one can free himself of the feeling that everything he eats this festival, the Passover of 1948, is soaked in the blood of his dear brethren who have risked their lives in order to bring food to besieged Jerusalem.

On Passover eve one could see bonfires blazing at the entrances to many houses. People were cooking their festive meal. The Rabbis permitted the consumption of pulses on Passover for Ashkenazim too[1]. I observed touching scenes of friendship when neighbors presented one

---

[1] Different ethnic communities among the Jews observe different dietary laws regarding the permissibility of eating pulses during Passover. (D.S.)

another with foodstuffs which they considered were 'unnecessary'. Not everyone though solely about hoarding.

We ate our Passover meal, the 'Seder', by candlelight and to the sound of the 'unfinished symphony' of rifle and mortar fire, though the news of the liberation of Haifa brought rejoicing to our hearts. A special 'Seder' for soldiers was held in the 'Shneller' camp. The Participants changed every hour, as they were called away to urgent guard duties. With their guns in their hands and their ammunition slung across their backs, they sat down to eat their Paschal meal in haste. The 'Seder' was conducted by Rabbi Jacob Berman, and David Ben-Gurion sat at the head of the guests. In his speech he said to the soldiers attending the 'Seder': "Let not thy spirit fall, O, Jerusalem. Our best boys have risked their lives for your sake. We shall not forget thee, O Jerusalem, and our right hand shall not forget its cunning".

*

This Passover the inhabitants of Jerusalem greeted one another with the phrase: 'A peaceful and happy festival'. The battle was resumed as soon as the first day of the festival had ended. Our men went out to conquer the blood-stained neighborhood of Sheikh Jarrah and had taken the center before dawn broke. The next morning our first unaccompanied convoy went to and from Mount Scopus.

Then the British ruler insisted that our men leave Sheikh Jarrah after having conquered it in battle. Our soldiers did as he bade, seething with anger. At midday that day British mortars fired with deadly accuracy at our men in Sheikh Jarrah, to make sure they left. Approximately thirty precious young lives had already been lost in conquering that neighborhood. That evening the dead and wounded were evacuated and the area was handed over to the British[2].

*

---

[2] Details of this operation can be found in Appendix 67, 'Liaison Officers Remember', the speech by Yitzhak Rabin.

During the first days of the festival of Passover 1948 Jerusalem was bombarded by enemy mortars situated at Nebi Samuel. On that same day one of the evening papers issued a special edition with the sensational headline: Ceasefire Agreement Reached. The inhabitants were thunderstruck. In their hearts they asked: will we be able to endure this too? And again, on the last day of the festival, when the streets were full of people celebrating, the mortars roared again and victims fell.

That Passover Jerusalem became a besieged and fighting city. Everyone, great or small, was a front-line soldier, silently obeying the orders issued by the 'Jerusalem Region Defense Headquarters', to 'build defense walls, do not walk about the streets unnecessarily. Remember that the noise of the mortars is worse than the damage they inflict'.

The residents of Jerusalem have been told to build fortifications. Anxiously though willingly they have begun to protect their houses. Sandbags have been placed at the entrances, and windows have been blocked with bags of earth or books. As if to mock them, the sun shone in all its glory while the people remained closed up in their homes, waiting for what the morrow would bring.

While the adults were busy building up the defenses, the children were sent to bring supplies from the stores. This involved mortal danger from the snipers' shots. Entire families have moved into cellars and underground apartments. 'For how long? God knows'. Youngsters have joined the field forces, while older people joined the Home Guard. Everyone was told to 'bring two blankets from home'.

*

During the days of the siege the inhabitants of Jerusalem learned three things: You don't get water just by opening a tap, you don't get electricity just by turning on a switch and you don't get food just by going to the corner store.

*

The Katamon quarter was a veritable thorn in our flesh. This week it was cleared of enemy forces. The first, and most difficult, step was the capture of the St. Simeon Monastery by the Palmah's 'Portzim' ('Breakthrough') Battalion. The Arabs (including soldiers from Iraq) fired on Jewish neighborhoods from this monastery. Both we and the Arabs knew that control of the monastery meant control of the entire Katamon quarter.

The battle for the monastery lasted several hours, which seemed like eternity to us. When our soldiers had conquered the monastery they went on to the houses, advancing from one building to the other. In their retreat, the Arabs tried to use the immunity of the Iraqi Consulate and entrenched themselves there. The force hesitated to bombard the Consulate building and tried to use official channels to stop the fire from the house. While this was being done, however, it transpired that the Consul and the officials had left the building long since. Our forces stormed the house and drove the Arabs out. Among the armored vehicles which the Arabs used were two of ours, which the Arabs had taken from us in the attack on the 'Nebi Daniel' convoy on its way back from the Etzion Bloc, three months ago. On the seventh day of Passover Katamon was in our hands. Through it contact was established with the Mekor Haim quarter, which had been cut off almost completely for several months.

Our forces set out from Katamon to conquer the German and Greek Colonies and Baka. A British officer told reporters, after visiting Mekor Haim, that he would not have believed that there were less than five hundred defenders in the quarter, and called them 'the five hundred members of the suicide squad who held out'. Everyone sang the praises of the residents of Mekor Haim (Fountain of Life), who had been gripped in the enemy's vise from Beth Tzefafa on one side and 'Allenby Camp' on the other. This pleasant little neighborhood bears the name of Haim Cohen from Krakow (and also the verse, 'For with thee is the fountain of life: in thy light shall we see light'. Psalm 36). It was founded in 1922 by Haim Cohen, a member of 'Mizrahi'. The British asked the

Jews to 'have compassion on the inhabitants of Mekor Haim, who are unable to withstand their assailants', and to evacuate the neighborhood. Their 'concern' even extended to offering their help in this evacuation...

*

Today we saw the soldiers and a handful of inhabitants of this quarter making merry and having a drink together, though their beverage was water mixed with a little wine. They had seen their enemy turn tail and flee. Operation Jebusite has succeeded, but Sheikh Jarrah has been handed back and the fruits of victory are not ours.

4.5.1948

Even in times of peace it is not good when several authorities 'look after' the same city. It is a hundredfold worse when this happens in a besieged and fighting city. 'Spheres of activity' have been defined as follows: the municipality, headed by Daniel Oster, is to deal with tax-collection, cleaning services, social welfare, etc., and The Jerusalem Committee, chaired by Dr. B. Joseph, will concern itself with affairs connected with the state of emergency. In actual fact, however, these spheres are not observed and there is needless and harmful duplication.

*

The position of mayor of international Jerusalem is being offered to the representative of the International Red Crosse. P. de-Rainier. According to the proposal there are to be two municipalities, one Jewish and one Arab, and de-Rainier will head both and coordinate between them.

*

Meanwhile we await the conclusion of lengthy negotiations about attaching the Bayit Vagan, Yefe Nof, Beth Hakerem, Kiryat Moshe, Hapoel Hamizrahi; Maimon, Etz-Haim and Givat Shaul quarters to the Jewish municipality. Till now they have been considered 'independent', mainly so that the taxes paid by their inhabitants are not used by the Arabs for their own purposes.

7.5.1948

The Arabs have cut the pipeline bringing water from Rosh Haayin to Jerusalem at Latrun, and the water supply has been cut off. Now they want to defeat us by thirst, since their attempt to defeat us by hunger has failed. The British authorities, in the process of disbanding themselves, have announced that they are unable to keep their assurance to hand over the pumps at Rosh Haayin to the Jews since in the meantime they have been taken by the Iraqis.

10.5.1948

Today, the first day of the Hebrew month of Iyar, is a great day for Jewish Jerusalem. Today the first Jewish post offices were opened and Hebrew stamps were used for the first time.

Since the morning crowds have thronged to the post offices in the Geulah, Mahaneh Yehuda and Rehavia quarters. Many did their utmost to be the first to benefit from the Jewish mail services. Everyone wanted to see and use the first Hebrew stamp, whose memory will be engraved forever in the annals of our independence. When the first man came out with the stamp in his hand, many people crowded around him looking with enjoyment and curiosity at the elongated stamp bearing the map of the Jewish State and the commemorative postmarks of the 'People's Administration' and the Post Office.

Every minute the line grew longer, comprising all ranks and walks of life, the sons and builders of Jerusalem, the simple laborer alongside the learned rabbi, the clerk with the merchant, the uniformed soldier and the housewife, for whom this line is the pleasantest of all those she has experienced. The line also included some professional stamp-collectors as well as a young man who did not know where and to whom to send his first letter by Hebrew mail, and finally sent it to himself.

There was one old man who found the moment ripe for some reminiscing. He recalled how he had stood up and danced upon hearing of the 'Balfour Declaration', which had been equated in its time to the edict issued by Cyrus, King of Persia. After that came years of suffering and pain, bloodshed and disappointments, bitter tidings of our brethren in the dispersion and the heroism of siege and enclosure in our land until this day, this stage in our path to rebirth.

One woman left the post office rather disappointed, holding in her hand the letter she had intended to send to her brother in the United States. She had been told that there was no way of sending it. The people in the line tried to cheer her up: 'Never mind, some day it'll happen, step by step, this is just the beginning'.

The babble of voices stopped when the old man took the stamp in his hand and, in a loud voice, pronounced the benediction: 'Blessed art thou, O Lord our God, King of the universe, who has kept us in life, and hast preserved us, and enabled us to reach this season'. All those standing there answered softly, 'Amen'.

*

The Red Cross delegation in Jerusalem has proposed taking the city under its auspices, provided all soldiers leave and the area is demilitarized. The entire city would be regarded as one great hospital. Before either side could analyse the proposal, which raises a great many difficult questions, the Arabs intensified their attacks on Jewish Jerusalem in an effort to create facts by force. It has been said that the armies of the neighboring Arab countries are about to invade the country in general and Jerusalem in particular.

The Jewish defense forces, the members of the Haganah, the Etzel and the Lehi, are making their preparations. A brave attempt is already under way to force the Arab attackers away from positions near Jewish neighborhoods in the north and south.

16.5.1948

It happened yesterday, the fifth of Iyar. Exactly one year after the U.N. Assembly approved the establishment of a committee of eleven representatives from different countries to study the Palestine question (UNSCOP), the Jewish State, to be called 'Israel', was proclaimed. Very few people in Jerusalem knew of or heard the proclamation, and only those fortunate few who possess a battery-run radio could tune in, since we have no electricity for most of the day. Actually, during the past two weeks there have been rumors that the U.S. has been demanding that the Jews defer the proclamation of the State. (Appendices 27-32).

From today we are our own masters. It is a wonderful yet terrifying feeling. British rule, which had continued for thirty years, ended when the representative who symbolizes this rule, the High Commissioner, Sir Allan Gordon Cunningham, entered his residence in North Talpiot on Friday morning. A little while later he left it, accompanied by a heavy guard, and made his way to the Kalandia (Atarot) airfield. From there he flew to Haifa, where he boarded ship together with the former Lord Chief Justice, William Fitzgerald, and the Chief Secretary to the Mandate Government, Sir Henry Gurney. They all stood to attention as the strains of the British national anthem were heard for the last time at an official event in Palestine. As their ship sailed away British rule in our country came to an end. In our hearts we hope that the prediction made by the British that 'chaos' will reign in Palestine will not be fulfilled.

*

The inhabitants of Jerusalem are busy translating independence into practise. A few of us journalists are in contact with officers and soldiers of the Haganah, Etzel and Lehi. Within the framework of 'Operation Pitchfork' they split up into three simultaneous fronts: the central force, consisting of members of the 'Haganah', hastened to the city center where several buildings controlling the area between us and the Arabs were taken on Friday morning. The first building to be occupied was the 'Generali' Building, which bears the effigy of a lion and dominates the crossroads leading to Jaffa Gate and the Commercial Center. Their colleagues gained control of the Russian Compound and the 'Bevingrad' area, named for Ernest Bevin, the British Foreign Secretary who was hostile to the Jews. The second force, comprising an Etzel company, turned north and occupied the Police School and the Sheikh Jarrah Quarter. Another fighting unit went south and gained control of the Greek Colony, the German Colony, Baka, Abu Tor, the railway station, the Jerusalem Electricity Company and the Allenby Camp.

The Arabs broke a promise given in their name to the Security Council by Jemal Husseini, as Moshe Shertok had done in ours, that from the moment the British left firing would cease in both the Old and the New Cities of Jerusalem. Our men confined themselves to occupying the buildings taken from us by the British.

Today we were informed that the Arabs have begun to attack the Old City, and that a hail of bullets has descended on the Jewish Quarter there. They have also destroyed a concrete defense wall which was erected in 1936, when Arabs attacked Jews, which served to separate the Jewish and Moslem Quarters. Unconfirmed reports stated that the Arabs had entered via Habad Street on one side and the 'Porat Yosef' Yeshiva, on the other. Old people and women had been assembled in the 'Misgav Ladah' Hospital building, and the International Red Cross flag raised on the top.

*

For two or three days the Chief Rabbi, Herzog, has been trying in vain to persuade members of the Committee of Consuls (the American, the Belgian and the French) to prevent the Arabs from destroying the

Old City and the Jewish holy places there. The Consuls themselves admitted in their reply that everything they said fell on deaf ears.

Yesterday an announcement was issued in the Arabs' name proposing that an agreement be made to refrain from using mortars in fighting in the Old City. We replied that the suggestion was ridiculous and that a general ceasefire should be declared. The Arabs refused to allow the dead and wounded to be removed from the Old City. The defenders of the Jewish Quarter, facing odds of ten to one, are preparing to repel the enemy attack.

*

My heart is racked with worry for the members of the Etzion Bloc. The rumor is that not one of the members of Kfar Etzion is left alive, all were killed in a stubborn and bitter battle. Many of the settlers of the other villages in the Bloc have been killed too and only a handful have been taken prisoner. It is said that we can expect heavy pressure from the Arab Legion, now that the Etzion Bloc settlements have fallen, since till now their valiant defense engaged considerable enemy forces. Now the Arab soldiers are free to direct their attention at the neighborhoods of Jerusalem.

*

Despite the joy in our midst at the establishment of the State of Israel, Jerusalem is left without aid or succour, its limbs severed, licking its wounds. The enemy is trying repeatedly to break through its defenses. Between one attempt and the other, when our soldiers repel them, the enemy does everything to destroy the spirit of its inhabitants by heavy mortar bombardments and a hail of bullets directed at every quarter and each street.

There is no real hunger although many items are in short supply. Fruit and vegetables are unobtainable. Milk and eggs are particularly scarce. Water is distributed in minute quantities. The movie-houses are closed and only a few cafes remain open.

The Jerusalem Region Haganah Commander has issued a special order of the day upon the proclamation of the State.

"The day for which we have waited for tens of generations has come. The State of Israel has arisen. The vision has become reality. Precious lives have not been sacrificed in vain. Our work has not been for nothing. Our efforts have born fruit. Henceforth we are no longer nameless, underground fighters, forced to conceal our weapons. We have become the soldiers of the free State of Israel, which takes its place within the family of nations. The battle will become even fiercer. We are now involved in the decisive struggle for the eternal capital of Israel and we are defeating the enemy. Difficult tests and days of trial still await us. Every Jew will be required to make a tremendous effort to preserve the priceless treasure which is ours. Today we will review with pride our achievements to date, drawing from them the strength and courage for what lies ahead.

"To mark this day I proclaim a pardon for all our soldiers who have been convicted of crimes. They are to be released forthwith, returned to their fighting units and allowed to participate in the battle".

*

Arab armies have begun invading our country in the north and south. Their attacks are intensifying, being directed primarily against Jerusalem. In Ezekiel we found the following verse: "For the king of Babylon stood at the parting of the way, at the head of the two ways, to use divination: he made his arrows bright, he consulted with images, he looked in the liver. At his right hand was the divination for Jerusalem, to appoint captains, to open the mouth in the slaughter, to lift up the voice with shouting, to appoint battering rams against the gates, to cast a mount, and to build a fort". (Ezekiel, 21, verses 21 and 22).

17.5.1948

Jerusalem is surrounded by mountains. In time of war these mountains breed fear and arouse anxiety in the hearts of its inhabitants.

The enemy fires shells and bullets bearing death from them. The city is surrounded by numerically superior enemy forces with better equipment.

Two days ago a carrier pigeon brought a cry for help from Atarot and Neve Yaakov to the north of the city. Both points were under fierce attack by Arab Legion forces. There are dead and wounded. In order to escape the bitter fate of the Etzion Bloc settlers, the defenders evacuated both these points. The road to Jerusalem is 'open' to the forces of the Arab Legion from both the north and the south. (Appendices 33 and 34)

*

Many of the Arab inhabitants of southern quarters of Jerusalem, such as Baka, the German Colony, the Greek Colony, etc., are fleeing from their homes. (Appendices 35 and 36)

At present there is a ceasefire in the city. Strangely enough, the sudden quiet disturbs many of the inhabitants, whose ears have grown accustomed to the roar of the cannon and the shriek of bullets. We are anxious as to what lies ahead, since this is just a momentary lull. The Bratzlav and Karlin hassidim sat and sang till after midnight, thanking the Lord for the ceasefire. Everyone knows that at present the city is 'no-man's land' and only those who live within it can save it from destruction. Meanwhile, with little food, no electricity and hardly any fuel, we survive and attempt to revive the city.

Our thoughts are with those in the Old City, a handful of defenders facing thousands of assailants. Both sides are digging in, both here, in the New City, and there, in the doubly besieged Jewish Quarter. At Jaffa Gate our men have reached the 'Tannous Brothers' building opposite David's Tower.

In the Valley of Hinnom, which separates Mount Zion from Abu Tor, members of the Palmah set up a steel cable from the top of Mount Zion to one of the houses on the outskirts of Abu Tor. They say that the cable will be used for transferring food and weapons to Mount Zion and for evacuating the wounded from the Old City.

18.5.1948

The thing that no one imagined could happen has in fact occurred in besieged Jerusalem. The newspapers of all the political parties and streams have merged. All the newspapers have united in producing and distributing a common daily called 'Jerusalem News'. ('Yedioth Yerushalayim'). And 'Hatzofeh' also shall dwell with 'Al Hamishmar', and 'Davar' shall lie down with 'Hamashkif' and 'Haboker'. Much hesitation preceded the appearance of the paper, but the discussions were short and practical. It was not to be a 'profit-making concern', and those involved tried to emphasize points of unity and minimize the divisions. Each journalist contributed some part of his information. Items which insulted one party or another or were potentially disruptive were ignored. Only reliable and well-founded information was published, without any exaggeration, as befits a paper put out by serious and responsible journalists. The inhabitants of Jerusalem gave it a warm reception. They did not know how much work had been invested in producing it but were glad to know that it was the outcome of a cooperative undertaking.

Yitzhak Ben Dor, the representative of 'Davar', was appointed the editor of 'Jerusalem News'. It soon became clear that the choice was a good one. Ben Dor was an upright, honest, reliable and devoted man, liked by everyone. He knew how to find and present material which interested and pleased the readers of all the papers. Associate Editor was Aviezer Goldstein (Golan), from 'Hamashkif'. I helped in collecting local material, proof-reading and other tasks. Other journalists lent a hand in producing the joint newspaper.

One of the first editions of the paper carried the sensational story that some of the scrolls discovered in the Qumran caves near the Dead Sea had been purchased and were in the possession of Professor Sukenik (the father of Professor Yigael Yadin).

Reports of military campaigns, fighting on the road to Jerusalem and in other places were supplied by the military correspondent, Azaria Rappaport. At the same time each evening one of the reporters was sent to the Palestine Post office to hear the 'news' on a battery-operated radio. Kol Hamagen HaIvri also provided reports of battles and information was sometimes supplied to the editorial office by Etzel or Lehi.

Ben Dor, the editor, was a master of the art of composing headlines. He attracted the readers' eyes and attention with apt headlines, such as: "Waves of Arab Attacks Break on our Fighters' Heroism"; "Prevention of Immigration and Independence in the Trusteeship Proposal". An item about unrest and demonstrations in Egypt was headed: "Let them Put their own House in Order"; a report that Agudath Yisrael had announced that it would have no part in any government established in opposition to the wish of the U.N. bore the heading: "Where Did They Get That Law"? Other examples were: "Magnes Has His Own Foreign Policy;" on the eve of the proclamation of independence: "They Boasted of Victory and were Defeated"; the report of the attack on the large convoy bringing food to Jerusalem was headed: "The Van Celebrates in Jerusalem and the Rear is Stalled in Shaar Hagai"; and when the Haganah position at the Yemin Moshe windmill was blown up: "Windmill Defeated".

It was almost a family newspaper. It contained items about day-to-day occurrences which were important locally, such as the announcement of Dr. A. Hareubeni's lecture on 'The Nature of the Bitter Plants Growing in Jerusalem Gardens', or the following item: (4th March 1948) "The inhabitants of Jerusalem are urged to refrain from alighting from buses or automobiles in Arab or mixed areas where there are no defense forces".

A typical Jerusalem announcement published by the paper during the first days of tension read as follows: "Residents of Jerusalem, look around you carefully as you walk through your city. If you notice a suspicious movement or package keep calm and call over the nearest member of the 'People's Guard'."

On 28th April 1948 the following piece appeared: "Censorship has ended. Yesterday censorship was lifted from the press and radio broadcasts. For the first time in twelve years the newspapers were published and broadcasts were transmitted without Government control".

Naturally, this referred to the censorship imposed by the British Mandate authorities. A few days later security measures were adopted, and later still our own military censorship was introduced.

In the 8th May 1948 edition, about a week before the proclamation of the State of Israel, a report appeared attributed to the 'United Press' correspondent in Tel Aviv, stating that the new State of the Jews was to be called 'The State of Judea', and that its 'Government', army, budget and national debt were already prepared.

The edition of 16th May 1948, the day after the establishment of the State, appeared with double spaces between the lines because it had been set by hand. The single headline read: 'The State of Israel is Reborn', and another heading, about the battles, went: 'And they Fled in Seven Directions'.

The 'chaos' which the British had expected and hoped would descend on the entire country, and on Jerusalem in particular, could be sensed in the announcements which appeared at that time, the first days of the War of Independence. In April 1948 Mr. Graves, the chairman of the committee appointed to act as the municipality of Jerusalem, announced that 'the use of water was to be limited'. Another announcement stated that there was a shortage of the solar oil used by the diesel pumps at Rosh Haayin, and that the water supply to Jerusalem had been cut off.

The 'idyll' between the Jerusalem representatives of the six morning newspapers in Tel Aviv was broken by the events at Dir Yassin. The fourth issue of 'Jerusalem News' carried the story of the attack launched by Etzel and Lehi against the village and its conquest.

The following day the newspaper published the Jewish Agency spokesman's reservations concerning the action at Dir Yassin. The editor gave it the headline: 'Let us not Follow the Example of Arab Cruelty'.

The Mapam party considered the tone of this too moderate. By the next day, 'Al Hamishmar' was no longer listed among the papers represented by 'Jerusalem News'. Discussions were held between the editor and 'Al Hamishmar' representatives regarding the newspaper's 'line'. 'Al Hamishmar', however, continued to dissociate itself from the newspaper after its sixth issue.

The latest edition of the paper, its 34th issue, appeared yesterdy, 17th May 1948, in a one-page, hand-set edition. (Appendix 37)

19.5.1948

The words of Uzi Narkiss, the commander of the 'Portzim' ('Breakthrough') Batallion of the Palmah, sounded like an ancient poem: 'You stand before the wall of the Old City, whence the Jews were expelled one thousand, eight hundred and seventy-seven years ago. It is your task to conquer the wall. Good luck!"

Night descends on Jerusalem, which is engaged in a fierce struggle for its liberty. The moon has risen, casting its pallid glow. Our young men have left the Yemin Moshe quarter and are now gazing towards Mount Zion, which they must take come what may. Young soldiers, the descendants of the kings of the royal house of David, pass between monasteries, mosques and graves, well equipped and armed. They carry with them not only weapons but also supplies for the defenders of the Old City, who have been cut off for several months. This time they are to fulfill a special and sacred mission, to break through the cruel barricade and establish contact with the fifteen hundred besieged defenders there.

Many inhabitants of Jerusalem are not asleep. They can hear the noise as the Old City is being shelled. A few know that 'we' are doing the shelling, and cast their eyes heavenwards, praying for the welfare of our brave defenders and soldiers. At headquarters the first report has been received of the conquest of the Armenian monastery on the top of Mount Zion. A company of only seventy Iraqis was on guard. The

'Portzim' Batallion's strike force drove the attackers away from their positions on Mount Zion and the seventy Iraqis were surrounded by the soldiers of the Palmah, who captured them together with their arms. Another strike force advanced from the Commercial Center and 'Tannous House', which had been captured that afternoon, towards Jaffa Gate. The diversionary actions at the Jaffa and Damascus Gates achieved their purpose and large enemy forces were kept there.

Arab Legion forces have been brought into the Old City to reinforce the enemy. We continue to bombard them with shells. The 'Davidka' plays its dull, roaring melody and the enemy is dismayed by the destructive power of this fatal weapon, the Jews' 'secret weapon'.

All at once the shelling stops. There is a strange silence all around. Only the dialogue of isolated rifle shots can be heard here and there. Somewhere a mortar shell explodes. The force is advancing towards Zion Gate. Our soldiers crouch downalong the wall of the church. They are tense with expectancy. 'The sappers take the lead'. They go ahead, explosives on their backs and their guns in their hands. With kangaroo bounds they jump to the other side of the alley. Now they are next to the wall itself, close to its stones. From here, thousands of years ago, the last of the Jewish fighters probably left Jerusalem. It is zero hour, 2.30 a.m. The push to Mount Zion itself lasted fifty minutes, under heavy enemy fire, directed to all sides in the confusion. Two young man, who had been cut off from their sacred, ancient city and their beleaguered brethren, go over to Zion Gate. Their commander softly voices his final order. Soundlessly the explosives are put into position. The two men leave the spot. Everyone buries their face in the ground and waits[3].

---

[3]   In his book, 'Chapters in the War of Independence', Mordekhai Yaakobovicz writes: "The two men were Blond Rafi and Dark Tibby. Ater the war they both joined the Israeli Merchant Navy, transferred to the Paratroops and continued side by side even after both had become family men.

The few moments that pass seemed like eternity. At 3.35 a.m. all Jerusalem shakes at the mighty explosion. Another thirty seconds pass before the soldiers raise their heads. A few leaps and our men stand before Zion Gate, which is still locked but has been breached by the blast. The soldiers pass through it in silence, with joy in their hearts. Undoubtedly those within are eagerly awaiting this moment. For so long they have hoped and held on, held on and hoped, believing that their colleagues would find a way of overcoming the enemy's obstacles. And they have succeeded. The sound of one of the old men of Jerusalem weeping softly for the destruction of Zion can be heard. His pleas are accompanied by a few enemy shots and our boys burst forward. Within a few minutes the great moment is here, there is covering fire and then the young commander of the Old City is shaking the hand of the first of the soldiers to break through. There is great excitement. Even though it is not seemly for soldiers to weep, here and there one can see them wiping a tear from their eyes. "We have been waiting for you", one of the Old City defenders says. "Had we not known that you were on your way to us, I doubt that we could have held on", adds Moshe, the young commander of the Old City since the beginning of the cruel siege.

Every moment is precious. Many wounded men need immediate medical attention. Some of the youngsters have been involved in heavy fighting for five months or more. They must be given a break. Another group examines the positions and starts making essential repairs to the fortifications. They know that the lull will not last and that it is merely a result of the enemy's immense astonishment, which the soldiers have used to their advantage.

When dawn broke all Jerusalem knew the glad tidings that a handful of our soldiers had overcome the enemy's troops and early on Wednesday morning, 19th May, the siege of the Old City had been broken and contact had been established between brothers praying for the peace of Jewish Jerusalem, the eternal capital of the Jewish nation and its reborn State.

The rejoicing was replaced by bitter disappointment. The Palmah forces which conquered Zion Gate left. How did this happen and why? We did not know. with sorrowful surprise people talked of 'The Palmah, which conquered and left'.

Etzel and Lehi fighters have failed in their attempts to conquer other gates to the Old City. (Appendices 38-46)

23.5.1948

At one of the press conferences we heard how, a few weeks ago, when the stranglehold around Jerusalem was tightening, representatives of the British High Commissioner, Sir Alan G. Cunningham, approached the famous Jerusalem painter, Ludwig Blum. They asked him to come to Government House on the 'Hill of Evil Counsel' near Talpiot, to paint the view, so that the high Commissioner could take it with him and remember the city in which he served as the representative of the Mandate Government.

Blum reached Government House under heavy guard. He sat and thought what picture he could paint to depict the struggles of the city for which a situation of 'chaos' was being prepared. His deliberations bore fruit and he conceived the idea of painting a storm over Jerusalem.

He began painting and after a few days the picture was ready. It depicted a modest, low-roofed Jerusalem, settled peacefully on hills and hillsides. In the skies above this quiet, tranquil city gathered the storm which threatened to engulf it. The High Commissioner looked at the picture, found it pleasing and took it with him when he returned to London.

A few days before his departure the High Commissioner asked Blum to come with him. Again he was taken to Government House in an armored vehicle. The High Commissioner said to him: 'Come with me to London. You cannot imagine what bitter and difficult times lie ahead for Jerusalem and the entire country. When we ieave there will be complete and utter chaos, and many of you will be killed. In London you will be given a studio where you can paint to your heart's content'.

Blum answered unhesitatingly: 'Thank you for your generous offer, High Commissioner, but I cannot accept. My place is in Jerusalem, in the city and among the people that I love'. The High Commissioner left with the picture and the artist remained[4].

24.5.1948

The sad news has reached us from the Old City that Rabbi Yitzhak Avigdor Orenstein, the Rabbinate's representative at the Western Wall, who discharged his task as guardian of our holy site with such devotion, was killed together with his wife by a single shell. Two days beforehand he had participated in the funeral of victims buried in a mass grave in the courtyard of Batei Mahseh and had even delivered a eulogy. He was recognized as a soldier after his death. An official document issued by the Government of Israel and signed by D. Ben-Gurion, asserted that he had fulfilled his duty with dedication, defending the homeland.

He was the life and soul of the Old City. During the siege he assisted the defenders and the man who organized military and civilian life there, Abraham Halperin, the commander of the Jewish Quarter, who was removed from his post apparently because of tale-telling.

*

---

[4] This incident had a sequel. After the British left, Jerusalem was placed under heavy siege. Every day there were fresh casualties. Blum remained in his studio in the courtyard of the 'Talitha Kumi' building off King George Street, and painted. This was one of the first places to be hit by the Arab Legion's shells, under the command of British officers, firing from Nebi Samuel. Shells came through the roof and splinters damaged several precious pictures. The following day Blum invited several reporters round, myself included. He showed us the results of the damage, which pained him very much. On this occasion he told us of his picture, 'A Storm Over Jerusalem', and of the High Commissioner's 'generous' offer, and the reasons for it. He then returned to his painting, immortalizing Jerusalem characters, at both the front and the rear. When the war was over he toured the country and continued to paint. He died in 1974, aged 83.

After long and bitter battles, Kibbutz Ramat Rachel is again in our hands. This is the third time that our soldiers have fought for this point. Ramat Rachel passed from one side to another three times during the last few days. In the course of the fighting several of its buildings were destroyed and burned. Legionnaires and Iraqis fought alongside the Egyptian soldiers. Our boys fought bravely and repelled them.

The Haganah spokesman announced that it is almost certain that the Government Hill area, where the Red Cross is situated, serves as a point for launching attacks on us.

This evening we were informed that the Arabs also tried to wrest the Notre Dame church, opposite the New Gate, from us. An Arab armored column approached from Damascus Gate, and while it was still climbing the hill was stopped by heavy fire from our forces and scattered to all sides. Many of the Arab infantry who followed behind the armored vehicles were killed.

*

During the last few days there have been an increasing number of power cuts. This affects private houses, but printing presses and cinemas suffer in particular. Newspapers which are published in Jerusalem are forced to appear in a two-page and sometimes a one-page format only. Newspaper reports about this aspect of Jerusalem life read something like this: 'For eight of the twenty-four hours of every day the inhabitants of Jerusalem are without electricity. The Jerusalem Electricity Corporation promised initially that the power cut would be in force only between 2 and 4 in the afternoon, but in fact this is the case for most of the day, and often large sections of the city remain without electricity at night too'.

Mr. D. Abulafiya announced at the municipal committee that arrangements have been made to ensure a minimal supply of electricity to Jerusalem. He announced that, 'the supply of electricity to hospitals, bakeries, printing presses, ice factories, the post office and the radio will continue. Electricity will also be supplied to national and local institutions of various kinds. The Jerusalem public has endured great suffering to ensure the supply of electricity to these institutions. There are chances that we will obtain fuel to enable us to supply electricity to the general public'.

*

Following repeated attempts by the enemy to conquer the city, the Jerusalem District Commander, David Shealtiel, published the following poster on 23.5.1948, which was read with interest by the inhabitants of Jerusalem.

"To the fighting forces and the Jewish inhabitants of Jerusalem:

"For the past seven days the enemy has been attacking Jerusalem with a regular army, armored corps and mortars, with the object of breaking into the city and destroying us. It is his heart's desire to conquer and rule Jerusalem. We have managed to repel the vast enemy forces and have even won additional territory which enables us to defend the Jewish sector more effectively.

"In this struggle we do not save Jerusalem alone, but aid the war throughout the country by pinning down large enemy forces and blocking the route from south to north and from east to west. Every bullet and shell fired at us is not fired at more exposed and less fortified parts of the country.

"We have made up our minds: the enemy shall not enter our city.

"The fighting forces and the entire population will fight for every stone in our holy city, and will make every house and street a fortress for the defenders and a grave for our enemies. Every inhabitant, without exception, must place himself at the disposal of the battle, wherever and in whatever capacity he is needed. The entire population of Jerusalem is called to defend the homeland, close ranks, fortify itself and draw on its inner strength.

"Consequently, I give the order that every individual can be called upon to fulfill any task at any time and place, in accordance with the instructions given him by the responsible security authorities; all property which has any value for conducting the war may be appropriated by the security forces, should they see fit to do so. No houses or neighborhoods should be abandoned by their inhabitants unless orders to do so are issued by the regional commanders; stores, houses of commerce, cafes and places of entertainment must not be closed. They will continue to remain open at the same hours as they were before the current state of emergency. The security forces have received orders to open these places by force if they are not opened by their owners; no citizen or soldier may walk about the streets of the city during a raid unless they are there on duty.

"Anyone who raises prices and engages in black market trade, whether as purchaser or seller, will be arrested and punished with all due severity for undermining the nation's war effort, in accordance with the laws of the Jewish military courts. The same applies to anyone who conceals goods and commodities required by the fighting forces for the continuation of the war".

25.5.1948

As the time for a political decision regarding the fate of Palestine drew nearer, and it became clear that the decision would be made on the battlefield, hosts of journalists flocked here, like bees to honey, from all four corners of the world. Some of them were well-known 'stars' of world journalism, while others were military correspondents who had served at various battlefields, crossed seas and land, interviewed heads of state, caused crises, toppled governments and made ministers lose their posts. The country is full of reporters, some of them anti-Semitic, others imbued with affection and admiration for an ancient nation which is renewing its independence in the land of its fathers.

Every single world news agency has opened a permanent office in Jerusalem, including Reuter, United Press, The Palestine Telegraph Agency, Associated Press, Palcor, the Jewish Telegraphic Agency, the French News Agency, the Polish Telegraph Agency, The Czechoslovak

News Agency, Exchange Telegraph, the Arabic Information Agency, International News Service, etc.

The foreign press was allocated special rooms in the British Government Press Office in David Building at the end of King George Street, opposite the windmill in the Yemin Moshe Quarter. For their convenience a post office branch was sited in the building, and through it they could cable their copy direct to their newspaper's offices or to their agencies.

About one hundred and fifty journalists thronged to Jerusalem, attmpting to witness what was happening and describe events in this city to the best of their ability. Some of them came for just a short term, like Daniel Clifton of the New York Times and Homer Bigart of the New York Herald Tribune, and remained here as their paper's permanent correspondent. Some of them were known as no great respecters of the Jews, but the daily heroism of Jerusalem's Jewish population led them to become our greatest admirers.

The foreign correspondents in Jerusalem were divided into two camps, one in the Pantiles Hotel and the other at the Saint George School. Mr.G.S.Hoover, chairman of the Association of Middle East Foreign Correspondents, visited Jerusalem and expressed the hope that these two camps (one in the Jewish sector and the other in the Arab part, both near the 'border') would be 'protected', in accordance with the Geneva Convention, and that both 'would be open to everyone who came, unarmed, to explain his stand'. In practise this was not the case. The Arabs did not know, or did not wish to know, what was written in the Geneva Convention and fired indiscriminately.

In February 1948 Guy Cox, the Exchange Telegraph correspondent, was killed in mysterious circumstances while travelling from Jerusalem to Tel-Aviv. He was found dead in his automobile at Shaar Hagai. There were various rumors as to the cause of his death. Some said he had simply been murdered by Arabs. Others claimed that he had been a British intelligence agent. Others asserted that he had been connected with the Jewish Institutions, and since he was found dead the night before trucks full of explosives were blown up in Ben Yehuda Street by the British it was suggested that Cox knew in advance about the plan and was on his way to Tel-Aviv to inform the Haganah commanders about it.

The journalist, A. Golan, told us that a few days before his death, Cox had asked him whether Etzel would be prepared to accept two British policemen and whether Golan would be ready to give them shelter in his apartment. The journalist and his friends lived near the Oranim Hotel in Beth Hakerem at the time. This pension served as a hiding place for several Britons who had deserted and gone over to the Haganah. Golan feared that these British policemen wanted to spy on what was going on at the Oranim Hotel. After consulting the Etzel commander, Golan told Cox that Etzel was prepared to accept the two British policemen but they would not be the ones to decide where they would live. At that point Cox cancelled his proposal.

*

The way our people deal with the foreign correspondents is not very successful. They told me they had been obliged to contact Ben-Gurion and tell him that they had been prevented from sending their vast readership information about the heroism of Jerusalem's Jewish population, and that the world was learning about the battle for Jerusalem only from Arab sources.

How have the foreign correspondents sent their copy abroad? Some of them have done it through the foreign consuls who are allowed to cross the border, or through U.N. observers. Through them they sent envelopes to associates in the Old City, and they in turn sent them abroad. Some of them transferred envelopes to Amman, whence they were sent abroad. Some of the reporters feared the censors in the Old City or Amman. In order to get the material past the censor the journalist would insert anti-Semitic or pro-Arab phrases, writing the piece in terms which were flattering to the Arabs, so that the censor would smile and pass the article for publication. The Reuter correspondent sent his despatches to London regularly via the British Consul in Jerusalem, whose office was near the Damascus Gate, by the border. (Appendices 47 and 48)

Yesterday the first of the people who were expelled by the British army returned to their homes in Rehavia and King David Street (formerly King George Street), to the area which was formerly called Security Area B. The buildings which are now empty and await their owners include Beth Meir (the building of the World Mizrahi Organization, named for the President of the movement, Rabbi Meir Berlin). A special Accommodation Committee is dealing with returning people to their homes and finding dwellings for people forced to flee shelled areas. The Mizrahi Teachers' Seminary will remain in its new home in the Italian Hospital building in the Street of the Prophets. The occupants of the Italian Hospital have been evacuated and an additional hospital for war wounded has been set up there.

*

Jerusalem is still suffering from an abundance of 'authorities' and from a confusion of responsibility among various committees.

Till now we have had a committee established by the National Institutions to deal with all the problems 'arising from the implementation of the U.N. resolution to internationalize Jerusalem'.

The 'Jerusalem Committee' appointed on 22nd April 1948 by D. Ben-Gurion has been more effective. It operates through four subcommittees: A. A legal-administrative committee to discuss adapting existing laws to the new regime which is about to be set up; B. A committee for economic development, which will set up a central economic company; C. A committee dealing with problems of ground for building homes, in the hope that new immigrants will be directed to Jerusalem; D. A committe for religious, cultural and scientific institutions, which will act to make Jerusalem a spiritual and cultural center for the Jewish nation throughout the world. Mention has also been made of establishing another committee, to prevent Jews leaving the city.

There were nine members on the 'Jerusalem Committee'; Rabbi Yehuda Fishman, Menashe Eliashar, Y. Ben-Zvi, Peretz Bernstein, Bernard Joseph, Dr. Werner Sentor, David Remez and Reuben Schreibman. The chairman was Dr. Abraham Garnovski and the secretary was Ephraim Forder.

The committee for religious, cultural and scientific institutions was headed by Y. Ben-Zvi and consisted of two sections. The religious one was headed by Rabbi Fishman (Maimon) and its members were Rabbi Simha Assaf, the representative of the Chief Rabbinate, Rabbi Z. Sorotzkin, the representative of Agudath Yisrael, and Mr. Bezalel Bijinski of the Mizrahi. There was also a general section.

Mr. Haim Salomon, the chairman of the Jerusalem Communal Council, sent an urgent message to the 'Committee of Six' appointed by the heads of the Jewish Agency and the National Council describing Jerusalem's difficult position. In his letter he wrote, amongst other things: "Jerusalem is completely surrounded by enemies. It is cut off from its essential source, Tel-Aviv. The road to Jerusalem is in constant danger of being blocked. The efforts to secure a stock of supplies for an emergency involve considerable expense and danger. The Old City is totally cut off from the Jewish neighborhods and almost two thousand people are living there in suffering. The new Commercial Center, 'Shema', has been razed to the ground. The buildings left after the fire are being destroyed by the Arabs. The latest disaster to hit Jerusalem, the destruction of Ben Yehuda Street, has brought tragedy to more than fifty families.

"In the Street of the Prophets there is a large building containing more than one hundred rooms, which belongs to the Ethiopian Government. The British are about to leave it and the Arab Higher Committee has proposed leasing it for ten years. If that building falls into Arab hands more than half of Jerusalem will be in danger. The building is the key to Meah Shearim and its environs on one side and the Street of the Prophets and Jaffa Road on the other. The link with Mount Scopus will also be endangered. Consequently, no effort is too great to obtain that building".

The Government appointed a special Ministerial Committee to deal with Jerusalem, consisting of D. Ben-Gurion, Eliezer Kaplan, Aharon Zisling, Moshe Shertok and Moshe Shapira. They travelled to Jerusalem and spent an entire day there, discussing the establishment of a 'central authority' for the city with the representatives of the inhabitants. They met with the members of the National Council, the Communal Council, the Jewish Agency, parties and economic organizations. One of the proposals was that the Government should appoint a Governor, who would work together with a Jerusalem committee whose members would include the Chief Rabbis, Isaac Halevi Herzog and Ben-Zion Hai Uziel, as well as Rabbi I. Dushinski (of Agudath Yisrael) and Rabbi Meir Berlin.

Another suggestion, made by Mr. Haim Salomon of the Communal Council, was that a wider forum, to be called 'The Jerusalem Council', should be established. It would include eleven representatives of the political parties included in the Communal Council, members of the municipal council, representatives of Agudath Yisrael, members of the National Council residing in Jerusalem and members of the Jewish Agency Executive in Jerusalem. It would set up departments for political, economic, education, health, religious, sanitation, transport, etc. affairs. The Government would include a Minister for Jerusalem.

There were two or three other suggestions, such as merging the municipal council with the Communal Council, appointing a Minister for Jerusalem from among the inhabitants of the city, etc. In the end the Ministerial Committee decided to establish a body of 13 members, including representatives of all the above institutions.

Meanwhile, Jerusalem continues to be an example of too many cooks spoiling the broth, to the detriment of the city and its residents.

*

The following article (one of many) appeared recently in the
Jerusalem paper 'Today' ('Hayom') (as well as in other papers) under
the heading: 'True Leadership for Jewish Jerusalem'. The passage
below is part of the article:

'Today marks the twelfth day, making one week and five days, of the
ceasefire. In other words, for twelve days the mortars of the Arab (i.e.
British) Legion have not shelled Jewish Jerusalem. That is the sole
benefit derived by the Jewish inhabitants of Jerusalem from the
ceasefire. During the first eight days not a single food convoy reached
the city, and only on the ninth day did convoys bringing food and fuel
begin to arrive, though not in sufficient quantities. In a few areas
inhabitants have been able to obtain small amounts of vegetables, and
have even been informed that a second delivery is due, but the residents
of other neighborhoods have received no vegetables at all. Industry is
paralysed. There is darkness everywhere. Minute quantities of water are
allocated for drinking and washing. Civilian and economic life has come
to a halt. Cultural activities and entertainment are neglected.

"We do not know whether it is because of the negligence of the
municipal institutions or the absence of 'neutral supervisors' that the
Jewish population of Jerusalem is forced to live this way. It would seem
that both sides are at fault. The municipal institutions have not exerted
sufficient pressure on the supervisors, and the latter do not grasp
statements couched in delicate language. This is a fact.

"The municipal institutions are rambling and diverse in their methods
and approaches. The very fact that in Jewish Jerusalem, which
comprises one hundred thousand inhabitants (may they increase and
multiply!), there is no umbrella organization which is responsible for
affairs requires an explanation. The situation is different in Tel-Aviv,
not necessarily because its inhabitants are more obedient to the
institution which governs the city and more loyal to the city itself.

"The last few months, during which the Jews of Jerusalem have
drunk the cup of bitterness almost to the dregs, proved that the
population is wonderfully disciplined. Jerusalem, however, lacks the

leadership it needs and deserves. It may be that the Communal Council, or more precisely, the members of the Communal Council, are not capable of governing the city during a time of emergency. If this is so other, abler people should be given the chance of taking over, rather than establishing another institution which is partly parallel, partly in competition with it, namely, 'The Jerusalem Committee'.

"Moreover, when the Jewish municipality was established in Jerusalem, would it not have been wise to follow the example set by Tel-Aviv and unite the two institutions, the Communal Council and the municipality? There would undoubtedly have been some who said: but in Jerusalem there is a separate community (Neturei Karta). That is indeed so. It is known, however, that for some days talks have been conducted with the separate community regarding its joining the Jerusalem community. These talks could surely have been held many weeks and months ago.

"Thus, there are in Jerusalem three official institutions and one unofficial one (the orthodox community and Agudath Yisrael), and now the Government of Israel has decided to set up a Ministerial Committee on Jerusalem. This item of information appeared in the press alongside the news that a supreme committee for Jerusalem is to be set up by the rabbis of the city. The Jewish population will doubtless welcome every useful deed undertaken for the benefit of Jerusalem, but they are entitled to ask, 'Is it absolutely necessary to have so many institutions for this?'"

30.5.1948

The thing we feared has happened. The Jewish Quarter has surrendered and there are no Jews left in the Old City. This phrase has been pounding through my brain, ever since we heard on Saturday night that the old people and the women left the Jewish Quarter and walked to Katamon. The handful of defenders, most of them wounded, have been taken captive. The Arabs pillaged and plundered their property, desecrating synagogues and scrolls of the law. We were told that the officers of the Legion could not tolerate the mob's cruel behavior and ordered them to stop.

Some of the old people wept as they told us, together with the Haganah radio operator who had maintained contact with the Jewish Quarter until the decision to surrender was made, that during the last few days they had been informed several times to 'wait for reinforcements' and 'hold on'. One of our planes dropped ammunition, which fell into the hands of the Arabs. More and more of our people were wounded. 120 of them were in the 'hospital'. About seventy corpses lay in the open. Only about thirty people were still at their positions, fighting with the last of their strength.

They also told us of the death of Esther Cailingold, who was just 22 years old.

I had seen her when I visited the Jewish Quarter. She was the daughter of a religious Zionist family in London, and had immigrated to Palestine in 1946. She had volunterred to teach in the Old City, in what she called 'a sacred Jewish environment', During the heat of battle she still remained calm.

A piece of shrapnel pierced her thigh. She lay wounded the Friday evening that the Jewish Quarter surrendered. My informants told me with tears in their eyes how an Armenian orderly had tried to ease her pain with the only drug he possessed, a cigarette. Esthi, for that was Esther Cailingold's pet name, shook her head as if to say, No, now it is the Sabbath. And so she died.

Two days ago, on Friday, two rabbis went out towards the Legion's positions, a white flag in their hands Resistance ceased at two in the afternoon. Our representatives signed the document saying that they were capitulating in Abdullah Al-Tal's headquarters. The last radio message sent from the Jewish Quarter said: We are surrendering. Inform Mount Zion to prepare to accept us and tell the hospital to prepare beds. It is not yet clear whether prisoners will be taken. Goodbye. Out. The station is annulled. (Appendices 49 and 50)

THE TORTUOUS CEASEFIRES

2.6.1948

Residents of Jerusalem under fifty years of age have been summoned to build fortifications today. Those responding have been promised food, clothing, wages and a grant for supporting their families.

The Jerusalem Committee intends to open restaurants which will provide equal portions of food at reasonable prices to everyone.

This week every adult will be allocated a carton of milk in exchange for a ration point. Bread will also be distributed in return for points as of today. Storekeepers are required to open their stores from 8.a.m. to 4.p.m. without a break. Anyone who disobeys this order will be punished.

Here and there one sees young boys and girls wearing leather gloves. With steel cutters they are dismantling barbed wire fences encircling entire areas which were British 'security areas' until two weeks ago.

The transport department of the Jerusalem Committee has announced that no further applications should be made for permits to leave the city, until it is possible to send at least two convoys to Tel-Aviv.

*

For a week there has been talk of a ceasefire, but each time a different date is given. Our Provisional Government in Tel-Aviv ordered our forces to cease firing at 3 a.m. today. At noon the inhabitants of Jerusalem joked that dawn had not yet broken for the Arabs and that 3.a.m. had not reached them.

153

The truth is that the inhabitants and defenders of Jerusalem are tired. Possibly our Institutions were in too much of a hurry to agree to a ceasefire and give the order to our troops, and that is why the Arabs have become intransigent. The Arab attacks are continuing. Haganah headquarters in Jerusalem have announced that if the Arabs do not stop firing by noon we will cancel our agreement to the ceasefire.

The U.N. informed the Jewish institutions that there has been a 'misunderstanding', that the order to cease firing has not yet been given on the Arab side, and that a new date for the ceasefire will soon be fixed.

*

The Katamon neighborhood has been handed over by the military police to civilian rule. Hundreds of families evacuated from the Old City, Neve Yaakov, Atarot and border areas have been accommodated there.

The military authorities have again published a grave warning against any attempt to damage church and monastery property.

*

Yesterday I was permitted to tour the defensive positions on Mount Zion. There were three soldiers with me, a driver, a radio operator and a quartermaster, as well as a young nurse from Tel-Aviv who had spent days and nights tending the wounded fighters in the Old City, saving many of them from death. She had been one of the last to leave the Jewish Quarter on the day it surrendered to the enemy. I was the only 'civilian' on that journey to Mount Zion.

With a feeling of complete freedom we drove, albeit in an armored vehicle, along a road which had only yesterday been within a 'Security Area'. Now the entire area was in our hands. As a souvenir of the cruel and oppressive rule there were notices in English here and there, forbidding entry and obliging innumerable identity checks at every step.

Now no one takes any notice. Jerusalem is beautiful in the calm of its nights. Unfortunately the snipers in David's Tower disturb the peace, declaring their existence by firing indiscriminately towards the Jewish part of the city.

*

The vehicl brought us to one of the forward positions near Jaffa Gate. The soldiers took with them regards from their comrades on other fronts as well as plenty of food. They did not pay the slightest attention to the enemy snipers, merely reassuring the 'civilian' in their midst, namely, me, that the night was 'quite quiet' apart from 'one or two snipers and shells'. The 'civilian' accordingly suppressed his astonishment and adopted the soldiers' confidence.

We soon reached Yemin Moshe (Mishkenot Shaananim), the 'oldest' neighborhood in New Jerusalem, which had withstood the enemy in exemplary fashion. Like every border area in Jerusalem, every position and stone within it is stained with the blood of fighters and defenders. The stones of Mishkenot Shaananim are silent, as are the soldiers whose shadows we saw hugging the walls of trenches and fortifications, their weapons in their hands, ready for whatever might happen. We walked silently along the narrow paths to the operations room, which maintains contact with the 'outside world', informing and being informed of everything going on. The soldiers in the next room sat and told cock and bull stories of a highly original nature, without copying them or translating them from any source whatsoever. It was time to change guard. Some came in and others went out, but this did not keep the raconteur from continuing for one instant. I listened to the shells falling nearby, but the people with me could not have cared less about them. They must have grown used to the noise.

We went back to the vehicle. As we swltched our engine on the snipers increased their fire and shells, and the light of a rocket preceded the flash of the shell and the sound of its explosion. Our automobile skirted the Sultan's Pool and parked below Mount Zion. From there we

climbed the hill stealthilyand on foot. At first we did not notice the
shadows of men on either side of us They were ours, seeing but unseen.
A few words forged a bridge of friendship between us. Again a single
shot cut through the air. 'Don't worry, friend', Jacob the quartermaster
said to me, 'this side is all ours', and waved with his hand towards New
Jerusalem. 'Only there', he added after a moment, 'in the Old City, is
where the enemy is'. 'And we'll go back there yet', said Tzippora, the
Tel-Aviv nurse from the Old City.

From the peak of Mount Zion Jerusalem lay in front of us. Its beauty
pierced us, contrasting with death by ambush. As if he could read my
thoughts, the driver said: 'That's the way it is, friend. Keep going'. We
passed through narrow lanes until we found ourselves inside a
monastery on the top of the hill, our objective.

We were filled with joy at the unexpected meeting. Aminadav ambled
among the statues and monks' cells as if he were walking along the
main street of his home town, Bnei Braq.Gershon Mashari Hased,who
had also come here not long since, had just solved the problem of where
to pray in this center of idolatry, and had found a place in one of the
long corridors which was bare of pictures.'Never mind', he replied in
answer to my question, 'one can be a good Jew even inside a
monastery'.The young commander of the position took us with him on a
short tour. He told us what an important role it had played for the
Palmah battalion which had burst through Zion Gate a week before the
Jewish Quarter had surrendered. Although there had been several
unsuccessful attempts to break through after that, the enemy had paid a
heavy price for the position we had been forced to abandon. Since we
had conquered the monastery Yemin Moshe he had gained a respite. It
would also serve as a jumping-off point for reaching Zion Gate in the
future.

Our people were in three houses on the way from here to David's
tomb. This building had served as the Christian school, built by the
missionary, Samuel Govatt, for the English mission in 1896; nearby
was the Protestant cemetery, where the English bishops of Jerusalem

are buried. Jews who converted are also buried here, with Hebrew verses on their gravestones.

Our tour had come to an end. On our return I knew that we had a foothold on Mount Zion. The day was not far off when the City of David would be in the hands of a generation which did not remove its gaze from the walls of the Old City, looking to the day when the prophecy: 'For I will defend this city, to save it', would be fulfilled. From the roof of the top storey the eyes of the man on guard pierced the darkness all aroind. He may have exceeded his command and cast longing glances at Jerusalem. He was a refugee, the sole survivor of a large family in Europe. From time to time he said to his comrades: 'Is there any privilege greater than being one of the defenders of Jerusalem?'

In my heart I said: Happy is the people that is in such a case.

6.6.1948

The Arab Legion continues to attack the neighborhoods of Jerusalem, trying to invade the New City, sometimes from the old Beth Yisrael Quarter or Batei Ungarin, and sometimes from Notre Dame, opposite the New Gate to the Old City. Today the Abu Tor district, which commands the road from King George Street to Talpiot, was the target of the attack.

In newspapers and in idle discussions (yes, even now these continue) the question of whether the Arabs will set up their own state alongside the State of Israel is asked. After all, people say that, Abdullah, the king of Jordan, will want to annex the territories he conquers to his kingdom. (Appendices 51 and 52)

*

The Almighty dealt kindly with us in arranging that the houses of Jerusalem should be built of stone, according to an order issued by the

Turks. The shells and bullets cause little damage, scratching the stones a little and falling to the ground.

It is strange but we seem to have become accustomed to the sound of shooting, to walking at the sides of roads, hugging the walls of houses, and to running for cover whenever we hear the dull thud of shells. The notice-boards are almost empty. There are no movies or plays, no shows and no entertainment. Jerusalem does not have the heart for that sort of thing just now. At present the pavements are covered in the broken glass of store windows which have not been repaired. Not only is it difficult to find workmen to do the job, it is well-nigh impossible to find glass.

Many families have organized themselves in cellars and shelters, living in crowded conditions, although no one complains. The shelters are full of brotherly love, even though beforehand, outside, everyone hated everyone else.

7.6.1948

Today we learned that the U.N. has appointed a Swedish Count, Folke Bernadotte, to mediate between us and the Arabs. People wonder precisely what is the role of a mediator; and which side he will favor. The journalists were told that a mediator works to achieve a ceasefire. Some believe he will succeed, others are doubtful. For more than a week the Security Council has resolved that the shooting should stop, but the fighting still continues. (Appendix 53)

8.6.1948

The enemy continues to bombard New Jerusalem with cannon and three-inch mortars. The city suffers greatly because of the siege, but the enemy has not advanced one step. There is no limit to the torments and readiness of the population. In fact, those words sum up these days in Jerusalem. My heart insists that I attempt to express something of the heroism of every man, woman and child in Jerusalem under bombardment. The phrase, 'things will turn out alright', is on everyone's lips, not as an empty phrase but in true belief.

*

This week our forces started shelling the Old City, though only for a few hours. The Arabs immediately announced that their shelling of the New City was only in order to defend the Christian churches damaged by the bombardment of the Jews. That is the only way to achieve a ceasefire and get them to talk about an armistice, dissuading them from continuing to shell us.

A glorious page in our history is being written by the youngsters of the Youth Corps (Gadna), organized in three divisions (Modi'in, Massada and Yehuda), who are working on the fortifications around Jerusalem. The youngsters are contributing their energy to the beloved city with joyful exuberance. They leave every day at dawn and return exhausted at dusk. Old people and adults too old for other duties work with them.

Three times this week a ceasefire has been declared for the area of the gates into the Old City. Twice when we returned Arab prisoners of war the Arabs kept the agreement and opened fire only after the appointed hour. The third time, when the Arabs returned one Jewish family, they deliberately broke the agreement and began firing before the time.

Jewish Jerusalem is approaching the thirtieth day since the start of enemy shelling. And although there is much destruction and heavy damage to life and limb as well as the bitter discomfort of the siege, neither sorrow nor the enemy shall enter Jerusalem.

10.6.1948

The journalists of Jerusalem accompanied their veteran and devoted colleague, the chairman of the Jerusalem Journalists' Association and director of the 'Davar' editorial office here, Yitzhak Ben-Dor, to his final resting place. He was killed in the bombardment of Jerusalem. He was 55 years old and left a wife and daughter.

He had been a member of the Second Aliyah, and had been a resident of Jerusalem from the early days of its rebuilding. He had owned a photography store and had gone into journalism by chance. He had once met Berl Katznelson and said to him: 'Give me an opportunity to work in journalism'. His wish was granted and Ben-Dor (formerly Bendar) did not let the side down. Even before that he used to publish articles in 'Kontrass'. He began as a reporter for 'Davar' in Tel-Aviv, later editing the 'Economy and Finance' section. A few years ago he was sent to Jerusalem to head the paper's office here. Here, in the city he loved, his vision had sharpened, the scope of his writing had expanded and his pen had been blessed. He had written under the pen-name, I.B.D. Ben-Zion.

The nation's ethical and moral values were very close to his heart. He spoke admiringly of 'Tirat Tzvi' and other undertakings of the religious Zionist movement. He was pure of heart almost to the point of disingenuity, treating everything with serious attention. For him human dignity was the most important thing. He was precise and simple in his ways, the first to answer every national call, whether it be to the Jewish brigade during the First World War or the British army in the Second World War, when he was above the required age and enlisted together with his son, Haim. A few weeks ago his beloved son fell near Yagur in one of the actions against the enemy. He conquered his tears and his sorrow and wrote his well-known piece, 'To the Mothers and Fathers in Israel'.

During the last few weeks I worked alongside him, producing 'Jerusalem News'. He willingly accepted the job of night editor of this paper, in addition to his work on 'Davar', rejoicing at every demonstration of unity and cooperation. With his modesty, his understanding approach to everyone, his genuine brotherly love and considerate approach to every issue, he bridged the differences between the various newspapers.

More than anything else he loved Jerusalem, touring its ancient institutions and modern undertakings. He was happy to express its desires and act as spokesman for its functionaries. He did not cover up failures or conceal errors. He admired every new enterprise in Jerusalem, encouraged beginners and beginnings, and aspired towards a Jewish Jerusalem which labored and supported its inhabitants as well as being a center of learning and Jewish culture. And in Jerusalem a piece of shrapnel killed him, fired by the same enemy which had killed his son, Haim.

One morning, when we returned after our work on 'Jerusalem News' and I tried to find shelter from the mortar shells, he said to me calmly: 'One has to be very careful these days. The enemy has a great many tricks up his sleeve, and we need a lot of patience to pay him back in his own coin. We will suffer many casualties, I fear, but anyone who sees the victory which will undoubtedly be ours will be fortunate'.

He did not see it.

11.6.1948

The Government of Israel has twice agreed to an unconditional ceasefire, but the Arabs have not.

During the negotiations for 'ceasefire arrangements' the Swedish mediator, Count Bernadotte, announced that his interpretation of the Security Council resolution (of 29th May 1948) that 'people of military age should not enter the countries at war', is that immigrants to Israel during the ceasefire should be placed in a special camp under the supervision of U.N. personnel. Otherwise he will order young immigrants to be returned to their countries of origin. We heard that Moshe Shertok, the Foreign Minister, reacted angrily when Bernadotte told him that the President of the Security Council agreed with him. Shertok said. That President is only the Syrian delegate, namely, the representative of one of the countries fighting against Israel. Bernadotte rejected Shertok's statement saying: 'He spoke as the representative of the Security Council, not of Syria'.

*

At ten this morning, after several postponements, the ceasefire came into force. The Government of Israel published an official announcement to this effect, warning that anyone who violated the ceasefire would be considered an enemy of the State.

The municipal institutions made sure that there was electricity for one hour this morning, so that people could listen to the broadcast of Kol Hamagen HaIvri and the announcements concerning the ceasefire. (Appendix 54)

Major-General David Shealtiel, commander of the Haganah in the Jerusalem region, published the following announcement at the time of the ceasefire:

"I address you on the day the thunder of the cannon around Jerusalem ceases and you are able to walk about the city without fear, to warn you that behind the wall Arab snipers await you and that at every moment you and your relatives are in danger of being shot and your homes of being shelled.

"On behalf of myself and my comrades in arms I wish to congratulate you today, inhabitants of the capital, on your steadfastness during the six months of the war. You are termed 'the rear', but in a besieged city the distinction between front and rear becomes confused. You stood firm, and your resolution was unwavering during this joint battle. Your heads remained unbowed throughout the bitter and barbaric bombardment by the enemy, which took its dreadful toll of your nearest and dearest. In silence you endured the sleepless nights, the dearth of water and the rationing of food. Your staunch perseverance enabled the fighting forces to fulfill their duty with confidence at the front line. You lived up to your proud heritage. You showed the world how an ancient, stubborn people fights for its home and its inheritance. ·

"Today we have reached the end of a chapter in the campaign. The ceasefire came into force an hour ago, but I must warn you that it will be in effect for only four weeks. I must caution you that the war has not ended. The war will continue, both for the State of Israel and for Jerusalem.

"Residents of Jerusalem, for nine years, since the publication of the White Paper, the eternal capital has suffered more than anywhere else in the country. The British forces rent it asunder and did their utmost to bring the city to its knees. Now hired mercenaries have been sent to destroy and ravage it, but ever since the banner of freedom has been raised in our country, on 14th May 1948, many restrictions have been removed. The gates of its stronghold have been opened and its pride and honor have been restored to it.

"Today, the day of the ceasefire, we honor the memory of the daughters of Jerusalem the capital to the north and south, which fell to the enemy. We remember the Old City, which was defeated by enemy forces, and we prepare to continue the battle. We will ready ourselves for the supreme effort that still awaits us when the ceasefire ends, and prepare for it physically and spiritually.

"We cannot yet return to our normal routine. We must continue our efforts in every sphere of life, in work, recruitment, fortifications and production. Carry on working as you have done till now, in a disciplined and responsible way, without any illusions. Every one of the twenty-eight days of the ceasefire, every moment, must be devoted to the campaign, and then we will win the battle to bring peace to the city of peace".

A special order of the day issued by the commander of the Haganah to soldiers in Jerusalem read:

"We have been ordered to cease firing for four weeks, starting at 10 a.m. today. If the enemy honors this ceasefire, another stage in the present war, in which we have been engaged since 29th November 1947, will have ended. When this war began, six and a half months ago, it was clear to us that we faced a difficult and lengthy struggle which would not end until our nation had been assured a just and lasting peace. Today, despite the order to cease fire for the moment, it is evident that our war will not end until freedom, independence and safe borders are guaranteed for the State of Israel.

"Soldiers of the Haganah, you have inscribed another glorious page in the ancient annals of the eternal city. Prepare now with fortitude and wisdom for the final and decisive stage of the battle, until victory is ours".

14.6.1948

On the eve of the festival of Weeks (Shavuot), the first festival to be celebrated in the State of Israel and the first on which there was no access to the Old City and the Western Wall, the army issued permits to forty soldiers and several journalists to conduct the night liturgy of Shavuot in the cave in David's Tomb on Mount Zion.

We ascended Mount Zion at night, so as to remain unperceived by the Legionnaires posted on the walls of the Old City. At first we hesitated to speak out loud, fearing that our voices would reach the Arabs, but gradually our enthusiasm grew and between one reading and another we sang Hassidic tunes and melodies, singing out loud so that our voices would carry to the abandoned and desolate Jewish Quarter.

Before dawn we climbed onto the roof of the building and, with the first rays of the sun, cast warm and longing glances towards the site of the Temple and the Western Wall. No one asked the question which was in all our hearts: For how long shall we stand and gaze towards the Western Wall from Mount Zion? We felt that the war for the deliverance of Jerusalem had not yet ended.

*

Until the very last moments, and even after the time fixed for the ceasefire, the Arab-British Legion tried to wreak death and destruction in Jerusalem and its non-combatant population. Several children were killed by enemy shells ten minutes after the ceasefire had come into force. Every night before that as well as on the Friday morning (the day of the ceasefire), the enemy made frantic efforts to conquer some of our positions, push us back and break through our lines, but without success. In a frontal attack by the Haganah and Etzel several Legionnaires were killed in the area of Sheikh Jarrah. Two houses next to the mosque there were blown up and destroyed. Enemy attacks on Ramat Rachel, Notre Dame and Musrara were repelled and three of the Legion's armored vehicles were made unserviceable.

At ten minutes past ten the last enemy shell was fired from Nebi Samuel at the city center, and only then did they lay down their arms.

On Friday and Saturday many people still hesitated to go out into the streets. On Saturday night we heard shooting from the direction of Beth Tzefafa, and there were rumors that one of the convoys to Jerusalem had been attacked. On the day of the festival people recovered, praying in private homes because many synagogues had been damaged or destroyed. In the afternoon many people walked about the city, looking at the damage which had been caused to buildings here and there. Many visited the hospitals and asked after the wounded. Professional and amateur photographers snapped ruined buildings. Journalists also roamed around, to inspect the city. They toured Beth Yisrael, Shaarei Pina, Meah Shearim and Geulah, an area which had been particularly badly damaged by enemy shelling from north Jerusalem (Nebi Samuel and Shuafat). In many apartments near the front we saw people who had not left their homes and had found shelter in cellars and temporary shelters.

The buildings which had been worst affected included the Great Yeshiva of Meah Shearim, which had received several direct hits, and the 'Hapoel Hamizrahi' building in the Street of the Ethiopians, which was pocked with shrapnel holes and whose synagogue had been hit by a shell and its windows shattered. Large holes gaped in many hospitals, schools and synagogues.

The children of Jerusalem sighed with relief and collected shells and shrapnel as souvenirs. Neighbors greeted one another with the benediction, 'Blessed is He that has kept us in life'. Friends and acquaintances met with rejoicing.

In one of the public buildings which had been badly damaged by shells, the following inscription remained untouched: 'And I will cause an alarm of war to be heard in Rabbah of the Ammonites; and it shall be a desolate heap, and her daughters shall be burned with fire: then shall Israel be heir unto them that were his heirs, saith the Lord'.

*

The daily ration of food for the inhabitants of besieged Jerusalem is 230 grams of bread per person, a small amount of cornflour (instead of flour), one kilo of carrots (at 130 mills), a kilo of potatoes (at 140 mills), fifty grams of margarine (at 20 mills) and one chicken per two days for every four people. (Appendices 55 and 56)

When the ceasefire began the reporters were taken on a tour of Jerusalem. We saw how similar were the conditions of the men at the front and the civilians at the rear.

In one place we asked one of the old men: 'What did you eat and drink during the raids'? He smiled and said: 'I read through the bible more than twenty times. What else did I have to do? When I was hungry or thirsty, I ate and drank the bible'.

*

Despite the cruel war, both the Arab and Jewish inhabitants of Jerusalem act according to local agreements. We read the following item in one of the local Jewish papers: 'Last night Ramallah Radio announced that tomorrow, Wednesday, workmen will go up onto the roof of St. George's Church in Jerusalem, on the road to Nahlat Shimon, to repair it befor the rains. You are requested not to shoot at them'.

There has been a lot of confusion in marking the borders in

Jerusalem. When the ceasefire began entire Arab families appeared with their children and said simply that they were 'going home', to houses in which our soldiers were already stationed. Our soldiers ordered them to return. The Arabs shrugged their shoulders and did not know what to do.

"We live there", they said, pointing at the house behind us.

Our men asked them: "Were you here last week"?

"No"! they said, shaking their heads.

"Then you must not come here".

It was hard to convince an old Arab who wanted to be allowed to cross, asking the 'simple' question: "What have we got to do with the war? We're simple working folk, other people fought the war. Now everything's over, isn't it"?

"Sir", our men answered him calmly, "whether everything's over or not we don't know yet. Go back to where you were the day before yesterday. When we find that everything really is over and there is peace, we'll see".

*

The regional commander of Jerusalem, David Shealtiel, appeared at a press conference in Jerusalem with the emblem of Jerusalem on his lapel. He came equipped with maps and diagrams, which he used to explain Jerusalem's difficult military position.

The major threat to Jerusalem was not from the north but from the south, he said. Egypt's armored corps was preparing to penetrate the city along an undefended route.

The reporters were unrelenting. Was it really only by 'chance' that the attack intended to rescue the Old City had been delayed and that the battle was abandoned so quickly, or was it the result of a defined policy?

Shealtiel tried to conceal his anger without much success, sighed and explained for the hundredth time what had happened.

At least two weeks were needed to complete the preparations for a campaign like that, he said. When the Security Council decided on the ceasefire we faced a military and political problem: was it worth attempting to storm the Old City nevertheless or not? Was there any point in losing additional lives in a battle whose success was doubtful, or was it preferable to gain additional salients elsewhere, such as Sheikh Jarrah in the north or Beth Tzefafa in the south? The decision was to try and take the Old City.

Sometimes, he added, even good planning and first-rate execution do not succeed. When the advance began, we were unable to take positions from which to attack in the Old City and were obliged to retreat when the ceasefire came into force. We had wanted to take the Old City on the 17th of Tammuz, the date on which the walls of Jerusalem had been penetrated by the enemy at the sieges during the periods of the First and Second Temples, but unfortunately we had not succeeded.

Why hadn't the Israeli army captured the Old City when the British left Jerusalem? one reporter persisted.

Shealtiel replied that on that day the Etzion Bloc had fallen and an armored column of the enemy's had been in position on the road between Hebron and Bethlehem. The southern part of the city had been open to the enemy. The British were still in Talpiot. "At that time we were very short of weapons, men and ammunition. We had a very clear commission, to defend the lives of the one hundred thousand Jews in Jerusalem, to link up the areas of Jewish Jerusalem and to eliminate the enemy pockets. We implemented our commission, but our limited strength prevented us from conquering the Old City at that time. There was no political reason for our failure to take it. An attempt was made to go in". Shealtiel showed us the order of the day which had been issued to the soldiers and which began with the words: 'Tonight you have been charged with the historic mission of conquering the Old City'.

Jerusalem was conquered by its inhabitants, the commander continued. "When the attack began there were very few soldiers in the city, hardly any trained men and insufficient and outdated arms. We began mobilizing the young men, though it was no easy task to get people out of Meah Shearim who had large families to look after, and send them to the front. There was no money to provide for the families nor any heavy guns. At any rate, we continued to mobilize because our objective was to save Jewish lives. Jerusalem remained without food or water, clothing or shoes, and was shelled by day and by night. The heroism of Jerusalem lies in its steadfastness rather than its conquests, for to remain day after day in the same salient and to stay calm and resolute, that is true courage".

Shealtiel devoted much time to rejecting the accusations made by breakaway groups. He described Lehi's 'attack' on the Old City and said that the first the Haganah headquarters knew of it was when they received a call for help from them. They had gone to save Jews, he said, but what was the point of attempting to conquer David's Tower when the Jews of Jerusalem were endangered by the threat of an enemy invasion? They may have merely wished to obtain for themselves the glory of being the ones to take David's Tower, he declared. "As commander of the city, I had one mission, to ensure the safety of Jewish lives. If I had gone along with Lehi in this attack and succeeded in conquering David's Tower I should have had to be court-martialled for endangering the entire city".

He recalled that at Sheikh Jarrah Etzel had abandoned its positions in the Police School, and added that there was no cause to be ashamed at making a necessary retreat, but that Etzel should not hurl accusations at others.

The breakaway organizations, he stated, "demand a share in commanding troops in Jerusalem, although they have not added much in the way of military strength to the city. Instead, they are too much concerned with political matters. Why should they have a share of the command? They may be specialists in underground fighting, but war is not fought in the underground. It is true that they are good soldiers, but that has nothing to do with command. I am the commander of Jerusalem", Major-General Shealtiel stressed.

17.6.1948

Through Mr. Neuhaus, the Belgian consul, a meeting was arranged
between the regional commander of the Haganah, David Shealtiel, and
the commander of the Jordanian Legion, Abdullah el-Tal. It was agreed
that during the two hours of the meeting both sides would refrain from
firing, so that the meeting could be conducted 'in a peaceful
atmosphere'.

The meeting place was a partly-destroyed building, which had been
the Christian St. Mary school before the war, in Suleiman Street,
descending from Notre Dame and the old Municipality building which
is in our hands towards the Damascus Gate, which is in the hands of
the Arabs.

Shealtiel was accompanied by auxiliary officers, Zion Eldad,
Yeshurun Schiff and Joseph Shnurman, as well as by two or three
journalists, including myself.

Both the Arab and the Jewish commanders brought deputies and
advisers with them as well as journalists and photographers. It was a
strange experience to walk along, a handful of officers and reporters, led
by a U.N. man with a white flag in his hand. We passed the courtyard
of Notre Dame and entered Suleiman Street, which was considered no-
man's-land but was in fact a battlefield. The street was lined with
broken glass and fragments of shells. Here and there lay the corpses of
Arabs who had been killed in the war, and who had not been buried by
their comrades. A few shots still echoed and the sound of automatic fire
could be heard in the distance. The shelling had stopped. as had been
agreed.

A similar 'procession' emerged from the Damascus Gate, with the
Arab commander, Abdullah el-Tal and his aides, led by a U.N. man.
He was accompanied by an Iraqi officer who had joined the Jordanian
Legion, and three officers, Tark Bey Askari, Muhammed Hazam Bey
and Haled Majali.

The members of the 'ceasefire commission' introduced Shealtiel and
el-Tal to one another, then their seconds-in-command and their aides.

The journalists did not wait to be introduced. As professional colleagues they went over to one another, shook hands and exchanged greetings, as if they had been serving in distant countries and had just met. The journalists were introduced to the commanders. We knew most of the Arab newsmen from the good old days. A few jokes were cracked and mutual smiles exchanged.

The meeting was 'chaired' by the members of the ceasefire commission, the Belgian Consul, Neuhaus (chairman), the consuls of the U.S. and France and the U.N. representative. The commanders sat opposite one another, flanked by their aides. The Jewish and Arab journalists stood behind them together with two or three foreign correspondents and photographers. The commanders spoke and the reporters took notes.

The subject on the agenda was 'no-man's-land' and the ban on either side exploiting agreed ceasefires for conquering areas or buildings. Shealtiel asked his counterpart, Colonel el-Tal, to allow the scrolls of the law to be removed from the ruined synagogues in the Old City and brought over to our side. Then the lists of prisoners of war were compared and the date and method of exchanging them was discussed.

The Jewish journalists had an opportunity to hold a friendly conversation with their Arab colleagues. The newsmen from 'over there' did not conceal their surprise (and disappointment) on hearing that no one was dying of hunger in Jewish Jerusalem and that we had suffcent food and water.

One of the reporters suggested suddenly that we commemorate the first joint meeting by having our picture taken, for who was to know if and when there would be another one. His proposal was accepted without demur.

We parted, once again exchanging handshakes, phrases and smiles. We turned our backs on one another and each group walked towards its own sector. Half an hour later shells were again falling on Jerusalem. The 'unfinished symphony' shattered the air and cast fear into our hearts.

Was it the same Arab commanders with whom we had sat and whose hands we had shaken who were responsible for that vicious attack? We knew, and they had hinted to us, that they were mere 'puppets' in the hands of their superiors. Jewish Jerusalem was not slow in paying them back, and fired its share of shells and bullets.

The next day we attended a similar meeting of commanders. While we were still on our way a heavy bombardment began suddenly. We jumped aside, hugging the walls helplessly. Shells exploded noisily beside us, their fragments scattering in every direction. Miraculously no one was hurt. When the shelling stopped we continued on our way to the meeting. Abdullah el-Tal apologized, explaining the incident as the consequence of his soldiers' lack of obedience and responsibility, half in jest half in earnest, using one word: 'Wallad' (children).

As was his way, he gave a pleasant smile which dispelled the tension.

18.6.1948

There have been rumors in the city that representatives of 'Neturei Karta' in Meah Shearim and Batei Ungarin went out into the street with a white flag in their hand saying: 'We'll go to the Arabs. We've had enough of war'.

When I visited these neighborhoods nobody had heard of the incident. On the contrary, we saw yeshiva students leaving the area to engage in building fortifications and to guard the city at night. (Appendix 57)

*

People who have returned from Tel Aviv report that serious claims were put forward by the citizens of Jerusalem at the National Council against the Institutions and leaders, who are not doing enough for the city. They said that the feeling in Jerusalem is that it would have been possible to conquer all of the city, but that this had not been done for political reasons.

Ben-Gurion replied that these claims were serious and if they were justified then the persons responsible should have been court-martialled. But they were unfounded, he asserted. Most of Jerusalem is in our hands, and what is not we could not have conquered. Much Jewish blood has been spilt for the liberation of Jerusalem, and such claims should not be made.

*

Although we were busy with our local problems, our hearts and ears were inclined towards Tel-Aviv, to hear what was happening there, where our leaders were.

A few days ago Ben-Gurion said, rightly, that 'the resolutions of 29th November are dead. Neither the U.N., the U.S.A. nor Russia established the State. The Jews and the Israeli army did'. He added that if the war was not decided one way or another, we would be faced with a situation when we would be told that the resolutions of 29th November would have to be upheld. We did not want war. We would not be 'stupidly correct', he said, "and to return the refugees would be folly. Those who made war on us will have to take the consequences. The Arabs disregarded the U.N. resolution, and if they had been strong enough there would be nothing left of the U.N. decision, and perhaps even of the Jews of Palestine, and no one in the U.N. would say a word".

B.G. cited the case of the expulsion of the Jews from the Old City. No state or individual protested against that violation of U.N. decisions. It would be good if the U.N. also ensured that its resolutions were implemented, but the fact is that the Jewish State was not established because of or with the help of the U.N., and the Israeli army, not an international force, faced the Arab aggressors[1].

---

[1]   This is outlined in greater detail in Ben-Gurion's book, 'When Israel Fought', published by Mapai, 1951 (Hebrew).

I was one of a group of journalists taken on a tour of a camp, 'somewhere in Jerusalem', where several Arab prisoners-of-war were being held. They were men between the ages of 15 and 55, ranged in a straight row in front of us, and we were invited to speak to them briefly. Most of them had been captured while fighting in and around Jerusalem. A few had been found here and there in buildings taken by the Haganah. One of these 'fighters' told us that until he had been captured be had had 'a first-rate American rifle'. Some reporters recognized former acquaintances among the prisoners: the secretary of the C.I. D. in Jerusalem, a man who had sold drinks in the corridors of the law courts, a well-known Arab lawyer, an Arab regional officer who had been captured during battle, an engineer, a merchant, etc. Many of them spoke English and one of them, a former cook in one of the capital's best hotels, spoke fluent Hebrew.

When the prisoners-of-war were asked how they were being treated they said that the food was good and they were satisfied. One of them complained that there was no variety to the food, and 'every day it's the same thing, beans and lentils'. Others announced that they did not want to return to the Arab sector, and that they were satisfied to remain here. One of them asked: 'when is the ceasefire going to begin'? They were very happy to receive a copy of the Palestine Post and were offended when we asked how many of them were illiterate. About ten of them could not read or write, and their comrades had undertaken to teach them. Some of them, on the other hand, were graduates of the American University in Beirut. They and others were studying Hebrew.

They all slept on good mattresses, received 2,200 calories of food each day, and had a clinic and a doctor who looked after them devotedly.

Mr. de-Reynier, the head of the International Red Cross delegation in Israel, visited the prisoner-of-war camp and said he was very satisfied with it. He claimed that it was on a par with the best European camps.

*

A few weeks ago the following notice appeared in the local press concerning 'the distribution of mail': 'Residents of the Beth Yisrael, Nahlat Shimon, Bathei Zibenbergen and Nahlat Yitzhak Quarters and the area in and around St. Paul's Street who have left their homes and gone to live elsewhere, should apply to the leader (mukhtar) of the Beth Yisrael Quarter, Moshe Alpert, at his home. Letters and cables have been given to him. Anyone who thinks that there may be mail for him should apply to the mukhtar'.

*

The foreign and local correspondents in Jerusalem heard that negotiations had been conducted, again via the consuls, with the Jordanians, to allow a group of orthodox Jews to go to the Western Wall to pray. The Jewish Agency spokesman admitted, in reply to a question, that secret negotiations had been held and that the Jordanians had initially stipulated that the people allowed through should not be under sixty years of age. Another of their conditions had been that the group should not contain more than twenty men. We were obliged to agree to both conditions, the spokesman added, but in the event the Jordanians cancelled the agreement. (Appendix 58)

20.6.1948

During these days of siege, considerable publicity has been given to Dr. Susskin's research on the need and possibility of growing potatoes and other vegetables by the hydroponics system (growing plants without soil in water). The research study maintains that the U.S. army used this method successfully in its war against the Japanese in the jungle.

At a press conference details were given of the pillage of abandoned Arab homes in the Sheikh Badr Quarter. The People's Guard hurried to the spot to prevent wanton robbery and looting, and some of them were beaten by their countrymen who thought that from now on 'anything goes'.

The 'unfinished symphony' of firing and shelling continues at night. Some people have such 'musical' ears that they can distinguish between 'our' firing and 'theirs'.

*

The most popular 'commodity' in Tel-Aviv is a reporter from Jerusalem. A few days ago the military correspondent, Azarya Rappaport, was there and was asked to speak about Jerusalem at the Journalists' Forum there. Azarya described Jerusalem's military and economic position, and the boost the inhabitants of the besieged city had received from the Palmah's actions. He stressed that Jerusalem could hold on but still needed support and supplies from Tel Aviv.

The inhabitants of Jerusalem see each other with fresh eyes, as if they have been born anew. When they go out into the streets it is as if they are saying, we shall not die but live, for nevertheless and despite everything we are still alive. On nights of suffering they say: 'Oh, what a night. Thank God it's over'.

Is it really over? We would like to believe it is, but the nights of suffering recur again and again.

*

During the ceasefire a group of journalists visited Rabbi Joseph Gershon Horowitz, the rabbi of Meah Shearim and the doyen of Jerusalem's rabbis. The rabbi addressed us, speaking in a spirit of belief that Jewish Jerusalem will be victorious. We began telling him how grim the actual situation is. Synagogues have been destroyed in the Old City, people are killed every day and who knows how things will end. The old rabbi, who had celebrated his 80th birthday not long before, stopped us and, like a seasoned soldier, said: "Never mind, our soldiers will conquer the Old City yet, and it shall be rebuilt by Israel".

*

Rabbis Ben-Zion, Hazan and Minzberg were permitted to return to the Jewish Quarter in the Old City to examine the damage caused to synagogues. They were accompanied by Dr. Abraham Bergman, a Belgian officer, and Abdullah el-Tal, the commander of the Arab Legion. They found everything devastated. There are no arks of the law, and nothing is left of the ritual appurtenances or the ancient synagogues, including the Porath Yosef yeshivah. The rabbis were not allowed to approach the Western Wall. The Arab commander said to them: 'Some other time'.

22.6.1948

The visit of a Minister from Tel-Aviv is an event which gets headlines in the local press. In large print we were informed that three Ministers, Eliezer Kaplan, Moshe Shapira and Aharon Zisling, have come to Jerusalem to discuss our pressing needs with the city fathers and to report to the cabinet in Tel-Aviv.

The newspapers tell us that the Foreign Minister, Moshe Shertok, has also visited Jerusalem. The sources are the foreign correspondents (U.P.), who state that Shertok met with B. Joseph, the chairman of the Jerusalem Committee, and discussed the city's problems with him.

Dr. Joseph assembled the Jerusalem reporters and spoke about the possibility that the war will be renewed, referring to 'a difficult discussion' with the intermediary, Bernadotte, about supplying food to Jewish Jerusalem. He also told us that the U.S. representative on the Ceasefire Commission, Bordat, supported Bernadotte's view that 2,800 calories of food per day was sufficient for the Jews of Jerusalem, stating that millions of people in China subsisted on far less.

Mr. Joseph informed the journalists that at present we have adequate supplies of food. The 230 drivers from Tel-Aviv who were stuck here for eight weeks, ever since bringing the large convoy of food just before Passover, had received all they needed from the municipal institutions, plus an 'idleness' benefit. Dr. Joseph expressed the hope that the

Government would recognize Jerusalem's special expenses and would reimburse the city.

*

The Ministers, Moshe Shapira and Rabbi I.M. Levin, participated in a meeting at the home of Chief Rabbi Herzog, at which Rabbis Dushinski and Dr. M. Buxbaum were also present. Amongst other things, it was decided at this meeting to set up a supreme committee of Jerusalem rabbis.

29.6.1948

The Arab Legion's intentions of attacking Jerusalem are clear to anyone who bothers to go up on one of the roofs of the houses near the border. The immense work on constructing fortifications in the Arab sector appears to be at its height. From one of the observation points I saw about one thousand Arab laborers returning in vehicles belonging to the Legion from building fortifications and digging trenches in the Sheikh Jarrah area. This work is done mainly at night. An employee at one of the consulates told us that this work of constructing fortifications includes building bases for heavy 100-pound mortars, which are being set up five or ten kilometers away from the city. Preparations are also being made on the Jerusalem-Tel-Aviv road, near Shaar Hagai. The Arab Legion is training its artillery ceaselessly north of Ramallah, in the famous Valley of the Thieves and elsewhere. Extensive preparations are also being made inside the Old City. The Arabs understand that if they attack New Jerusalem the Old City will come under attack too, and they are preparing it to absorb lead and steel.

During the last few nights women and children have been evacuated from the Old City and moved to Jordan. The general impression is that the battle for Jerusalem could be reopened at any moment. The number of British officers in the Arab Legion has grown during the past days. 14 officers who were under General MacMillan's command have gone over to the Arab Legion.

It has been learned that the Arab Legion's manoeuvres which were held on Saturday to the north of Ramallah were intended to serve as an exercise in undertaking an infantry advance under cover of mortar fire. I was told that the Legion had been accustomed to this method of warfare in the desert or on flat terrain but not on mountains, and was now practising this.

In addition to cutting off our water supplies, the Arabs are now attempting to limit Jerusalem's food still more. The Ceasefire Committee, which is a consular committee, has informed the Jewish authorities that it cannot permit the amount of food which the Jews demand to be brought in to the city during the ceasefire. Our calculations were based on allotting 4,200 calories per person each day, which is 700 tons of food for the entire city, while the committee permits only 2,800 calories per day. There are serious differences of opinion on this point. This quantity does not include fuel or medicines. Negotiations are still going on regarding water, and the Belgian Consul is still discussing the water supply with the Arab Legion but has not yet received any answer.

The American-Belgian colonel is meanwhile conducting special negotiations on behalf of the U.N. with the commander of the Arab Legion in Jerusalem about the demilitarization of Mount Scopus and the complete neutralization of the Hebrew University and the Hadassah Hospital, which are registered as American property.

At a ceremony to mark the 'swearing-in' of the soldiers, Major-General Shealtiel showed us a map of Jerusalem, the 'ceasefire map', signed by the U.N. representative, the Arab commander, el-Tal, and himself about two weeks ago. He took the opportunity of telling us that he had prepared some 'surprises' for Abdullah el-Tal if and when the fighting was renewed.

7.7.1948

The intermediary, Bernadotte, has published his proposals for 'resolving the conflict' between us and the Arabs. Most of the Jews of Jerusalem have reacted with anger. There is no shortage of 'proposals'. There have been innumerable deliberations and the U.N. passed a resolution, which we accepted for lack of anything better. Why should the tiny area allocated to our country by the U.N. be restricted even more?

Bernadotte proposes that Jerusalem should be given to the Arabs (while the U.N. suggested that it be 'internationalized'). Most of the Negev, he says, should also be given to the Arabs (to King Abdullah). Western Galilee will be within Israel, there should be unrestricted Jewish immigration for two years and economic federation between Israel and Transjordan. Haifa will become a free port and Lydda a free airport.

*

The official ceasefire will come to an end in another two or three days. Meanwhile there is no break in the unofficial attacks, and the toll of dead and wounded continues.

In an article in 'Davar Yerushalayim', Yitzhak Ben-Zvi writes that in three weeks Jerusalem has been the target of more than twenty thousand shells, and the number of its dead has exceeded one thousand. He claims that the pain and suffering endured by the spiritual isolation of Jerusalem's Jewish population is no less than that of its material isolation.

Ben-Zvi concludes his article with the following sentences: 'For many weeks we have not seen a Tel-Aviv newspaper. We have not seen our Government's official gazette either and do not know what new laws and arrangements have been introduced by the Government.

9.7.1948

Our expectations that the ceasefire would continue have been dashed. The ceasefire has ended. Already today we felt a fundamental change in the situation, as shells whistled past from our positions to the Arab bases. Many people smile, hoping that the conquest of the Old City is not far off. May their hopes be fulfilled.

The municipal committee of the Communal Council, with the participation of members of the Municipality and representatives of the neighborhoods, assembled to hear Count Bernadotte's proposals. They rejected them unanimously, defining them as an 'obstacle' to any agreement. They all called on the Government of Israel not to allow Jerusalem to exist in 'a political vacuum'. In their resolution they urged the Government to annex Jerusalem to the State of Israel and declare it as its capital. The representatives of Agudath Yisrael were the only ones who did not support the resolution, claiming that this is not the time for 'provocative resolutions'.

*

Rumor has it that a water-pipe has been laid in secret from the coastal plain to Jerusalem. The censorship has banned any reference whatsoever to it. The pipe was laid at the same time as the 'Burma Road', the secret road which by-passes Latrun, was built, and now there is water in our taps.

*

The leaders of the Jewish population of Jerusalem acted like the patriarch, Jacob, in the verse, 'Why do ye look one upon another?' They did not reveal their victory over the enemy, who wished to kill the residents of Jerusalem by thirst, and the fact that water flows through the new pipe to Jerusalem. One of the items in the ceasefire negotiations with the Arabs, through the mediation of the foreign consuls, was that the flow of water from Rosh Haayin be resumed and that the pumps at Latrun be enabled to work. What did the Arabs do? They bombed the pumps at Latrun and were 'sure' that the Jews of Jerusalem would soon surrender.

In former times rainwater was collected in cisterns, in the courtyards of the houses, for the use of the inhabitants of the houses. This is still the case in the old neighborhoods, where every house was built with a cistern, just as every house is built with a shelter these days. In order to ease the shortage of water the British laid pipes from King Solomon's Pools, to the south of the city, and from Maayan-Farrah to the north. Later on, a more efficient water system was built, and a special pipeline was laid from Rosh Haayin, near Petach-Tikvah, to the reservoirs in Jerusalem. During the siege the Arabs stopped the pumps at Rosh Haayin and on the way to Jerusalem.

The Arabs cut off the water supply to Jerusalem about a week before the State was established, when they closed the pumping station at Latrun. Two weeks before they left the country, the British informed the leaders of the Jewish population:

"We regret that we are unable to honor our committment to transfer the pumps and machinery in the plant at Rosh Haayin to you, because they have been seized by the Iraqis".

When the Jewish representatives protested the British told them not to get so excited as the pipes were anyway starting to get rusty and could not be changed in present conditons.

The city fathers appointed a special team, headed by the engineer, Zvi Leibovitz, which quickly cleaned and repaired about two thousand empty cisterns in the city, under the noses of the British and the Arabs. For several days and nights the employees of the Municipality ran water into the cisterns and filled them up. On one occasion the British engineer expressed his surprise to his colleagues at the increase in the consumption of water. The Jewish employees of the Water Department immediately showed him reports of 'faulty pipes' and an abundance of 'leaks' which needed to be repaired. The conquest of Katamon at

Pesach brought additional water as full cisterns were found in the courtyards of many of the houses there. The ration of water for drinking and washing could be increased accordingly.

When the pipeline from Rosh Haayin was cut off and both the Arabs and the British were sure that the inhabitants of Jerusalem would start to feel its effects, everyone in Jewish Jerusalem was promised about ten liters of water per day. This amount was distributed by special vehicles, which went through the neighborhood centers. The drivers often had to do their job under a hail of bullets and shells. The People's Guard accompanied them, to keep order and protect them from sudden attacks. Some of the people doing this work were killed while doing their duty, saving the residents of Jerusalem from thirst, until the new pipe could be laid.

12.7.1948

For the first time in Jerusalem's history it has experienced an air raid. An Egyptian plane dropped bombs on Jewish Jerusalem, killing two people. It was some consolation to us to know that our cannon, which are newly installed in the city, are giving as good as they get. Time and again, in the morning and the afternoon, the Arabs tried to break into Jewish Jerusalem from Suleiman Street towards Notre Dame and from the Zion Gate towards Mount Zion. The assailants were repelled by the heavy fire our defenders opened on them, and turned back in confusion.

Jerusalem is gradually breaking the vise of the enemy and overcoming the siege. To the north east of Jerusalem the Jordanian army was deployed in a long, doubled-over crescent with its center at Sheikh Jarrah, while the Egyptians were dug in to the south-west of the city.

The conquest of the village of Malha which is at the far end of Emek Refaim (Baka) and controls the Tel-Aviv-Jerusalem railway track, Beth Tzefafa and Mar Elias, where the Egyptian army is deployed, will provide a 'jumping-off point' for taking Ein-Karem. The village is already isolated and surrounded.

14.7.1948

Haganah headquarters have announced that another ceasefire is to come into force at 3.p.m. on Sunday. The consular Ceasefire Committee has requested that the ceasefire be observed. Nevertheless, the Arabs have attacked our positions in Musrara. A hail of bullets was fired from the wall of the Old City, killing several Jews in the first hours of the ceasefire.

The Jewish Agency spokesman registered a protest against the cables the consuls had sent to the U.N. stating that 'the Jews have violated the ceasefire', whereas it is the Arabs who continue firing.

It was suggested that the aid given to the observers by special Haganah 'liaison officers' should be stopped, but it was concluded that this would harm us, and so their activity continues.

18.7.1948

Another attempt to take the Old City has failed. For some days we warmed ourselves with the thought that we would soon return to our ancient city and the remnant of our Temple, the Western Wall, but it was not to be. When another ceasefire (the second) was discussed, on 17th July, the decision was made to break into the Old City, and the word was passed around that this was to be within the framework of operation 'Kedem'. The Etzioni Brigade went towards the Zion Gate and Etzel approached the New Gate. The city shook to the sound of mortars and cannons, but the wall was not breached. Etzel succeeded in getting through the New Gate, but the wall at the Zion Gate stood firm. Daylight put an end to the operation before it could get under way, and the second ceasefire came into effect.

BETWEEN BOMBARDMENTS

20.7.1948

After the commanders of the Arab Legion and the Egyptian troops refused to meet the Jewish commander yesterday, and it was said that there were differences of opinion between the Jordanian and Egyptian commanders, the three men met twice today to determine a border-line between the sides.

The second meeting was at Ramat Rachel. The commander of the Legion, Abdullah el-Tal, came accompanied by three British officers. Lieutenant-Colonel Ahmed Abd al-Aziz, the commander of the Egyptian forces in south Jerusalem, attended the meeting after all. The meeting was chaired by the U.N. observers, Colonels Bagley and Andronovitz. While the discussions were going on in the conference room, we Jewish, Jordanian and Egyptian journalists went outside and had our photograph taken together.

At the meeting the border was agreed on and all sides accepted the ceasefire proposal. We'll wait and see.

22.7.1948

May the grace of the city be granted to its inhabitants. I have just returned from a lightning tour of the borders of Jewish Jerusalem and the outlying neighborhoods, which have received a heavy 'baptism of fire'.

185

The starting point for our tour was the Nahlat Shiva Quarter, one of the first to be built outside the walls of the city by seven Jews on the 2nd of Iyar, 1869.

To the south the neighborhood borders on the Moslem cemetry, and to the east on Princess Mary Street (Queen Shlomzion today), areas which were a source of trouble for the residents of the quarter untill 15th May. But that is the source of Jerusalem's strength and vitality, its inhabitants did not leave.

We went down Jaffa Road. We saw Russian nuns going in and out of the Russian church and the adjoining buildings, which in the past had served as hostels for Russian pilgrims who used to come here before the First World War. The entire area, including the buildings of law courts, the C.I.D. and Apac are now controlled by the Military Governor as occupied territory. the fine Central Post Office building has been re-opened, and entry to it is from Princess Mary Street.

We reached Allenby Square, named for the commander-in-chief of the British forces which conquered Palestine in 1918. It makes one think when one sees the square covered in broken glass and surrounded by ruined buildings.

We did not go far. The enemy was peering at us through the apertures in David's Tower, his gun at the ready. In the distance we could see the block of Arab buildings which our people had blown up and destroyed in the last few days.

It grieves one to see the enemy entrenched in David's Tower. It is some consolation to know that he is not free to move, as our snipers are constantly on guard. Our guide, who seasoned his words with memories from the recent and the distant past, reminded us of the Jewish revolt against the Romans, when this citadel was an extremely important defensive point, which fell only after all Jerusalem had been conquered.

From Allenby Spuare we turned right into Mamilla Street. On our right was the cemetry, and on our left the Palace Hotel, where several British commissions had sat 'to discuss the rights of the Jews in

Palestine'. We went towards Jaffa Gate. On our left was the large building of the nuns of the Vincent de Paul order. Facing us was the house in which Dr. Herzl and his entourage had stayed when they visited Jerusalem fifty years ago.

We walked along Julian Street, named after the Roman emperor who had given the Jews permission to build a temple on Mount Moriah in the year 362, althogh the building had never been erected. On our left was the Jewish Commercial Center, where we had learned how 'neutral' the British were in dealing with Arab opposition to Zionism, and where the battle for Jerusalem had begun, finding us 'between the hammer and the anvil'. Near what had been the Arab vegetable market and the bus-stop for the Arab buses to Hebron and Bethlehem was a large, imposing building. That was the 'Tannous building', which had served as the center of Arab activities in Jerusalem, such as the offices of the Arab Higher Committee, the embargo on Zionist products, etc. Now it was a defensive position for us and a point from which to advance further. From here it is only a few meters to the Jaffa Gate and David's Tower.

We continued walking along Julian Street towards the Y.M.C.A. building on our right and the King David Hotel to our left. A fine hill commands the entire area. Now we could see how and from where the British 'guardians of the law' had stabbed the Jewish quarter of Yemin Moshe in the back, as it faced a frenzied and well-armed (already then!) Arab mob on the hill adjoining the city wall on the other side. Our soldiers on this hill play an important part in restricting the movements of the enemy at the Jaffa Gate and David's Tower.

The railway station stands at the end of Julian Street. This was the first railway track to be laid in Israel (between Jerusalem, Lydda and Haifa), at the initiative of Joseph Navon, one of the Jewish residents of Jerusalem. Sixty years ago, after consulting Dr. Herzl, he obtained a firman from Sultan Abed al-Hamid, giving him the right for 71 years to build the track. Trains began running in 1894, and in 1922 the Mandate Government purchased the track for six hundred thousand Palestine pounds. The Government Printing Press building is situated next to the

188 JERUSALEM UNDER SIEGE

railway station, and our men have been occupying both buildings for several weeks.

Another important position is the Arab quarter of Abu Tor, above the Government Printing Press. The houses are built on a ridge overlooking the Valley of Hinnom. At the bottom of the hill is the village of Silwan, where the enemy is still situated. From the mountain to the right, Mount Zion, our soldiers restrict the movements of the Legionnaires, who are entrenched behind the city wall, only 19 meters from the Zion Gate.

From the eastern front we made our way to the southern part of the city. We were told that at Ramat Rachel the front was 'very hot'. The kibbutz buildings had been seriously damaged and the Egyptians had managed to occupy it twice, but our forces drove them out each time. The defenders of Ramat Rachel saw clearly how the enemy was digging in during the first ceasefire. Each night their soldiers would come a few meters nearer, until our soldiers gave them a clear warning.

When the ceasefire ended the enemy was thrown into confusion within less than three hours. The initiative of shelling passed to us and for every shell they fired they got several in return. That same night, as if from beneath the ground, Israeli soldiers advanced towards Ein Karem, to the west of the Mar Elias monastery, where the Egyptians were massed. One salient after another was taken in the Ein Karem area, and the enemy's cannon were diverted from Ramat Rachel to that side. The enemy's positions were being heavily bombarded by our side, however, and they had not expected that, it seems. All at once the enemy's dream of surprising us on the 'Burma Road', which was nearing completion in the hills between Bethlehem, Beth Jallah, Malha and Tzuba, came to an end. Now their forces were within the range of our cannon.

To the north of the city lie Shuafat, the Police School, French Hill and Sheikh Jarrah. In each of these positions there was a battery of cannons aimed towards the New City. That is the Arabs' sole route from Nablus and Ramallah, via the American Colony, where the Red Cross flag flies, to Herod's Gate.

The enemy cannot reach the New, Jaffa and Damascus Gates, and is unable to use these important positions, which come under the fire of the Israeli soldiers. They have, nevertheless, put up a battery of cannons on one of the hills near Damascus Gate, under the protection of the British consul, who has taken over the large German house which formerly served as the offices of the British army. Now, however, this is a doubtful benefit, as our shells have silenced the battery and harmed the enemy, who hoped that the British consul would protest at our firing towards his residence.

The defensive strip around New Jerusalem has not been penetrated anywhere and our forces are advancing towards the complete liberation of our capital. The first steps have been taken, and the next will not be long in following.

23.7.1948

David Shealtiel is a riddle to us journalists as well as to many of the inhabitants of Jerusalem. We were summoned to a meeting with him, as there were firm rumors that he was about to be replaced. It is said that he is introverted and uncommunicative. The civilian and military leaders claim that he does not involve them in his considerations and decisions, whether because he does not wish to worry them unnecessarily or because he does not know them well enough to trust them.

At another meeting with him this morning it seemed that he was trying to modify the tough impression he had made on us at previous meetings. (Appendix 59)

David Shealtiel began by saying that his first meeting with the journalists had been against his will. 'Then I gave in to the pressure of certain people and institutions', he said, 'Today I am meeting you willingly'.

Each reporter introduced himself in turn. Then the Jerusalem regional commander spread out a large map of the city. It was the original map which bore the signatures of the Belgian consul, the member of the U.N. ceasefire commission, Consul Berenson, Bernadotte's representative, our regional commander and his 'colleague', Colonel Abdullah el-Tal, the commander of the Arab-British Legion. The map was printed in three colors. The enemy territory was in green, and included Sheikh Jarrah in the north of Jerusalem and the Old City, an area which was far smaller than the blue which denoted the area in our hands and accouted for about three-quarters of the entire city. To the north-east, like an island in enemy territory, was the blue area of Hadassah and the Hebrew University on Mount Scopus. The Red Cross center near the King David Hotel formed a small dot at the corner of the map. To the north was our border, north of Sanhedria. To the west was the border of municipal Jerusalem, at Lifta and beyond. To the south, the border was at Ramat Rachel and to the east it ran along the wall of the Old City. At some spots the distance between the enemy's positions and ours did not exceed ten meters. At Ramat Rachel the Egyptians had moved forward during the ceasefire.

Pointing at the map in front of us, Shealtiel said: 'Our military position today is far better than it was a month ago. I am absolutely sure that Jerusalem will never be conquered by the Arab armies. The enemy appears to realize this too, and does not dare bring armored forces into Jerusalem, as here they will meet their end. Our most serious problem is to assure supplies for the large civilian population, but we will overcome this too.

'Militarily we failed grievously at Sheikh Jarrah, when Etzel abandoned its positions at the sight of the Arab Legion's advancing armored column. Since Menahem Begin has given his word several times that there was no alternative I believe him, and possible any other unit would have retreated in a similar situation, but it was a failure'.

He was asked whether it was correct, as Etzel claimed, that on that day they had warted for anti-tank weapons to be brought to their positions at Sheikh Jarrah, but that they had not arrived. Shealtiel replied that he did not know anything about that. The Haganah there had provided covering fire, but a cover unit is not strong enough to face the enemy. Our plan had been to link up with Mount Scopus, and we had failed.

Another question referred to the statement made by Mr. Oster, the mayor of Jerusalem, based on 'reliable sources', that if we were shelled by the enemy again we would shell the Old City indiscriminately. In reply Shealtiel stated that he was not the person to which that question should be addressed. "Mr. Oster did not participate in the making of my military plans", he said, "but I will tell you that when I met the commander of the Arab Legion I promised him a 'military surprise' when the battle is resumed".

'And how did Abdullah el-Tal react?' he was asked.

"He smiled like the noble Beduin he is and remamed silent', Shealtiel replied, 'but I assure you that I will keep my promise. We react differently to shelling than the Arabs', he continued. 'The bombardment of Jewish Jerusalem united the inhabitants, reduced the number of shirkers, increased the readiness to fight and led to many cases of mutual help. When we shelled the Old City in the last few days we created an atmospers of panic and confusion among the population there. Many Arabs ran away and it was necessary to declare a curfew several times and use force in order to stop people leaving the Old City'.

'What were the reasons for the fall of the Old City'? was another of the questions he was asked.

'The inhabitants of the Jewish Quarter had been through four months of difficult siege', Shealtiel said. 'The age and character of the inhabitants were such that most of them were passive. The Arabs held positions on all sides. The Armenian Quarter, which is adjacent to the Jewish Quarter, is on higher ground and only after the Arabs entrenched themselves in the Armenian churches and monasteries were the Jews there really endangered. We had enough food but not sufficient ammunition. We tried to break through from the New City to the Jewish Quarter four times. We succeeded only once, and then only for a few hours. On the day they surrendered we were about to embark on a more extensive attempt to break through and there were chances that we would have succeeded, but the people could not hold out any longer. For two weeks our military plans to aid the Old City were under the constant pressure of calls for help on the grounds that 'the situation is critical'. That inevitably influences the planning of any military undertaking. We did not have enough time to calculate everything, to consider every detail and aspect, because we wanted to respond immediately to the urgent calls for help from there, and that pressure did not help us.

"Historians will write one day about the defense of Jerusalem and its brave stand. The inhabitants have no cause to complain, however, that the Yishuv has abandoned them. Jerusalem neglected the Haganah. Very few people know with what arms we faced a strong and well-equipped army in the first few days. Not many know what our stores of weapons were. My first concern was for the immediate danger, and I made sure that the approaches to the city on all sides were fortified to prevent the enemy from advancing with armored columns. Only on 16th May, when we had dug ourselves in around the city, did we begin advancing towards Jaffa Gate. We penetrated as far as the Commercial Center, conquered 'Great Tannous House', and hoped to take David's Tower too, but the enemy put several of our armored vehicles out of commission. We went through a lot, although Leningrad went through more. Jerusalem is wounded, though by no means destroyed, and will be able to withstand its enemies. The fear of danger is greater than the danger itself. I am not a resident of Jerusalem, but I feel like singing the praises of the city. Don't forget, the men fighting in Jerusalem are close to their homes. They have to cope with the day-to-day problems of their families. They are involved in their wife's concern to ensure her children's food and their own anxiety to support their families, and we cannot provide regular help for the soldiers' families. We do not have clothing for our army, and did not even have mattresses until a few days ago. Last winder, during the freezing cold nights, we did not have enough blankets. I am not blaming anyone for this. Israel fights with what it has. We did a lot with hardly any weapons and very little training. This is what conquered Jerusalem. Everyone did his duty, the Palmah did what it was supposed to and so did the field force, the old men, the soldiers trained by Yaakov Patt, everyone'.

A journalist asked whether it would not be advisable, in order to make the fighting easier, to evacuate the civilian population from Jerusalem.

Shealtiel replied: 'That is primarily a political-Zionist problem. We did not hold on to the Old City for military reasons either. Sentiments sometimes turn into military considerations of the first order. The immense tradition which surrounds ancient Jerusalem was a decisive incentive. There is no point in removing the women and children from Jerusalem and making it a military position in an Arab sea. There is a value to Jerusalem which continues its life despite everything, and to which the whole nation is attached.

'How can the population be calmed regarding the future?' he was asked.

'Be calm, but not indifferent', Shealtiel said. 'By that I mean that you should be unruffled, engage in training and build fortifications. The population should continue fortifying the city. There will be no repetition of what has gone before, however. I hope that as a result of the new road from Tel Aviv there will be no siege and complete blockade, as there was before. The Yishuv will break through to us and we will break through to it'.

Question: What were the reasons which led us to hold on to a place like the Etzion Bloc?

Shealtiel: 'First of all, it had considerable political-Zionist value at a time when we emphasized and proved that we had not abandoned a single settlement. The main point, however, is that there was a military argument which maintained that the defense of Jerusalem should not be undertaken at its approaches but at some distance from the city. To the east, at the Dead Sea; to the north, at Atarot and Neve Yaakov; and to the south, at the Etzion Bloc. I am not giving my opinion, but it is a weighty military strategy. We hoped that with time our forces would become stronger everywhere. We based many activities on that hope. We expected to grow in manpower and arms, but the arms arrived only some time later'.

Question: What did we learn during the shelling of Jerusalem?

Shealtiel: 'We learned that most of the casualties occurred among people who were walking about the streets during the bombardment. We learned that we need a great number of shelters, and, most important, that we need to provide 'surprises' for our neighbors, as I promised my 'colleague', the commander of the Arab Legion'.

Question: What about the University and Hadassah? Are negotiations being held with the Legion about this site?

Shealtiel: 'I have heard that there are negotiations between the representative of the Government of Israel and the U.N. representative on this issue. It is a civilian, not a military, affair'.

Question: The people of Ramat Rachel maintain that they were neglected, and that if the defenders there had been given the forces which arrived later on, Ramat Rachel would not have fallen in part. Is this true?

Shealtiel: 'What does it mean, 'neglected'? Undoubtedly if we had more forces things would be better. We had to hold on everywhere with the forces at our disposal. We were called to many fronts. We have to divide up the forces we have and cannot concentrate them all in one place. We assessed that the force at Ramat Rachel could withstand the enemy. It is not always the number of defenders which is the decisive factor, sometimes it is the readiness for attack that night, the general mood, and so on. It may have been that the self-same force could have withstood the self-same enemy the next day or the day before'.

Question: What happened to the units which were supposed to enter the Old City after the conquest of the Zion Gate, and for some reason members of the auxiliary forces were sent instead of combat soldiers.

Shealtiel: 'The people who went in, did so because that was their task.

Some of them were very brave. For the Old City we needed older men
who had sticking-power, rather than strong young men. The men of the
field forces, for example, held on admirably, till the last man'.

Question: What is the status of our soldiers in Jerusalem vis-à-vis the
State of Israel?

Shealtiel: 'From today the soldiers of Jerusalem are also part of the
Israeli army. All areas of Israel which have been conquered by the
Israeli army and which we hold come under the jurisdiction and
responsibility of the State of Israel, and all the laws, restrictions and
instructions pertain to them. We will not hold on to them for ever in
opposition to the U.N. resolutions, but today they are in our hands and
under the State's authority. The Jerusalem police force will also be
organizing shortly within the framework of the national police force'.

Major-General Shealtiel concluded by saying: 'Today the army was
sworn in. It was a great event. One needs perspective, it seems. We are
too near events and should not concern ourselves too much with details.
We have been through a difficult time, but it was a grand period
because we endured with small forces and little equipment. Imagine
how things will be when training has been increassed. The army will
continue to train and receive arms, and its numbers will also increase.
The Yishuv will not abandon us if the difficult times return, though we
might have to eat small amounts of rationed food again. I saw children
from Buchenwald here whom I brought with me from the camps then at
the end of the war. They have grown and toughened and are soldiers in
our ranks'.

28.7.1948

Jerusalem hungers for a festivity, and today there was a bright spark
in the general grimness. The city fathers, civilians and soldiers
assembled in the Yeshurun synagogue to offer up a prayer of
thanksgiving. Chief Rabbi Herzog said: 'If the prophet Jeremiah were
to rise from his grave, he would undoubtedly say, 'I remember thee, the

kindness of thy old age', instead of 'the kindness of thy youth', and 'when you wentest after me in the diaspora' instead of 'in the wilderness'. The prophecy, 'and the sons shall return to their borders' is fulfilled in us, and Jerusalem shall also be our capital'.

Then the first military parade of its kind was held in Jerusalem. David Shealtiel, the Jerusalem regional commander, was on the saluting dais. He was flanked by the two chief rabbis, Chief Rabbi Halevi Herzog and Rabbi Ben-Zion Meir Uziel, the U.N. representative, Colonel Bronson, and the members of the Ceasefire Committee, the American and French consuls, and others.

Chief Rabbi Herzog handed the Jerusalem regional commander, David Shealtiel, a standard made of silk on which the symbol of the sword and the olive branch were embroidered, together with the words: 'Jerusalem, the Sixth Brigade' in gold thread. The Chief Rabbi said: 'Keep this standard carefully, and God will be with you and your men'.

The commander took the standard and declared: 'I will cherish this standard, which symbolises sleepless nights, days and nights of heroism,. We face the renewal of hostilities, and we will fight bravely without retreating. We will use all the weapons and means at our disposal. We now have better equipment than before. Onward, to victory'.

We journalists had already seen the 'better equipment', and because we also knew what weapons the enemy had we sighed and said: "Never mind, in the final event it's the men not the tanks who determine the outcome of the battle".

Afterwards the soldiers marched in a victory parade through King George Street, Ben Yehuda Street, Jaffa Road and Mahane Yehuda. They wore tattered khaki uniforms and carried Czech rifles, a few mortars and machine-guns. Radio operators carried small receivers on their backs. The 'Davidka' was pointed out to us, and noted by the foreign correspondents with interest, as till now it had been considered Israel's 'secret weapon'.

Jerusalem received a new lease of life after 19th June, in the middle of the first ceasefire, when our contact with the coastal plain was renewed via the Burma Road. The city which had undergone a grim siege began to receive supplies, first of weapons and then of food.

The 9th July, the day the first ceasefire ended and the fighting was resumed, marked a turning-point in the war for Jerusalem and the beginning of Israel's victory.

*

Funds were again collected for the J.N.F. (Keren Kayemet) in the streets of Jerusalem today. Once again we saw the blue boxes in the hands of young boys and girls. Passers-by were asked to donate money and wear a ribbon bearing the portraits of Herzl and Bialik.

Towards evening a few Jerusalem journalists accompanied one of the officers on a brief bour of 'our' prison. We found nine Jewish prisoners there. My friend tapped me on the shoulder and said: 'They need a tenth man to make up the quorum for prayer' (minyan). Most of them were in jail for profiteering. When we asked them how they felt, they answered: 'As long as there are only a few prisoners the conditions are very good'. We joined them in hoping that their numbers would remain low. One of my colleagues told us, in the presence of the prisoners, what Bialik had answered when asked when the Jewish State would be established: 'When a Jewish policeman arrests a Jewish thief, brings him before a Jewish Judge and places him in a Jewish prison', The prisoners laughed, but assured us that they were not thieves.

*

Last night the journalists were invited to a 'State Day Assembly' held in the copse of the Schneller camp. There were hundreds of soldiers of both sexes there. An order of the day issued by the regional commander, Shealtiel, was read out. It said that the comradeship of the men in arms had brought us victory. The Brigade's Education Officer, Eliezer Passkin, said briefly: 'We willed it and it is no dream. We did not receive our State as a gift. We bought and conquered every inch with blood and sweat'. Songs were sung and extracts from the writings of Herzl, Bialik, B. Katznelson and Alterman were read.

A march written by Asher Heter in memory of Moshe Salomon, the commander of a company in the Moriah Battalion, was read out. He had volunteered for the company which had failed to break into the Old City through the Jaffa Gate. When Mussa and his companions left the Tannous building they were the target of heavy fire directed at them from David's Tower. He was seriously wounded, and died two or three days later, aged 28. The commander of an auxiliary company, Yoseph Grintal, composed a melody for the words. Here are some of its verses:

MARCH

We're off to fight again,
Once more we mount our tanks,
The auxiliaries are led by Mussa,
Moriah's bravest man.

We shall come back,
Battle-weary and proud,
The gates of the camp
Will welcome us,
The huts will greet us,
The guards will look at us with pride,
On the second watch.

Mussa will never return,
But the auxiliaries will go out without him.
Sir, lead us out again,
That's what Mussa always said.

1.8.1948

It is a strange coincidence, but two governors were appointed. this week. The Arabs appointed Ahmed Hilmi the Military Governor of the Old City, which is still in the hands of the Arabs and under the rule of the Jordanian Legion. We appointed Bernard Joseph the Military Governor of Jewish Jerusalem.

A special command, signed by D. Ben-Gurion, the Minister of Defense, was issned.

'By the authority of the Israeli army's rule of the occupied area of Jerusalem I, David Ben-Gurion, Minister of Defense, in the name of the Supreme Command of the Israeli army, hereby appoint Dr. Dov (Bernard) Joseph the Military Governor of occupied Jerusalem'. (Appendices 60 and 61)

The new regional commander of Jerusalem who took Shealtiel's place this week is Lieutenant-Colonel Moshe Dayan. All the reporters know about the new regional commander is that he is the son of Shmuel Dayan, one of the founders of Nahalal, that he was one of the 33 Haganah members imprisoned in Acre gaol by the British and that he recently returned from the U.S.A., where he attended the funeral of Colonel David Marcus, who was killed in an accident. (Appendices 62 and 63)

A festive parade and brief farewell ceremony was held at the Schneller camp, in honor of the outgoing regional commander. In a special order of the day Shealtiel wrote:

'It has been my privilege to head the Israeli army in Jerusalem during the last six fateful months. The day has come when I must part from you, officers and soldiers.

'Not only has it been a privilege, it has also been an honor to command soldiers like those of Jerusalem, who displayed their heroism by standing firm in times and conditions which would have defeated any other army in the world. During the great conquests that you made in Jerusalem you displayed immense courage, and you won.

'You succeeded in turning the members of an illegal organization into first-rate soldiers. As I leave Jerusalem today, I am confident that the city will endure because now it has sufficient arms, trained men and, most important of all, the spirit and justified self-confidence of the soldiers.

'During my term in Jerusalem I learned that all its inhabitants are soldiers without uniform. They were all full partners in our victory, becauce of their forbearance, their readiness to do as they were bid and their willingness to fulfill the needs of the army and the war. An army which is supported by a population like this is sure of eventual victory.

'I send my best wishes to the army in Jerusalem and its new commander, and wish Jerusalem and the entire country ultimate victory, true peace and justice, the object of our war'.

2.8.1948

Today the Jerusalem reporters were informed that henceforth, instead of the 'Religious Section', there will be a 'Military Rabbinate'. The 'Religious Section' was established when the Haganah was organized in the struggle for pioneering settlement, illegal immigration and the first steps towards political and military independence. The Religious Section was headed at that time by Nathan Gardi, a member of the Hapoel Hamizrahi organization and one of the pioneers of religious settlement.

With the establishment of the State the need was felt for a religious-military institution, led by a talented and energetic man. Rabbi Meir Berlin (Bar Ilan), who headed the world organization of Hamizrahi and Hapoel Hamizrahi, had his eye on a young man, a pupil at the Merkaz Harav yeshiva in Jerusalem, who was full ot energy and very talented. The name of Rabbi Shlomo Goronchik was mentioned already then as someone destined to become Chief Rabbi in Tel Aviv one day, Rabbi Berlin spoke to Ben-Gurion about the need for a chief rabbinate for the army, even mentioning the name of the candidate. Goronchik was summoned to an interview with Ben-Gurion, who realized that the man was suited for the job. This week Goronchik was appointed chief rabbi of the army, and soon afterwards Hebraicised his name, to Goren.

3.8.1948

'This is the headquarters of the artillery corps in Jerusalem'. This sentence, spoken in Hebrew in an offhand way by a young Jewish officer, made our hearts swell with pride and admiration. In front of us was a Jewish headquarters, with military maps in Hebrew. Was it not incumbent upon us to recite the blessing, 'Who has kept us in life'?

The young officer showed us round the secret camp (near Beth Hakerem), with our cannon, which the Arabs have begun to feel. The gunners, he said, respect and like their weapons, and hence they have been given girls' names. Bertha is a fat, brassy type, Katyusha a brave Russian girl and Ditza a charming Israeli lass.

The task of the artillery corps in the Israeli army is twofold, the officer told us. "On the one hand it must defend the city against the enemy and liberate the approaches to Jerusalem, and on the other it must prepare the ground for a counter-attack on the enemy's positions and artillery batteries. The first step was to locate the precise position of the enemy' batteries and find the point of origin of the enemy's fire. This task was not difficult for several reasons. First of all, the enemy's artillery batteries were almost visible, being situated in an open field, on hills which could be seen from afar. When the shelling began again, however, fire was not returned immediately for tactical considerations. First we tried to find out the precise positions of the enemy positions, and when we had discovered the enemy's batteries, we hailed shells of different sizes and increasing destructive force on them. During the nine days of the renewed battle for Jerusalem we managed to destroy a considerable number of enemy artillery batteries and put them out of commission. The Jews of Jerusalem were well aware of that. A large armored convoy was destroyed by our gunners five minutes before the ceasefire came into force. Our observations showed that we scored many direct hits, causing havoc and destruction to the Arabs. The attack which was intended to conquer all of Jerusalem was stopped at 5.30.a.m. on Saturday morning. It's a great shame that the ceasefire spoiled things. It disturbed all our plans, but if the battle for Jerusalem is resumed, our victory will be quick".

The artillery unit in Jerusalem had suffered no losses. Although the Arabs shelled our positions, the gunners could continue their work efficiently thanks to excellent engineering planning and the conduct of the civilians, who worked 24 hours a day under fire. The batteries of Israeli artillery were directed from one central place, from where the order was given to fire. Had it not been for the ceasefire, our artillery could have destroyed Ramallah.

At the beginning of the battle the enemy had about 80 cannon. How many of them are left? It is difficult to say. But it is clear that most of them have been put out of commission and have been silenced. The enemy's gunners are not good, the officer said, because they are mercenaries who waste a lot of shells without having a specific target. We have long-range cannon and mortars of various sizes.

The officer was very happy with his work, he told us. The inhabitants of Jerusalem are also pleased with his work. Primarily because most of the enemy's batteries have been silenced, and still more because our cannon fire at the enemy's artillery, vehicles and armored vehicles. The officer concluded by denying the accousations put forward by Etzel and Lehi that they had not been given the promised cannon cover during the attack on the Old City. The officer regarded this as a personal affront. He was a soldier and a Jew, who took no interest in political and party affairs, and as far as he was concerned all the soldiers, whether Haganah, Etzel or Lehi, were Jewish soldiers. He was prepared to prove that the program was implemented by his men to the letter. He stressed that the low number of casualties in the attack on the Old City was due to successful planning and the coordination between the artillery and the infantry, and that the infantry had been able to advance without losses because of the artillery's accurate firing. The artillery of the Israeli army had stunned the enemy from the rear.

We chatted a while with the gunners. They were a regular ragbag, some had been born in the country, whilst others had immigrated from western and eastern countries. The representative of the journalists thanked the officer of the unit and wished the young gunners and their commander good 'playing' on their instruments until the enemy lost the will to continue killing and destroying, and until Jerusalem dwelt in peace.

10.8.1948

The ceasefire exists only in theory. In practise, the sniping, shooting and shelling has not stopped. The shelters are full of people from other neighborhoods, who have decided to live there until matters improve. Entire sections of the city are plunged into darkness and electricity is supplied for about one hour each night.

The monthly rations are being distributed in the stores. They consist of 750 grams of white sugar (till now there was only brown), (children get one kilo), a kilo of flour and 400 grams of margarine per person, a piece of soap, 330 grams of Australian cheese per child and 600 grams of frozen fillet of fish.

The Jerusalem Municipality has announced that henceforth the custom of 'Muharram', namely, arranging contracts according to the Moslem calendar, 'from Muharram to Muharram', is cancelled. From now on the sides will be free to sign contracts for any period they choose.

*

The committee of five cabinet ministers from Tel-Aviv is still in Jerusalem trying to reach a decision on the number of members to be included in the Advisory Council which is to work alongside the

Military Governor of Jerusalem. David Remez and A. Zisling proposed that the Council consist of 13 people, according to the composition of the Government, with the addition of representatives of the Revisionists and the Communists. Ben-Zvi suggested that a Council of 27 people be established, in which all groups are represented. Rabbi Fishman and Yitzhak Greenbaum supported this idea, but many people in Jerusalem oppose it, fearing that this will make for a large, clumsy organization and that the Military Governor, who is a member of Mapai, will do as he pleases.

The Sephardic Committee claimed that members of oriental communities comprise more than half of the population of the city, and that the composition of the Council should reflect this. The Yemenites announced that they are not 'just Sephardim'. The representatives of the religious groups, Mizrahi, Hapoel Hamizrahi, Agudath Yisrael and Poalei Agudath Yisrael said that the religious character of Jerusalem should be taken into consideration.

*

At a press conference Nahum Lipschitz complained that Jerusalem is neglected by Tel-Aviv, that there is no employment for industrial laborers in Jerusalem and that the prices of commodities are high. Before there was nothing to buy in Jerusalem, now there is nothing to buy it with, and some people cannot afford even their rations. The neglect of Jerusalem, Lipschitz said, is reflected in the allocation of raw materials and fuel and in the need for import permits, as if we were some foreign country. It is enough that we have to request aid from the Government and Tel-Aviv. Funds are required for developing and expanding enterprises.

A special commercial-financial committee has arrived in Jerusalem from Tel-Aviv, in order to find out what Jerusalem needs as regards raw materials, credit, etc.

11.8.1948

For the first time Jerusalem's new military commander, Lieutenant-Colonel Moshe Dayan, and the Arab commander of the Old City of Jerusalem, Abdullah el-Tal, met in the school building in Suleiman Street, near the Damascus Gate.

This meeting should have been held some day ago, but the Arabs did not keep their side of the agreement and continued firing. The commander and his aides, as well as we journalists, had to turn back on their tracks.

Moshe Dayan came to the meeting accompanied by two staff officers, a liaison officer and journalists. Abdullah el-Tal brought along three officers. Three Egyptian officers also attended the meeting. During the discussion we felt — and the Arabs made no attempt to conceal this — that not only was there no coordination between the Jordanians and the Egyptians, who held the Ramat Rachel front at that time, but the Egyptians did not have any idea where the Jordanian positions were and the two sides were hostile to one another, each desiring the downfall of their 'comrades'.

While the commanders were continuing their discussions behind closed doors, Arab and Jewish journalists conversed together and even had a group photograph taken.

From our Arab colleagues we learned that the Arabs on the other side of the border, in the country in general and in Jerusalem in particular, were confused and bewildered. The intervention of the Arab States had placed the Palestinian Arabs on the sidelines. They felt 'out of the picture', and all initiative had been taken from them. Every Arab country issued pronouncements and declarations about the Jews and their State, only the voice of the Palestinian Arabs was not heard.

Some went even further, claiming that ever since Britain, for reasons of its own, had established the body known as the 'Arab League' (founded by the British Foreign Secretary, Eden, in 1935), consisting of seven member-States, the chances of attaining peace had been substatially reduced. Had it not been for the intervention of the Arab countries, the Arabs and Jews in Palestine would have found a solution for their conflict long since.

15.8.1948

1878 years have passed since our Temple was destroyed, and three months since the Jews were expelled in our day and before our eyes from the Old City. Ten people, veteran inhabitants of the Old City who now live in Katamon, were permitted to ascend Mount Zion and look from there towards the ravaged Jewish Quarter and the remnant of the Temple, the desolate Western Wall. "The ways of Zion do mourn, because none come to the solemn feasts". The Jews of Jerusalem mourn doubly, for the distant and recent tragedies, and from all our hearts the question goes forth: "How long shall there be weeping in Zion"?

20.8.1948

Our Foreign Minister has sent the following cable about the situation in Jerusalem to Count Bernadotte, who is at present in Stockholm:

'The situation in Jerusalem obliges me to write to you. On 10th August, when I had the honor of entertaining you in my home in Jerusalem, you informed me that you had asked both sides to stop firing for three days. I drew your and your colleagues' attention to the fact that the Arab Legion, despite its written commitment, had not left the salients it had occupied in no-man's-land during the ceasefire. I emphasized that there was no point in a new agreement, assuming that the Arab side was prepared to act in good faith, as long as the Arabs continue to violate the ceasefire. I thought that our agreement not to fire in those circumstances meant that the Arabs would make additional conquests, which we woul not be able to prevent.

'You told me then that my stand was logical, and immediately promised to do everything you could in order to persuade the Arabs to vacate no-man's-land, and I told you that we would then be prepared to discuss the next step. I was, therefore, somewhat surprised when Dr. Dov Yosef received a letter from you asking us to agree to a new ceasefire not for three days but for an unlimited period, without your even hinting whether the Arabs had vacated or were about to vacate their positions in no-man's land. These positions were not in fact vacated, and are still in the Arabs' hands. We nevertheless replied in the affirmative to your letter, making only one reservation in that we distinguished between sniping and shelling. We stated explicitly that if our positions were to be shelled and in danger of being destroyed, we would consider ourselves free to return fire.

'It has since been published that you announced that the Arabs complied with your request while the Jews gave no answer at all. As a result, because the Arabs were praised for their good will, even though they had violated the agreement they had signed regarding no-man's land, there were new developments in Jerusalem. On the nights of 12th, 13th, 14th and 15th August the Arabs launched heavy attacks along the entire front, like those made during the worst part of the war. They shelled us with two and three inch mortars from the Mount Zion area, they threw incendiary material over the wall of the Old City, they shelled our positions in Sheikh Jarrah and in the region of the Police School with 20-liter cannon and they directed heavy machine-gun fire from their positions in Dir Abu Tor.

'In the same area the Arabs threw grenades at the Jews. We suffered four killed and seventeen wounded. The way in which the ceasefire agreement works is thrown into a tragic light by the death of our liaison officer, Zeev Herzog, who was killed by a sniper's bullet when he was accompanying the American Consul-General and was about to remove a road barrier. From the press I learned that you informed the Security Council, on the basis of reports you received from your observers, that the Jews in Jerusalem tended to perform acts of aggression. I would be very grateful if you would be so kind as to attach this declaration to your additional report, together with any comments you should see fit to make'.

*

Another of our attempts to conquer Government House, from where the Legion attacked our men in Yannait Ben-Zvi's Training Farm, has failed Our soldiers retreated, several of them were killed and wounded and five were taken captive by the Jordanians[1].

22.8.1948

Once again I was present at a meeting of commanders Dayan and el-Tal, who are fighting one another with all the forces at their disposal, firing vast quantities of bullets and shells at one another. At the meeting they shook hands and smiled broadly, as if they were close friends.

General Riley, the head of the U.N. observers in Jerusalem, took the chair at the meeting. Abdullah el-Tal was accompanied by three Egyptian officers, Ahmed Abed al-Aziz, Hassan Fahmi and Tallah Salam, and a representative of the Arab irregular volunteers, Tark al-Afriki. Dayan brought along his usual aides.

They met for about five hours, without results, being unable to reach any agreement about the 'map of the borders' between the sides. An intermission was called and Dayan and el-Tal went aside and were served coffee. They returned after a few minutes, the agreement was reached and the maps signed, to the surprise of the chairman.

*

Mr. Moshe Kolodny asked the following question at the provisional National Council: Is it not time to annul the siege of Jerusalem and eliminate the need for a permit in order to leave or enter the city?

---

[1]   In his book, 'Memories', Abdullah el-Tal once again let his imagination run wild, writing about this attack: 'In the Jewish attack more than fifty men were killed, including two senior officers, one of them a Brigade Commander and the other the deputy commander of a division. At least 100 Jews were wounded and 12 were taken captive'.

Zeev Sherf, the Secretary to the Cabinet, said that the road to Jerusalem was under the supervision of the army, and that therefore the Minister of Defense would reply.

The Minister of Defense, D. Ben-Gurion, replied: "For military reasons free entry to and from Jerusalem cannot yet be permitted, though this does not constitute a 'siege' of Jerusalem. It is merely one of the ways of defending the city, although it causes considerable inconvenience to many people".

25.8.1948

Dayan has had another meeting with the Jordanian commander, Abdullah el-Tal, and the commander of the Egyptian forces in southern Jerusalem, Ahmed Abed al-Aziz, in the Assyrian monastery next to the Jaffa Gate. All the participants came equipped with maps, and they discussed the borders and positions of each side in the Government House area. The head of the U.N. observers, General Riley, who chaired the meeting, wanted to demilitarize the area, where he and his team are situated.

26.8.1948

To whom will the Jewish policemen of Jerusalem swear allegiance? Half in earnest, half in jest someone suggested that they swear allegiance to an undefined international government.

Reuben Schreibman, the chairman of the Standing Committee's police committee, which has just concluded its work, informed us that the Mandate Government deposited the salary of every policeman for three months in advance from mid-May in the police fund. On 18th August 1948 the Israeli police force was established.

Today the policemen of Jerusalem were sworn in at an official ceremony. The commander of the Israeli police, Yehezkel Sahar,

announced simply: The Jerusalem police force is an integral part of the
Israeli police force, and the policemen here swear allègiance to it.

At these words both we and our policemen swelled with pride.

*

We toured several summer camps, where the children played and
lived as Snow White and the Seven Dwarfs, Alice in Wonderland,
butterflies and flowers. the counsellors are yong girls as the older ones
are involved in security tasks. During these days of siege and scarcity,
when many fathers are at the front. the one thousand and two hundred
children in these summer camps are managing to enjoy themselves.

While the U.N. observers and the consuls of the Ceasefire Committee
are holding talks with the Jordanian Legion and the Egyptians in an
attempt to persuade them to clear a 'security area' around the Red
Cross region in south-east Jerusalem, the Arabs are shelling the
neighborhoods of Jerusalem. The worst damage has been inflicted on
the Meah Shearim, Beth Yisrael, Shaarei Pina and Bukharan quarters.
The inhabitants of these areas laugh at anyone who mentions the word
'ceasefire'.

*

Moshe Dayan, the commander of Jerusalem, has declared that recent
events have raised doubts regarding the effectiveness of the means
employed by the U.N observers to maintain the ceasefire in Jerusalem.
Jewish soldiers entered the training farm, he said, only after the U.N.
observers had been warned several times that Egyptian soldiers were
advancing on the area from the south.

This is the first time that the observers have favored one of the sides,
in defining our forces' penetration of the training farm as 'a flagrant
violation of the ceasefire'.

*

If any dubious item of news is swallowed eagerly in times of peace, how much more is this the case in these days of siege and tension, when newspapers are a rare commodity. In consequence, an additional 'source' of news, or rather of rumors, has developed in Jerusalem. Sometimes these rumors are totally without foundation and both the public and the journalists call this source, the S.W.S. Agency, 'Some Woman Said'.

News from this 'source' spreads like wildfire all through the city: 'Have you heard? A convoy arrived last night from Tel-Aviv along a secret road'. 'We caught a British officer who came here to spy for the Arabs'. 'We have discoverd a new kind of weapon'. 'We're digging a tunnel from the New City to the center of the Old City'. And so on.

Once the journalists were told in confidence that soldiers led by Nimrod (the code name of Yehuda Lapidot), the commander of one of the Etzel companies in Jerusalem, had in fact begun digging a secret tunnel from our forward positions on Mount Zion in order to reach the Old City wall, place explosives there and blow a hole in it. The Etzel complained that after they had got half way they were ordered to desist and a Haganah unit took over.

The French news agency once reported that 'Lieutenant-Colonel Moshe Dayan and eight senior Israeli army officers have been killed in Jerusalem'. People contacted Jerusalem from Tel-Aviv to find out if the news was true. The journalists investigated and found that at that moment Dayan was attending a meeting of the Society for the Study of the Land of Israel and its Antiquities, and was sitting in a lecture given by Dov Joseph on annexing Jerusalem to the State.

27.8.1948

The Zionist Executive is convening at the moment. Its opening session was in Jerusalem, and the rest of its meetings are in Tel-Aviv.

During the course of the discussions it was said that Jerusalem 'is seething with fury at Tel-Aviv', and that although the residents of Tel-

Aviv send food packages to the inhabitants of Jerusalem, they themselves are enjoying life and profiting from the situation.

Someone even went so far as to write acrimoniously: 'The people of Tel-Aviv are having a good time at the expense of the population of Jerusalem, and salve their consciences with a few miserable food packages'.

The Jerusalem delegates addressed the members of the Zionist Executive bitterly.

Haim Salomon, the head of the Jerusalem Communal Council, said that the transfer of the central Institutions from Jerusalem to Tel-Aviv caused no less damage to Jerusalem than Abdullah's cannon.

Daniel Oster, the mayor, said that Tel-Aviv had made of Jerusalem 'a poor, old woman', leaving it closed up, distant and alone. Feivel Meltzer, A. Almaliah, Y. Tahon and N. Lipschitz also accused Tel-Aviv of 'gradually emptying Jerusalem of its sources of income'. Reuben Schreibman was even more vehement, claiming that Tel-Aviv 'has undermined the capital's credit'. Professor Ben-Zion Dinburg expressed the fear that Tel-Aviv wanted to be the capital itself, and was deliberately turning Jerusalem into a province, a process which should be stopped.

I. Shprinzak, the chairman, replied that Jerusalem was dear to everyone, and that everything would be done to restore the city to its former glory. He stressed that even though non-members were not usually permitted to address the Executive, he had come to Jerusalem for the express purpose of hearing its leaders.

Yitzhak Ben-Zvi said that Jerusalem contained Jews from every community, and that this was a very significant symbol. He added that Jerusalem was the front of the State, and that the battle for Jewish Jerusalem was the battle for the State. The sixty cannon which had shelled us from French Hill and Shmuel Hanavi would have come to the Tel-Aviv region if the front at Jerusalem had collapsed. Everything that had been transferred out of Jerusalem would have to be brought back. The Burma Road was not a sufficient link with the city. The connection had to be by a main road, by an airfield, by factories and industry, so that the population of Jerusalem would not have to go to Tel-Aviv for every little thing.

29.8.1948

We have begun using our own system of defense against the Arabs' frequent and dangerous sniping. For lack of any alternative, we have begun building 'inner walls' along several main streets (such as King George Street) and in some neighborhoods, like Talbieh, to conceal the open area from the snipers. A wall has been built near Notre Dame, opposite the New Gate, and in Jaffa Road not far from the Post Office, on the way to the Jaffa Gate.

*

Private parties have been held for the U.N. observers in several homes in Jewish Jerusalem. Some people have criticied this, particularly since the commander of the army has announced that we have no faith in these observers.

2.9.1948

The Egyptian commander, Lieutenant-Colonel Ahmed Abed al-Aziz, was again present at the meeting between Moshe Dayan and Abdullah el-Tal.

At these meetings ties of friendship have been created between the Jewish reporters and el-Tal, the good-looking, well-mannered Beduin commander. He once promised to send a special messenger to my house in the Nahlat Shimon quarter which was abandoned at the beginning of the war, in order to bring the diaries and notebooks I left there in my hasty flight. But for some reason his promise was not kept. At one of the previous meetings Abdullah el-Tal asked the Jewish journalists not to write nice things about him. 'Write against me', he said. 'Every time you praise me you do me harm'.

Today's meeting lasted five hours. The chairman was the American Consul, John MacDonald, the chairman of the Ceasefire Committee, and he was accompanied by American and French observers. The main subject was the signing of maps marking the borders. The discussion of the border in southern Jerusalem took a whole hour. The Egyptian commander gradually softened and agreed to take his forces out of the Ramat Rachel area. His bodyguard, an Egyptian soldier with a keffiyah on his head, shouted at him once or twice: 'Don't you dare give in! Back home they won't forgive you'!

The Egyptian gave him an angry look, but the discussions continued and later the Egyptian forces withdrew. Soon afterwards we heard that Ahmed Abed al-Aziz had been murdered and that his bodyguard had been arrested as the suspect.

WE WILLED IT AND IT IS NO LEGEND

2.9.1948

Today the district law courts were opened in Jerusalem. The ceremony was held in the hall in the Russian compound where the Supreme Court had sat during the Mandate. The emblem of the State of Israel has taken the place of the 'british Crown'.

The lawyer, Moshe Dukan, conveyed the good wishes of the lawyers and expressed the hope that Jerusalem would shake off its sufferings and troubles and that a new chapter of encouragement and rebuilding would be opened.

At this ceremony Bernard Joseph (Dov Yosef) appeared for the first time in his capacity as Jerusalem's Military Governor. He stated that his main function was 'to annul the military rule of Jerusalem' and to bring about Jerusalem's integration within the State of Israel as its capital. The mayor of Jerusalem, Daniel Oster, noted the symbolic aspect of opening the Israeli law courts in the very place where foreign judges had passed sentence on our countrymen in our holy city. The lawyer, M.H. Jinio, speaking on behalf of the Jerusalem Communal Council, said that during the siege and the shelling we had learned something which had not been doubted before, namely, that neither the Moslems nor the Christians had the right to Jerusalem, and it belonged only to those who had fought for it and defended it.

Yitzhak Ben-Zvi, the chairman of the National Council for the Israeli parliament, stated that for 28 years the National Council had led the

Jewish population of Palestine and it was now handing over 'the helm' to the nation's institutions.

The President of the district law court, Dr. Benjamin Halevy, thanked the various speakers for their wishes and honored the memory of jurists who had fallen in battle. He expressed the hope that the district law court would not remain in that hall for long, and that the Supreme Court would return to it. Dr. Halevy noted with satisfaction that the Minister of Justice in Tel-Aviv had begun eliminating undesirable elements, which had raised their heads under the auspices of the Mandate, from Government offices and the juridical network [1].

5.9.1948

Dayan and el-Tal met again, although this time they asked the reporters to wait outside. The meeting ended soon afterwards, when they reached deadlock. The commanders and their aides, as well as the U.N. observers, went outside 'to take the air and smoke a cigarette'. Dayan and el-Tal went to the side, as they have done in the past, and conferred in secret. When they returned to the meeting room they informed us that they had decided to set up a direct telephone line between them. The news took us all by surprise and was very

---

[1] One of the first suspects to be brought before a judge in Israel was Yehezkel Eliyahu David, who was accused of receiving stolen property. When he heard the charge against him he said: 'Your Lordship, I was a judge like you in Rangoon, Burma. I judged criminal offences. After I came here to Jerusalem my luck changed. Now I have to shine shoes for other people in order to make a living. My wife was killed six months ago by a shell, and I was left alone with three children'.

The judge said: 'That does not concern us. A bath that is not yours was found in your house. You took it from another house. Is that correct'?
In fluent English the accused explained how difficult his situation was and how hard it was to live whit children without a bath.

The judge sentenced him to a fine. The accused turned to the reporters with a wide smile and said: 'That's jusfice. The main thing is to be healthy'!

encouraging. The foreign correspondents hurried off to tell their readers throughout the world of the unexpected arrangement[2].

7.9.1948

The Sixth, the Jerusalem, Brigade, and the Portzim (Breakthrough) Battalion of the Palmah, which presented the inhabitants of Jerusalem with a fine gift — the conquest of the Katamon quarter — last Passover, have been honored as was their due. At a ceremony held in their honor this week, the brigade commander awarded them a special medal for bravery. The soldiers of the Palmah and five families whose houses had come under enemy fire in a neighborhood invaded by Iraqi forces stood side by side, equal in dedication and readiness to make sacrifices, brothers in heroism. These civilians had stood firm throughout the days and nights of the siege, until the enemy had retreated. Decorations were also awarded to the members of the Rehavia, Kiryat Shmuel and Neveh Shaanan neighborhood committees, for not leaving. It was noted that the inhabitants of these areas had rejected the 'good advice' of British officers, who had tried to convince them that they would be unable to withstand the Arabs, and had remained in their homes even when subjected to incessant sniping from Arab positions. They were joined

---

[2]   In his book on Dayan, Shabtai Tevet writes of these meetings: 'The direct telephone line was also an early expression of Dayan's view, which crystallized during his term as Chief of Staff, that the U.N. is a divisive rather than a binding influence between Israel and the Arab countries. Accordingly, the meetings between him and el-Tal became more frequent, eventually becoming a regular event, reported in the press. Announcements were made before and after each meeting concerning the agenda and the progress made on topics for discussion. Thus, Dayan and el-Tal, without U.N. intervention, reached conclusions on many issues, such as bringing Israeli laborers to the Mount Scopus exclave, the demilitarization of areas, the exchange of prisoners-of-war, permits for pilgrims to cross the border and finally the division of no-man's-land.'

by British soldiers, who had set up a cannon on the roof of the
Biberman buildings in Katamon. Comrades in the war and the victory
were awarded medals together.

14.9.1948

The Supreme Court was opened in Jerusalem today, in the same
building and hall where British judges had sat during the Mandate. Our
hearts swelled with pride at the sight of the impressive hall, with the
emblem of Israel where the British crown used to hang. The judges are
our own and were chosen not long ago by secret ballot at the eleventh
session of the Provisional Council of State. The guests included the
Military Governor of Jerusalem, Bernard Joseph, the Jerusalem
regional commander, Lieutenant-Colonel Moshe Dayan, Jerusalem
public figures and a group of reporters. Everyone fixed their gaze on the
emblem of the State of Israel, above the seats of the five judges of the
first Supreme Court in Israel, Dr. Joseph Zmorah (President), Rabbi
Professor Simha Assaf, Y. Olshan, Dr. H. Z. Heshin and Dr. M.
Dunkelblum.

The Minister of Justice, Pinhas Rosenblit, swore in the five judges,
who wore their caps and placed their right hands on the bible. Each
judge said: 'I hereby swear on my word of honor to serve the State of
Israel and its laws, not to divert the course of justice, not favor anyone
and to mete out justice fairly'.

Dr. I. Zmorah gave an impassioned speech, saying that our hopes
and prayers 'Return our judges as before', and 'In justice shall Zion be
redeemed', were being fulfilled.

The reporters whispered to one another that the five bibles on the
judges' desks had been printed by a Christian publisher in New York,
and immediately commented on the need for a Jerusalem edition of the
book of books.

18.9.1948

Yesterday afternoon Count Folke Bernadotte was shot and killed as he was passing through Jewish Jerusalem (the Katamon area). The French colonel, Saraut, was killed with him. There is no doubt that this is a foul deed and not the way to settle arguments. Those who hate Israel will undoubtedly utilize this against our young State, our wounded city and our embarrassed nation.

An organization which appears to be part of Lehi or more extremist than it has accepted responsibility for the assassination. The Government has taken vigorous steps to find the murderers and those who helped them. A curfew was imposed on Jerusalem for fifteen hourse, and many people were arrested in Tel-Aviv.

The Government of Israel issued the following statement:

'The Government of Israel is shocked by the dastardly deed perpetrated in Jerusalem yesterday, the murder of Count Bernadotte, the U.N. emissary, and his aide, Colonel Saraut, within the area under Israel's control.

'This murder is a horrifying violation of the authority of the U.N., a flagrant encroachment of Israel's sovereignty, a stab in the back for the Israeli army and a desecration of the name of Jerusalem, the holy city.

'The Government of Israel will reject the insane attempt to destroy its relations with the U.N. by shooting and killing its representatives.

'Those who committed this crime are enemies of the nation and its freedom. The Government will do everything in its power to detect and punish the murderers and those who helped them with all severity, and to eradicate the criminal gang responsible for the murder.

'The Government calls on the nation to rise up as one man against the enemy within. Every individual is required to give active and unflinching assistance to the army and the police in revealing the murderers and their accomplices and in annihilating the evil of terrorism from the land of Israel'.

29.9.1948

Today, a few days after the murder of the mediator, Count Bernadotte, the report he prepared has been published. His main conclusions were:

The interim ceasefire should be converted into permanent peace or at least an armistice; the U.N. should make the final decision about the borders between the Jewish and Arab parts of Palestine; the Negev should be given to the Arabs (contrary to the resolution of 29th November, Y.C.); the entire Galilee should be given to the Jews (also contrary to the resolution of 29th November, Y.C.); Jerusalem should be placed under international supervision; the Arab parts of the country should be given to the Arab States; the Arab refugees should be allowed to return to their homes; a compromise committee should be set up by the U.N. to attain permanent peace between the parties. (Appendices 64 and 65)

8.11.1948

Jerusalem is under curfew. It is a strange feeling to be subject to a curfew imposed by our own people, and not by an alien ruler. Our police have imposed the curfew and also maintain it. Jerusalem is experienced in curfews, but this time everyone obeys willingly as the object is to enable a population census to be taken. Journalists have been given a 'curfew certificate', as the Mandate authorities used to do.

16.11.1948

It seems that our leaders have also gradually realized that the heads of the various powers who claim to be concerned about Jerusalem and its sanctity are being hypocritical. This week Ben-Gurion declared in the Council of State: 'The Government no longer considers itself bound by the resolutions of 29th November'.

The Foreign Minister, Shertok, explained that 'only the new reality will be considered'.

Appearing before the State Committee of the U.N. as a guest, because Israel is not yet a member of the U.N., Shertok expressed Israel's reservations concerning the suggestion to internationalize Jerusalem.

He explained to the representatives of the nations at the U.N. that the State of Israel constituted a natural right and a historical necessity. The State was established in accordance with a U.N. resolution, despite the attempts of the Mandate Government to foil it and the Arabs' efforts to drown it in blood. He noted the general disappointment with the failure to implement the decision to internationalize the holy city. In agreeing to this kind of rule, he said, the Jewish representatives had not for a moment thought that the Jewish population of Jerusalem would be endangered, and certainly not that the Christian world would comply with the conquest of the city by the Arabs.

After describing the siege, the attacks and the shelling, as well as the hunger and thirst suffered by the Jews of Jerusalem, Shertok said: 'Jewish Jerusalem faced the cruel dilemma of surrendering to Arab rule and dying or fighting to defend itself. It chose to take up arms in self-defense. The world stood on the sidelines and did not lift a finger'.

*

We, the inhabitants of Jerusalem, know perfectly well that if we are alive and free it is only because of our own courage and sacrifice. The stone houses of the city were scratched and scarred by the enemy's shells, but not destroyed. The hearts of many inhabitants of Jerusalem were similarly marked, but their spirit was not broken. It is doubtful whether non-Jews, or even Jews who have not lived this year in Jerusalem undergoing siege, hunger and want, can understand the endurance of the population, which 'dances on the altar of sacrifice'.

7.12.1948

Today, at an official ceremony, the 'Heroism Road', linking
Jerusalem with the coastal plain was opened. It does not pass through
Latrun, which we were unable to conquer and where we lost many men.
We have known for some time of the new road, just as we have known
of a 'corridor' linking Jerusalem with the rest of the country.

Few people knew that scores of men and women went out in the
darkness of night, ignoring the hail of bullets and shells the enemy fired
from all sides, to the rocky mountains separating besieged Jerusalem
from the towns of the coastal plain. They secretly removed heavy
stones, cleared, dug, raked earth and levelled a road in the valleys and
the hills under the enemy's nose. Workers started out from the Tel-Aviv
end too. Older men and women, who were not taken for the war, fought
tenaciously here against rocks and stones. While Israel's representatives
were holding discussions in the institutions of the U.N. and were
laboring to persuade the Arabs of the justice of our claim to allow a
convoy of food through on the regular road, the Latrun Road, the
rocky scenery was changing. The work was completed after days,
nights and weeks of intensive effort and the workers from Jerusalem
and Tel-Aviv embraced one another with tears of joy in their eyes.

Few people knew that a few days beforehand a section of the new
road had been dubbed the 'Burma Road' by the New York Star
correspondent, A. P. Stone, who was one of the first people allowed to
travel on the road from Jerusalem to the coastal plain. He sent a long
report to his paper, describing with admiration the work of building the
road, and comparing the road's rocky, winding panorama to that of the
'Burma Road', which was built from Burma to China when China came
under heavy attack from the Japanese at the end of the 'thirties.

The dignitaries present at the inauguration of 'Heroism Road'
included David Remez, the Minister of Transport, Mrs. Golda Meir,
Israel's Ambassador to Moscow, and David Ben-Gurion, who cut the
ribbon stretched across the road. When the road had been opened a

company of soldiers of middle age and over, some with beards and sidelocks, marched along it. They were the ones who had done the work. 'Primuses' (light planes) flew overhead. The men marched ahead, followed by tanks, cannon and buses, which had hastily been given armor-plating so that they could be used to maintain contact with Jerusalem during the siege, and inging up the rear were mules. Some people remembered the Mule-Drivers Battalion in which the first men of the Jewish Brigade had served at Gallipoli during the First World War.

At a festive dinner held to mark the event, Yitzhak Levi (Levitza) waxed enthusiastic and declared that the next step should be to decide that Jerusalem was part of the State of Israel. The Israel army commander in Jerusalem, Moshe Dayan, told him to calm down and let things take their course.

At the dinner we heard that during one hard night's work, when the laborers were tired and were working with the last of their strength, the manager told them that they had to finish building the road that night. He also promised to give them extra pay for the special effort. The workers summoned up their strength and finished the road that night, but refused to accept the extra pay. 'Never mind', they said, "It was worth making the extra effort for the sake of Jerusalem'.

5.1.1949

Today it was made public that for several months Jerusalem has been getting its water through a new pipeline from the coastal plain. When the pipeline and pumps near Latrun were blown up by the Iraqis on 7th May 1948, this operation was begun in absolute secrecy. The Israeli leaders did not put their trust in promises made by the U.N. and the Arab Legion or in 'the justice of the nations', and began laying the pipe at the same time as the 'Burma Road' was being built and the 'Nahshon' campaign to open the road from the coastal plain was being implemented. Six months ago, on 22nd July, at four in the afternoon, hot water began to flow through the taps of every kitchen in Jerusalem.

Today the role and existence of the institution known as the 'National Council' came to an end, after thirty years of activity (from November 1917, when the 'Founding Meeting' was held in Petah Tikvah).

The chairman of the closing meeting was Eliyahu Berlin, eighty-three years old, who was chairman of the founding meeting, 30 years age. David Ben-Gurion said that the destiny of Jerusalem had been determined three thousand years ago, when David the son of Jesse decided to make it a Jewish national center. David Remez, the Minister of Transport, gave a speech of one sentence, as is his custom. He said: 'Like a river flowing into the sea, so the parliament of Israel flows into the State of Israel, which will endure for ever'.

Today was a great day for Jerusalem. The President, Chaim Weizmann, came to the city. The main streets, which have known pain and suffering, want and siege, took on a festive appearance. A gate of honor was set up at Romema, bearing the inscription: 'We have a strong city'. (Isaiah) The President cut a ribbon that was stretched across the street and the mayor, Daniel Oster, handed the President the key to the city and a scroll. In the square in front of the Jewish Agency buildings, the President reviewed a military guard of honor. To the sound of a shofar (ram's horn), the President entered the temporary assembly hall of the Knesset (Parliament) in the Jewish Agency building and swore an oath of loyalty to the State of Israel. Rabbi Abraham Haim Zwebner of the Mizrahi stood up and pronounced the benediction: 'Blessed art Thou... who hast given of thy glory to flesh and blood'.

At the end of the President's speech of thanks, the sole surviving member of the 204 delegates who participated in the first Zionist Congress, of which Herzl was president, held in 1897, Isidore Shalit aged seventy-eight, went over to him and spoke to him. 'It has been a long, long way', Shalit said.

21.2.1949

135 Arab prisoners-of-war have been released from the camps and returned to the Arab side. Some of them refused to go back, preferring to remain in Jewish Jerusalem. This group of prisoners-of-war is the first to be returned under the agreement made by Moshe Dayan and Abdullah el-Tal to release all the six thousand Arab prisoners held by Israel. The Arabs will release the 650 Jews from Mafrak in Transjordan.

The Arab prisoners-of-war are people from the Baka and Katamon areas in Jerusalem who moved to Arab parts of Israel, and Arabs from Hebron, Nablus and Ramallah. Zadek Darwish al-Jabri, the brother of the mayor of Hebron, was among them. Muhammad and Said, members of the Djani family, as well as Yani Butrus and Hanna Nazel, the brother of the lawyer, Nazel, were also returned. Nazel was going to be exchanged for the engineer, Gottlieb, who died of a heart attack while a prisoner-of-war.

I had a long talk with Faiz Rasas, formerly a resident of the Baka quarter and a clerk in the Central Post Office of Jerusalem, who was very reluctant to believe that most of Jerusalem was in our hands. We asked the Arab prisoners what it had been like in the camp run by the Israelis and they replied: 'To tell you the truth, everything was alright, except for the fact that every day they gave us potatoes and beans, until we grew sick and tired of them'.

2.5.1949

Moshe Dayan has announced that the Ceasefire Committee has agreed that an area of eight kilometers of the railway track, near the village of Beitar, will be handed over to Israel and the railway line from Haifa and Tel-Aviv will go through this area. In return for this and the promise that the area will remain peaceful, Israel has handed over the village of Beth Iksa, near the Jerusalem-Tel-Aviv road at the exit from Jerusalem. Beth Tzefafa has been split in two. The northern part of the neighborhood is included in the State of Israel, while the southern part remains within the Arab State. (Appendix 66)

4.5.1949

It is the first Independence Day in Jerusalem and, there are no limits to our joy. For some reason it seems as if many years have passed since the British 'left us to our own devices'.

Everyone in Jerusalem is sincerely happy, celebrating this Independence Day in his own way. Some people have decorated their balconies with flowers, carpets and the portraits of the first to dream of and fight for a Jewish State. The wall of the Hapoel-Hamizrahi restaurant in Strauss Street has been adorned with pictures from the struggle for independence. Someone has pasted slogans onto his balcony, such as: 'We were born to freedom'. 'Make us glad according to the days wherein thou hast afflicted us, and the years wherein we have seen evil'. 'Jerusalem — we have a strong city'. And so on.

For some days the 'Orion' movie-house has been showing, free, newsreels made by the Carmel company, depicting the struggle to build the State. The Maariv newspaper agency screened movies about the nation and the State on a wall in Ben Yehuda Street. Prayers were said in the synagogues for the souls of those who fell in the War of Independence.

At midday the population of Jerusalem gathered to watch the army's festive parade. No one remained at home. All the sidewalks along the city's main streets, the roofs and the balconies were black with people. Some people had been invited as guests of honor to the celebrations in Tel-Aviv but preferred to remain in their city, where they had suffered and were now being repaid for what they had gone through.

In the Valley of the Cross, in the field which had been Jerusalem's airfield during the siege, when the 'primuses' helped to support its defenders and inhabitants, the army started its parade. The hills all around were full of people. To the strains of the police band the army set out along Ramban, Ussishkin, Keren Kayemet, King David and Strauss Streets, through Meah Shearim and Turim Street. The saluting dais was near Histadruth House, and on it were the Chief of Staff, Yaakov Dori, the commander of the army in Jerusalem, Lieutenant-Colonel Moshe Dayan, the commander of the front, Zvi Ayalon, Major-General David Shealtiel and the former Military Governor of Jerusalem, Dov Yosef.

The parade lasted about an hour, and was saluted by the officers on the dais. A company of motor-cyclists rode ahead, followed by the standard-bearers marching on foot, with the commanders of the Sixth Brigade and the district in open cars. Behind them marched the Moriah Battalion, the communications unit, which maintained contact with isolated companies and distant settlements in the Jerusalem area, saving them from a sense of being cut off, using primitive equipment. They were followed by a mine-detecting and flame-throwing platoon, veterans of the Haganah, with the flag of Jerusalem at their head, the People's Guard, the youth corps, which played an important part in repelling the enemy, the women's corps, the medical corps and the 'Red Star of David'. Then came mule-drivers with their mules, which had carried strecthers for evacuating wounded men and arms, armored vehicles and the auxiliary battalion's troop-carrier, heavy and light mortars, the jeep unit, and the heavy cannon, wich were greeted with cheers by the Jerusalem public. They were followed by the engineering corps, with its heavy vehicles, the transport unit, whith its mobile repair unit, the Fire Brigade and, in special vehicles, a group of soldiers who had been wounded in combat. Bringing up the rear were the settlers from the villages around Jerusalem, their trucks decorated with greenery, flags and slogans: 'We willed it and it is no legend'.

In the afternoon a sports display was given by the army in the Y.M.C.A. sports ground.

Many guests came in the evening. Foreign consuls, the heads of institutions and mayors were received by the district governor, Dr. A. Bergman (Biran). The police band played, and the guests spent a pleasant time in a festive atmosphere.

In the evening thousands flocked to the Valley of the Cross, beacons were lit and the district commander, Yitzhak Levi (Levitza) welcomed the people who had come to celebrate. The Army Entertainment Group amused the audience, members of the Youth Corps displayed their ablity at sports and the evening ended with folk dancing by the Harel Troupe, members of the women's corps, etc.

*

At a modest though impressive ceremony, the foundation stone of a 'Memorial for the Defenders of Jerusalem' was laid at Nordau Square (in the Romema Quarter). A scroll was placed within the memorial stone, and its signatories included the Chief rabbis, Herzog and Uziel, members of the municipal council, the executive of the Jewish Agency, army officers, etc.

At a modest though impressive ceremony, the foundation stone of a 'Memorial for the Defenders of Jerusalem' was laid at Nordau Square (in the Romema Quarter). A scroll was placed within the memorial stone, and its signatories included the Chief rabbis, Herzog and Uziel, members of the municipal council, the executive of the Jewish Agency, aemy officers, etc.

The scroll read as follows:

'1879 years after Jerusalem fell to its oppressors and in the first year of its redemption and liberation by Israel, we laid at the approach to the city the foundation stone of a memorial to be erected for the pure and innocent, the defenders of Jerusalem, its fighters and guardians, its redeemers and liberators, who gave their lives for it in its siege and suffering and did not live to see this time of its rejoicing.

'Let this stone be a witness to the heroes who cast their lives aside and withstood the onslaught when Ishmael and Edom rose up against us, to take Jerusalem from us. To the heroes of a hide-and-seek war, who were not recognized as soldiers and were not allowed to wear uniform or raise their flag, all that we can give is a soldier's death.

'Let this stone be a witness to those who fell in the defense of Jerusalem in 1919 and 1920, to those who formed a living wall around it for three years, between 1936 and 1939, and to those who fell for it during the War of Independence in 1948 and 1949. Let this stone attest that Jerusalem has not been and will not be severed from the body and heart of the State of Israel, for which we died together, its sons and builders, those who were born here, those from Israel and those who came from the diaspora to help it and break through the way when the enemy placed his siege around it.

'By their blood we have reached this day, when we lay the foundation stone of the memorial, for Jerusalem belongs to Israel in the light of the sun, in the eyes of Israel and in view of all the nations.

'Let this stone and this memorial be a witness to what has not yet been done and must be done, to the heroes who fell while fighting a lost battle, few against many, unarmed against those well-equipped with arms, defending the Old City and the isolated settlements in the Judean and Jerusalem Hills. In their death they commanded us to complete the liberation of the holy city, the City of David, the heart of Israel, and of all the Jewish settlements in the Land of Israel which fell into the enemy's hands'.

*

The diary has ended. The sage of Jerusalem's struggle for life, liberty, unity, greatness and grandeur continues and will continue until God establishes it permanently, the joy of the world, the city of a great king.

APPENDICES

1. The amount of arms possessed by the Haganah on the eve of the War of Independence.
2. Ben-Gurion on the sincerity of the desire of the British to leave Palestine.
3. The death of the 35 on the way to the Etzion Bloc.
4. An anti-Jewish leagflet of the (fascist) British League.
5. Bernadotte on the hostile attitude of Britons in the Arab Legion.
6. Christopher Sykes on the undermining of law and order by the British regime.
7. Discussions of Jerusalem's status: internationalization or annexation to the State.
8. The attitude of Rabbi Meir Berlin on the Jerusalem question.
9. Dov Joseph on Halperin's removal from the Old City.
10. Mrs. Rivka Weingarten on Halperin's arrest.
11. What Halperin said about Weingarten.
12. What Alhanani said about Weingarten.
13. The Schneller Camp is transferred to us.
14. From Tel-Aviv to Jerusalem via the Dead Sea., 15. Dov Joseph on the conquest of Dir Yassin.
16. Etzel's version of Dir Yasin
17. The communiqué issued by Lehi on Dir Yassin.
18. What Abdullah el-Tal wrote about Dir Yassin.
19. The Israeli army's report on Dir Yassin.
20. An eye witness account of the slaughter of the Hadassah convoy.

231

21. Abdullah el-Tal's account of Golda Meir's meeting with King Abdullah.
22. Shabtai Tevet's description of Moshe Dayan's meeting with King Abdullah.
23. Yigael Yadin's account of his meeting with King Abdullah.
24. An agrement with Abdullah was near.
25. Y. Galili on the Nahshon Campaign and its significance.
26. Y. Raphael on the distribution of fuel.
27. The State of Israel was not created by the U.N.
28. The U.S.A.'s intentions of abandoning its support for partition.
29. Moshe Sharett on the fear of a shift in the U.S.A.'s attitude.
30. The U.S.A.'s stand on the partition question.
31. Y. Galili on the attitude of the People's Administration.
32. The decision to proclaim the State without delay.
33. The resistance and retreat of the inhabitants of Neveh Yaakov and Atarot.
34. Abdullah el-Tal on King Abdullah's attitude towards the Old City.
35. Why did the Arabs flee their homes?
36. Roy Carlson on the Arabs' flight.
37. Newspapers which appeared in Jerusalem during the siege.
38. — 46. Statements made by Uzi Narkiss, A. Sela, Y. Yadin, el-Tal, Yannait and Adina on the attempt to break into the Old City and the reasons for its failure.
47. W. Lacquer on the inadequate treatment of foreign correspondents.
48. Roy Carlson on the inadequate treatment of foreign correspondents.
49. The surrender of the inhabitants of the Jewish Quarter in the Old City.
50. A medic's account of the Jewish Quarter's resistance and surrender.
51. Areas of Judea and Samaria annexed by the Kingdom of Jordan.
52. The plan to establish a separate Arab State.
53. Bernadotte's account of his meeting with King Abdullah.

54. Abdullah el-Tal's opposition to the ceasefire.

55. The shortage of food in Jerusalem.

56. The request for a 'permit' to bake on the Sabbath.

57. Yaakov Orland's play on the demonstration by the Neturei Karta.

58. Permission for Jews to pray at the Western Wall in 1949.

59. The appointment of David Shealtiel as District Commander of Jerusalem.

60. For and against the appointment of Bernard Joseph as Military Governor.

61. The annulment of the post of Military Governor of Jerusalem.

62. Moshe Dayan as District Commander of Jerusalem.

63. Moshe Dayan's approach.

64. Bernadotte's aide on the assassination.

65. Bernadotte's support for the Arabs.

66. The railway line to Jerusalem.

67. Liaison officers remember.

68. What is the 'Mandelbaum Gate'?

[1]

In the Haganah Bulletin for 1973 we read that in December 1947 the Jewish defense forces in Jerusalem possessed the following weapons: two three-inch mortars with a few shells; thirty-three two-inch mortars with about two thousand shells, two anti-tank rifles; six 'Schwartzlose' medium machine-guns; 16 'Bren' machineguns; five 'Louis' machine-guns; 160 rifles; 196 'Sten' sub-machine-guns and nine other sub-machine-guns of various kinds; about 6,000 hand grenades made by the Military Industry; about 3,000 hand grenades and 402 revolvers. (7.12.1947)

[2]

In 'The History of the War of Independence', published by Marachot, p. 49, David Ben-Gurion writes: 'The administration of Palestine was crumbling, but still tried — whether directly of indirectly — to prevent or at least restrict the Yishuv' self-defensive capacity. In opposition to the U.N. resolution, Britain refused to release Tel-Aviv port on 1st February, and even though its police and army had left the Tel-Aviv area, British war ships continued to sail in the waters off Tel-Aviv. In effect, a naval blockade was imposed on Palestine, being directed against the Jewish population, since the borders in the north, south and east were open to the Arabs'.

In the same book, on pp. 47 and 49 he writes: 'On 7th December 1947 the High Commissioner summoned me and informed me that he had been instructed by His Majesty's Government to tell us and the Arabs that the British wished to leave Palestine as soon as possible. There were considerable difficulties, he said, because the army had many stores and stocks which would remain here. The army would take only those things which belonged to it. When I asked him why the stores should be left here, he evaded giving an answer. I told him that the U.N. resolution made it clear that from 1st February at the latest we were to have the use of one port, to enable immigration on a large scale. He told me that that was a recommendation, not a resolution, and

234

that it was a matter to be decided by the U.N. and H.M.G., not the Palestine Administration. I asked him why he was discriminating against us in the Arabs' favor, since the Arab People's Guard was being given Government arms, while the Jews were not. He answered: "The Jews have plenty of arms, and the Arabs do not'.

[3]

In his book, 'When Israel Fought', Ben-Gurion gives the evidence of two Arabs regarding what happened to the thirty-five young men. One of the Arabs concluded his statement by saying: 'They fought to the last man. When the Arabs thought they had all been killed and started advancing, one of the Jews stood up, badly wounded, and threw a grenade. The Arabs shot him and the youngster tried to throw a stone at his attackers but fell dead with the stone in his hand. If one has to die, then let it be like those heroes'.

[4]

The newspapers in Jerusalem received a manifesto signed by the Palestine branch of the (fascist), 'British League', saying:
'We have given our holy oath that we will embark on a crusade against the Jews. Consequently, on 22nd February 1948 we attacked the main Jewish Quarter in Jerusalem with explosives, causing heavy losses to the street mob. More than one hundred were killed and two hundred wounded, all of them Jews. We are proud to announce that we did not discriminate between the cowardly and odious Haganah groups and the murderous Stern gang. Jewish women and children, old and young, will all be wiped off the face of the earth. We will finish Hitler's work.
'British soldiers and policemen! Join the British League. We will all join in this war, from the most senior representives of the British Empire to the lowest'.

[5]

In his book, 'To Jerusalem', Folke Bernadotte, the U.N. mediator between the Jews and the Arabs, wrote on p. 31:

'I had an interesting conversation with the corespondent of the 'Stockholm Todningen', G. Kumlin, who had been in Palestine a month, during which time he had seen fighting between Arabs and Jews. I was particularly impressed by the description of his experiences with the Arab Legion. He had seen for himself that the Legion's attacks on Jerusalem were led by British officers. There were several other elements in the Legion, such as Yugoslavians who did not accept their present government, Poles from Anders' army and a considerable number of German officers, who had managed to enter Palestine in a variety of ways. Kumlin had spoken to them and could say that they remained firm adherents of Hitler's doctrine'.

[6]

In his book, 'From Balfour to Bevin, Struggles for Palestine', by Christopher Sykes, published by Marachot, 1966, the author, who is British, accused the British Government not merely of negligence but also of undermining law and order in Palestine. (p. 303)

[7]

On p. 98 of the 'Haaretz' calendar for 1949, under the heading, 'The Question of the Status of Jerusalem', we read: 'The Government should also find a solution to the political status of Jewish Jerusalem in the present situation. The Jews of Jerusalem raised the question themselves, because there was no single Government authority responsible for matters pertaining to the city. Many circles in Jerusalem and outside it have demanded the city be annexed to the State of Israel, and vehement propaganda in this direction is being issued by Etzel, Lehi and the Revisionists. Our Government, however, is not inclined to imperil its relations with the U.N. by acting in opposition to a resolution passed by the General Assembly. Consequently, for the present, Jerusalem has been declared occupied territory, headed by a Military Governor, Dr. Dov Yosef, who has been appointed by the Government. As a result of the extended siege and the disconnection from the coastal plain, Jerusalem's economic life has come to a standstill, and an extensive development plan and many investments will be needed to revive Jerusalem once more and replace the part played in its

economic life by the Government and the National Institutions which have
been annulled'.

[8]

Both Jews and non-Jews realized that the proposal to internationalize
Jerusalem was unrealistic. Rabbi Meir Berlin also abandoned the approach.
Below is part of a letter he wrote to the Mizrahi Council in Jerusalem in July
1948:

'I am writing this letter in order to express my opinion on one of the most
important questions to be discussed at this Council, the question of Jerusalem,
our capital and holy city.

There are individuals and parties amongst us who, by their declarations
and decisions, create the impression both internally and externally that there
are differences of opinion regarding the desire and right that Jerusalem should
be not merely part of the State of Israel but the capital of our State. These
declarations and decisions do more harm than good.

'The disputed issue is only whether it is possible to relinquish part of
Jerusalem, and in the present situation this part is the holiest, to an Arab
government to form the seat of an Arab king. For if we demand only our own
rights there is a chance, many people think, that a 'compromise' will be
reached which is to our detriment in that we will have to recognize foreign rule
in part of the holy city.

'The foreign Minister, Shertok, was right when he said to the General
Assembly: "We do not regard ourselves morally bound by the resolution of
29th November regarding Jerusalem.". In my letter to him I wrote:

'A. The holy city of Jerusalem has been and will be the spiritual and political
center of the revival of Judaism. The city in which David resided has always,
whether in the times of the kings of Israel or during the years of the dispersion,
been considered the capital of Israel and of the State which would one day be
established.

'B. During the negotiations leading up to the U.N. resolution of 29th
November the Jewish Agency representatives agreed, on behalf of all Israel, to
accept the U.N. demand that Jerusalem become a special, international area
under the U.N. This agreement reflected our desire to do as we had been asked

by the nations which had agreed to the establishment of the State of Israel with the same readiness with which they had agreed to the narrow borders of the new State of Israel, even though they do not accord with the borders laid down by our holy Torah or with the nation's political and economic needs.

'C. To our regret, the U.N. has not kept its word, neither in helping to establish the State nor in implementing the internationalization of Jerusalem, and hence there is no obligation, either moral or political, to agree to the internationalization of the city. On the contrary, the bitter struggle waged by Israel's army in and around Jerusalem and the many who fell in order to free the city from the Arabs and Moslems who wished to conquer and rule the holy city, and the fact that most of Jerusalem is in our hands, requires that the city remain the capital of the Government of Israel and an integral part of the State'.

[9]

In his book, 'The Faithful City', Dov Yosef wrote of A. Halperin and his valiant efforts in the Jewish Quarter of the Old City (pp. 63-68). Amongst other things he said: 'Later there were rumors that Halperin had been arrested and expelled from the Old City as a result of taletelling, and that Mr. Weingarten, the chairman of the committee of Jews in the Old City, had 'cooperated' with the British'.

At a press conference held to mark the publication of this book, it was announced that a committee had been set up to investigate these rumors. For some reason the committee stopped its work almost at the beginning. It consisted of Gideon Hausner, Abraham Arst, a member of the Jerusalem municipality, and Hanoch Givton.

[10]

I asked Mrs. Rivka Weingarten, the daughter of Mordekhai Weingarten, what she knew about the circumstances of Abraham Halperin's arrest and the accusations against her father, whom I knew as an energetic and dedicated official. I drew to her attention the description which had appeared in Dov Jeseph's book ('The Faithful City', pp. 66 and 67) on this score. Although it

grieved her very much to recall it, since she was convinced that the accusations
were unfounded, she acceded to my request and jotted down what she knew.
Below is a summary of what she wrote:

'Halperin came into the Jewish Quarter during the siege of 1948 at the request
of my late father, who declared his presence essential as an anaesthetist.
Halperin was known to the British and was wanted by them for 'troubles' he
had caused them.

'He often came to our house and his relations with my father were very good,
for as commander of the Haganah he was a frequent visitor. The relations
between him and my father deteriorated when Halperin realized that he would
not easily be able to control affairs in the Jewish Quarter which did not pertain
to his sphere of activity, namely, security. Halperin did his utmost to restrict
the activities of my father, who had headed the community for many years and
dedicated his life to the Jewish Quarter and its inhabitants.

'With regard to his arrest, this was due to a coincidence which Halperin had
used to his own advantage. He got into trouble with the British army because
members of the Haganah stole 400 new sacks, which the army had brought to
the Jewish Quarter for preparing barricades. The British officer in charge,
whom we called One-Eyed-Dick, wanted to lynch the inhabitants of the Jewish
Quarter. Realizing that he was in earnest, Halperin promised to return the
sacks, but did not keep his word. The British kept a watch on him and
unfortunately, when he left our house after one of his usual visits, arrested him
about a hundred meters from our house.

'When Halperin was arrested, the British army officer was about to take him
out by the Zion Gate and deposit him by the Jaffa Gate, where it was feared he
would be handed over to the Arabs. Father was called to deal with this, as he
had with hundreds of cases when Jews had been arrested for a variety of
reasons, and he insisted that Halperin be transferred to Jewish Jerusalem. The
officer refused and Father got into the automobile in which Halperin was
sitting and declared that he would not leave Halperin and that whatever they
proposed to do to Halperin they should do to him. Only then did the British
officer give his word that he would personally hand Halperin over to the Jewish
Agency. Quarter of an hour later Father was informed that Halperin had in
fact reached the Jewish side in safety.

'Halperin was saved. My late father went through all the suffering and pain

which the inhabitants of the Jewish Quarter endured until the surrender. He did
not leave it for a single moment, and like a devoted captain went into captivity
together with my mother and my four sisters, one of whom was wounded.
When Father returned he heard about the shameful 'affair' of the accusations
against him, but was never given the chance of getting at the truth'.

[11]

In his article on 'The Jewish Quarter on the Eve of the War of Independence',
in the internal bulletin of the Haganah in Jerusalem, 1973, Abraham Halperin
wrote about Mr. Weingarten, the leader of the Jewish Quarter in the Old City.
Below is an excerpt:
'There was no official body in the Jewish Quarter representing the inhabitants.
The leader (the appointment to this position was always made by the rulers,
and in this case by the British), Mr. Mordekhai Weingarten, had established
the 'Committee of Jews in the Old City' from his supporters, and a rival
committee had been set up by those who opposed him. What they had in
common was that both were formed by dignitaries who had no real support
within the community'.
The same bulletin contained an account of the activities undertaken by
Rabbi Yitzhak Avigdor Orenstein (he and his wife were killed by a shell on
23rd May 1948, a few days before the Jewish Quarter fell), after Halperin was
expelled from the Old City, to mobilize help for the besieged population of the
Jewish Quarter. In a letter to Hanoch Tempelhof, who took Halperin's place
maintaining contact with the public institutions, Orenstein wrote, amongst
other things:
'From your letter I realize your loyalty and dedication to the Jewish population
of the Old City. I would like to draw your attention to the fact that the people
here have not been paid and are discontented. I have managed to see the
devoted labors of Raphael Abulafiya, the Director of Misgav Ladah Hospital,
and Mrs. Yogal, the secretary of the Council for the Old City. In one of my
letters I mentioned the problem of supplying kerosene to the Old City. The
situation has deteriorated since then. I am not referring to the fact that in most
of the houses there is no electricity, but they cannot even prepare themselves
food for the Sabbath. It should be stressed with all gravity that we require
kerosene in order to ease our situation'.

[12]

In his book, 'Jerusalem and its Inhabitants', published by Reuben Mass, A. H. Alhanani writes:

'There were several attempts to slander Weingarten for supposedly glorifying his position in the Old City, aggrandizing himself as the representative of those who were left, 'chairman of the committee of Jews of the Old City' or 'leader'. But the man paid no attention to idle talk, walking uprightly, as he had always done. He drew his authority from his deep desire to regard the Old City as the perfection of glory forever, and his moral strength from his immense love of every alleyway.

'The old City fell. The courtard was a pile of rubble benearh which people and scrolls of the law were buried, together with ancient writings and precious memories. Weingarten took his wife and two daughters and went into exile in Jordan, together with the other inhabitants of the Jewish Quarter.

'When the State was established and the prisoners-of-war released, Jews throughout the world were ecstatic with joy, but Weingarten walked about as if in permanent mourning, uncomforted. He lived in 'exile', in Rehavia, wrote laments and fasted every year on the anniversary of the fall of the Old City.

'Several people asked him to recall the events which had occurred in the Old City. 'The time is not yet ripe', he would say, surprising many by his silence. Even when he was attacked, verbally and in writing, he fought with himself not to reply. Someone published a book in which he was criticized, and the press made the most of it. Weingarten was asked to reply, and there was general rejoicing when, after consulting a friend, he was advised not to speak until the time was right.

'And he took his great secret with him to the grave'.

[13]

Yitzfik Abrahami, one of the editors of 'The Book of the Haganah in Jerusalem', wrote (Volume , p. 98) about the Schneller Camp:

'On 17th March the British left the Schneller Orphanage building. On the same day I summoned to the camp at Schneller the commander on the People's Guard, Zeev Avnat, the head of the Mekor Baruch community committee, Mr. Neiman, and the headmaster of the Tachkemoni School, Mr. Ilan, to affix the mezuzah at the gate. After the ceremony I handed over the camp to the district command and it became a training camp. It contained primitive laboratories for preparing explosives, under the supervision of Aharon Katzir, and also served as the central food store for the entire city'.

[14]

Yaakov Tzernovicz (Tzur) gave the following report of his journey to Jerusalem, via the Dead Sea, which took 23 days in March 1948:
'At that time, mid-March, the blockade around Jerusalem was tightening. The blowing up of the Jewish Agency buildings, the ruined houses in Ben Yehuda Street and the barbed-wire fences of the British, gave the city the appearance of a battle-field. The Arabs did not stop sniping at the narrow pass in the Judean Hills, the Castel was in the hands of the gangs and armored vehicles made their way slowly in convoys towards the coastal plain. There was still electricity in Jerusalem and the Mandate radio gave laconic information about clashes and casualties in the Valley of Jezreel, in Galilee and on the border between Jaffa and Tel-Aviv. The increasing shortage of supplies and the sense of siege in Jerusalem accompanied by the firing of the Arabs and the aggravation of the British, created an atmosphere of being at the front. One day I decided to go and see what was happening in the Negev, promising to be home in a day or two, in time for the Sabbath. I made the journey from Jerusalem to Tel-Aviv in an armored vehicle.
'Next day I set out in another armored vehicle, sitting on a fuel barrel, for Rehovot and thence to Nir Am. On the way, near the village of Barbara, we came under fire and one of the vehicles hit a mine. Somehow we reached Nir Am, where I was 'stuck' for several days, without any way of contacting the north. After a few days the fields dried and I was summoned to the commander and allocated a place in the small plane which stood on the improvised landing strip.
'I was introduced to the young pilot, who was standing and tying some rope round the wing of the plane, and we went in. Soldiers started the propellor of the 'primus' by hand, and it bucked and rose. When we were in the air the wind blew the map out of the pilots hands, and he shouted: "Hell, now I don't know which airfields are ours".

'After a very brief flight of less than a quarter of an hour, we landed at a former British military airfield, not far from Beer Tuviah, and I reached Tel-Aviv in an armored convoy. There I learned that the chances of reaching Jerusalem were as remote as ever. For a few days I wandered around Tel-Aviv, while the road to Jerusalem remained closed.

'One evening, as I was walking along Dizengoff Road, I saw Golda Meir deep in conversation with one of the Zionist leaders from abroad. She asked me what I was doing and I told her of my adventures. I showed her the order from the Jerusalem headquarters, saying that I had to get back with all possible haste. She said; "Since it's urgent, I'll give you a note for headquarters. It is still possible to get to Jerusalem from the Dead Sea, because British soldiers accompany the convoys of the Phosphates Company to safeguard the exports. Some of our colleagues have returned to Jerusalem that way. At headquarters they will arrange a flight for you from Tel-Aviv to the landing strip at Kalia, and the day after you will be able to join a convoy going up to Jerusalem".

'I thanked her, hurried to the office she had mentioned, received a ticket for the flight and presented myself next morning at the airfield near the Reading Station, on the other side of the Yarkon River. An eight or ten-seater plane was standing on the strip. The doors were closed, the engine started and a few minutes later we found ourselves flying over the Judean Hills, seeing below us Arab villages, camps of the Arab Legion and encampments which appeared to be training bases for the gangs in the hills. Within less than an hour we began coming in to land. Soon we could make out beneath us the white houses of kibbutz Beth Haarava and the camp of the men who worked at the Dead Sea and the Phosphates Company.

'When the noise of the propellor had died down and the doors of the plane were opened to the burning heat of the Dead Sea, we found ourselves surrounded by dozens of young men who worked at the Dead Sea Works, members of the Haganah without uniform, and some old friends from Jerusalem. Not far from the strip stood a row of trucks loaded with sacks of phosphates, next to jeeps and tenders in which uniformed British soldiers were sitting. Someone spoke excitedly with the officer in charge of the convoy. From afar we saw him shaking his head, signifying 'no'.

"Why have you come here"? one of the boys asked a passenger who had just alighted from the plane.

"What do you mean, why have we come? To get to Jerusalem, of course". Everyone burst out laughing.

"To get to Jerusalem? Very nice. You'll have to sit and wait with us. For three days we have been arguing with the British, who refuse to let any passengers join their convoys. They say they can't be responsible for passengers. The Arabs around Jerusalem are angry because the Haganah killed Abed Al-Kadr Huseini at the Castel, and they haven't calmed down yet".

'With us were several Jerusalem dignitaries, including Yitzhak Ben-Zvi whose younger son, Eli, had been killed in the battle at Beth Keshet. Now he was stuck here on his way back from his son's funeral. He walked among us sad and downcast by the tragedy that had befallen him, though from time to time he would recover and join in the endless discussions we held about our approaching victory, the State that was to be established and our problems.

'One day we were called to the commander and told that the next day a 'plane would come and take us back to Tel-Aviv. And so once again we found ourselves flying over the Judean Hills on our way to Tel-Aviv. After another few days of tension and waiting, we were put into an armoured vehicle together with Y. Ben-Zvi, Abraham Garnovski and B. Joseph.

'Late at night the convoy reached Kfar Bilu, where we were told to leave the vehicle and wait for information as to whether and when we could get through. We waited for news from the hills around Jerusalem, as the battles on the road to Jerusalem had not yet ended. After a few hours we were told that the rest of the journey was postponed, and it was not likely that we would continue before morning. The passengers from our armored vehicle were accommodated in one of the classrooms of a school in Rehovot. We lay down on the desks and tried to doze until there was a knock on the door and we were called to return to our vehicle.

'Once again the convoy began its journey from one village to another, and from one station to another. At Hulda forest a small plane joined us, flying above the vehicles, drawing near then going far away. Near Latrun and Bab el Wad we could see the stocking caps of the Haganah soldiers between the rocks. Although the vehicles kept close to one another, the convoy stretched out for several kilometers, and when the first truck had reached the Castel, the rear of the convoy was still at Latrun. At the top of the Castel our boys waved to us with their hats, and the blue and white flag was flying over the fort.

'We drove into Mahane Yehuda market, surrounded by crowds of people, who were laughing and crying at the miracle which had befallen the inhabitants of Jerusalem. The city was at starvation point and our convoy guaranteed it supplies for the months of the siege, but it was the last convoy to reach Jerusalem without any problems. Two days later, when the trucks made their way to Jerusalem again, they were attacked by Arabs, soldiers were killed and vehicles burned. A few trucks managed to break through and reach Jerusalem, but after that the road to the coastal plain was totally cut off. The Castel was conquered by the Arabs again, the Legion entrenched itself at Latrun and Jerusalem was completely under siege.

[15]

In his book, 'The Faithful City', Dov Yosef wrote the following about the Dir Yassin affair (p. 74):

'We suffered a defeat of a different kind when, on 9th April, Etzel and Lehi units mounted a malicious and unprovoked attack on the Arab village of Dir Yassin. There was no reason for this attack on a quiet village which had not allowed companies of 'volunteers' from across the border to enter its territory. This was an act of terrorism, implemented apparently for political reasons. Information of their plan leaked out, and two senior Haganah officers tried to dissuade them, demanding that they help us instead in our battle for the Castel. Their behavior and methods were such, however, that apart from arguing with them we had no way of stopping them.

'The battle, which should have lasted one hour, lasted all morning. The assailants had not been adequately briefed, and some Arab snipers in one of the houses held them up for a long time. The women and children were not given enough time to leave the village, even though warned to do so over loudspeakers, and many of them were among the figure of 254 dead published by the Arab High Council. It was a tragedy in every respect. The dissidents held the village for two days and then left. Most of the Jewish population of Jerusalem despised them and the Jewish Agency absolved itself of responsibility for them in a sharply-worded public declaration. Nevertheless, the Arabs were given a strong argument to use against us, and the name 'Dir Yassin' was used by them many times to justify their acts of violence and persuade villagers to join the growing flight from Palestine'.

[16]

A very different, in fact completely contradictory, description of Dir Yassin is given by a member of Etzel, I. Ofir, in his book, 'On the Walls', (Etzel in the Battles of 1948 in Jerusalem) which notes that there was cooperation between the Haganah and its commander, Shealtiel, rejects the accusation of 'slaughter' and decries, as did many others in the country during the siege, what he calls the exaggerated self-indictment which gripped us afterwards and which is expressed still today by those who hate and oppose us.

Below are passages from this book:

'The conqest of Dir Yasin constituted a turning-point in the military situation of the country, and exerted immense political influence on the political front, marking the beginning of a chain of Jewish victories over the collapsing Arab forces. It was only by chance that the conquest of Dir Yassin became part of the Haganah's extensive military operation, the 'Nahshon' campaign, which was intended to lift the siege of the city by conquering the salients in the hills which controlled the road to Jerusalem.

'Dir Yassin was a danger because it formed a wedge within the Jewish settlement to the west of the city. The constant sniping from the direction of Dir Yassin and Ein Karem bothered the Jewish population, particularly since Dir Yassin served as a transit point for Arab forces on their way from Ein Karem to the Castel.

'When Haganah headquarters in Jerusalem heard of Etzel and Lehi's plan to conquer Dir Yassin, the Haganah asked the Etzel commander in Jerusalem to time the attack on the village with their own attempt to recapture the Castel. (The letter sent by the Haganah commander, Shealtiel, to the Etzel commander on this point is quoted here, Y.C.)

'Before the battle the question of treating prisoners was discussed, and we decided that our men should separate the population involved in the fighting from the rest. Consequently, the element of surprise was eliminated, and a special armored vehicle equipped with a loudspeaker was prepared in order to inform the villagers before the battle began that the place was surrounded and that the fighting men should be separated from the women, children and old people.

'The start of the battle did not go according to plan. The Arabs discerned the attackers and opened fire and the armored vehicle with the loudspeaker did

not reach the village. The fighters were forced to advance under heavy fire
from the Arabs. The men on the scene reported that the Arabs tried to deceive
us by coming out of their houses dressed as women. In the heat of the battle it
was difficult to distinguish between a 'fighting woman' and a genuine one, and
that may explain why some Arab women were found among the dead.

'The commander of the Haganah in Jerusalem showed an interest in what
was happening in the battle for Dir Yassin, came to Givat Shaul, met the Etzel
commander and asked him if he needed help. Shealtiel thought that in
undertaking to conquer the village, Etzel and Lehi had taken on more than
they could manage, and was prepared to come to their aid. The Etzel
commander rejected his offer.

'The conquest of Dir Yasin brought a spirit of rejoicing to the Jewish
population of Jerusalem, which had been depressed for some weeks. There was
exultation throughout the country, but this met the disapproval of the leaders
of the Jewish Agency, who feared an increase in the popularity of the fighting
underground, and during that time of bloodshed embarked on a campaign of
horror stories concerning the organizations which had conquered Dir Yassin.
This propaganda was also intended to influence the discussions of the Zionist
Executive, which was about to reach a decision regarding the agreement
between the Haganah and the Etzel. The chairman of the Jewish Agency
Executive, David Ben-Gurion, was not satisfied until he had sent a cable of
condolence to Emir Abdullah, 'The wise ruler who seeks the welfare of his
people and his country', expressing his regret at the Arab victims who had
fallen at Dir Yassin'.

[17]

'Lohamei Herut Yisrael.
'Communiqué on the Dir Yassin Affair.
'Reply to the Haganah's yellow leaflet (paralleling the yellow star).
'We have explained the military reasons for holding Dir Yassin. We herewith
publish the letter sent by the Haganah in Jerusalem, without any additional
explanation:
"To: Shapira
"From: The District Commander

"I have been informed that you intend to attack Dir Yassin.

"I would like to point out that the occupation of Dir Yassin is one stage in our general plan. I have no objection to your undertaking the action provided you are capable of holding on to the village. If you cannot do this I must warn you that the village will be blown up, leading to the flight of its inhabitants and the occupation of the abandoned dwellings by foreign forces. This will hinder rather than help the general campaign, and the reconquest of the village will involve heavy losses on our side.

"Another factor I should like to draw to your attention is that if foreign forces are brought to the spot, our plan to establish   (these words have been omitted for security reasons) will be upset".

'After we conquered Dir Yassin and held it for three days, we had achieved the objectives we set ourselves:

'A. We had destroyed the criminal Arab forces which had entrenched themselves there, threatening Jerusalem's western neighborhoods.

'B. We had confiscated all the arms and ammunition in the village and transferred it to the fighting nation.

'C. We had demonstrated that a relatively small Jewish fighting force could implement a strategic military operation of the highest importance, if it worked according to a bold and well thought-out plan'.

*

In the Etzel handbill pasted up on the walls of houses at that time (and also in Ofir's book), the fact was emphasized that a representative of the Medical Association, Dr. Avigdori, accompanied by Dr. Droyanov, visited Dir Yassin the next day, conducted a thorough examination of the bodies and the houses and affirmed that, apart from shell and bullet wounds, there was no evidence that the bodies had been mutilated.

[18]

In his book 'Memories', Abdullah el-Tal wrote the following about the Dir Yassin affair:

'On 9th April 1948 Jews from the Irgun Gang (his term for the Irgun Zvai Leumi) and Stern (Lehi) surprised the peaceful villagers of Dir Yassin, to the west of Jerusalem, killing women, children and old men indiscriminately, mutilating their bodies and throwing them into the village well. Three hundred people were killed, most of them women, children and old people. The British did not dare send their forces, and simply despatched a Jewish policeman to investigate what had happened. The attack was launched on the basis of a pre-arranged plan, and was undertaken with the knowledge of the Jewish Agency and the Haganah organization. The objective of the Jews in this action was a far-reaching, one and they succeeded in achieving it to a considerable extent, sowing terror throughout all the Arab villages, whose inhabitants began leaving them. The Arab press unintentionally helped the Jews to achieve their aims by giving detailed reports of the barbaric crime.

'...The Jewish Agency, which feared the rebuke of King Abdullah, sent His Majesty a letter condemning the crime and placing the responsiblity on the Zionist gangs.

"On 13th April the Arabs took revenge for the innocent victims of Dir Yassin. They attacked the convoy making its way to the Hadassah Hospital and the Hebrew University, killing many important people".

[19]

A few years later 'The History of the War of Independence', (Hebrew) published by Marachot, gave a brief report of the affair which was very different from those given above (p. 117):

'On 9.4.48 Etzel and Lehi attacked Dir Yassin. The battle for the village was an easy one, but the attackers nevertheless suffered losses, particularly in the assault on the Mukhtar's house, which dominated the village. During the conquest about two hundred villagers were killed, including women and children. The Dir Yassin affair was reported throughout the world as the 'Dir Yassin Slaughter', damaging the good name of the Jewish population of Palestine at that time. All the Arab propaganda channels publicised it, and still do so today, although there is no doubt that it helped in leading to the collapse of the Arab rear in the period which followed. This was achieved more by the publicity given it by Arab spokesmen than by the deed itself. They wanted to prove how cruel the Jews were and in this way spur their people on to engage in a holy war against them, but in fact merely demonstrated their cowardice. Today they admit their error'.

[20]

At one of the memorial services for the people killed in the convoy, I collected eye-witness accounts from people who were there at the time, in addition to what I had seen myself:

I was standing together with a group of journalists and defenders on the roof of a high building in Jerusalem, looking anxiously towards the convoy of physicians and scientists which had been trapped by Arab mines in full view of the British soldiers, in the Sheikh Jarrah neighborhood. No one thought then how terrible and bitter the end would be. No one believed that, just a few meters away from the Haganah positions, unarmed nurses, doctors and scientists who had cared for and saved dozens of sick Arabs from Jerusalem and its environs would be murdered in such a cruel and base way. Arab ministers and dignitaries from the neighboring countries used to come to the Hadassah Hospital, which had a notable reputation.

Soldiers stood in the Beth Yisrael quarter begging their superior officer to give them the order to go and rescue the people trapped not far away from them. Many people were watching the heroic action of the two dozen youngsters who, with light arms, were fighting off the hundreds of Arabs firing from the houses all around. No one was sent to help them because Dr. Magnes, who was in his house in the city, phoned the British commander-in-chief, General MacMillan, and asked for permission to send a Haganah detachment to their aid. The General, of course, objected, saying: "No, the situation is quiet. The arrival of the Haganah will only inflame the situation and increase the danger".

The request was repeated several times, and rejected. For five full hours the defenders stood by the convoy and fought off the mob. Not far away from there British soldiers stood idle, although their task was 'to safeguard the road to Mount Scopus', in accordance with assurances given by the British High Commissioner to Magnes and by the British Minister for the Colonies to Mr. Leon Simon, etc.

This slaughter was implemented, it seems, on the basis of a deliberate plan prepared with the knowledge of the British soldiers guarding the road to Mount Scopus.

[21]

In his book, 'Memories', Abdullah el-Tal writes about Golda Meir's meeting with King Abdullah:

'King Abdullah had many contacts with the Jews. This was known to the inhabitants of Amman, particularly those who visited the palace.

'In many cases the King would travel secretly to the border with Palestine, where he would hold meetings with Jewish leaders. I will describe two of them:

'At the beginning of April 1948 Abu Yosef (the name given by the Arabs to Daskel, the manager of the elecricity plant at Gesher) contacted his friend, Muhammed al Zabati, the court chamberlain, and informed him that Shertok wished to meet the King at the electricity plant. His Majesty was very pleased to hear this and arranged to hold the meeting on 12th April 1948, the day he moved from al-Shuna (the winter palace) to Amman.

"When they reached the Jordan Valley the King went to al-Zabati's farm to dine. At the farm the King's tracks were lost and the guards at the farm kept quiet about the fact the the the King had eluded them among the trees and gone towards the Jewish settlement which was being built on Transjordanian land for the employees at the plant. Shertok and Abu-Yosef were waiting there, and they all sat down to lunch together. After the meal the King and Shunkeiti conferred together secretly with Shertok and Abu-Yosef for over an hour. Nothing was made public about what was discussed between them, apart from what the King said later, namely, that the most important decision reached at that meeting was that both sides agreed to the partition plan and the ways of implementing it.

'The crisis in Palestine reached its peak in mid-May, a few days before the end of the British Mandate. The Jews wanted to be sure that King Abdullah would keep his promise to support the partition plan and refrain from using force. They contacted Jordan, exchanged views and reached an agreement that the meeting would be held in Amman. The King knew that this time Golda Meyerson, one of the most prominent figures in the Jewish Agency, would come to the meeting. The King sent Muhammad al-Zabati in a pick-up truck which could be relied on as regards speed and strength. The King told al-Zabati to go to the Jordan Valley in order to collect Golda Meyerson, who was waiting at a certain spot between the trees. Al-Zabati reached his farm in the Jordan Valley at 9 p.m. and found Golda waiting for him, wearing a keffiya and an akal. He sat her beside him and placed her companion, the interpreter, in the back. On the way back al-Zabati drove at top speed, reaching Amman within less than two hours, during which time Golda sat beside him without saying a word. He turned in at a villa on the road between Mahta and Amman, where dinner had been prepared. When al-Zabati entered the room where the meeting was to be held and informed the King that his guest had arrived safely, the King was very pleased and told him to bring her in, as he had been waiting ever since the automobile had set off to collect her. Golda entered the room, the King stood up, they shook hands and His Majesty invited her to dinner. Golda did not eat much as she seemed to be tense and ready for a fight. The King, who noticed this, spoke to her gently and tried to put her at her ease until the meal was over and they went to the room where the meeting was to be held. 'There was a long discussion between His Majesty and Golda, who raised demands made by the Jewish Agency which seemed to him to be rather extreme and difficult to implement in the way they asked. The essence of what she said, as told to me later by people who were at the meeting, was: that the King should declare peace with the Jews, refrain from sending his army to Palestine, and send a governor to rule the Arab part of Palestine, in accordance with the partition plan; in exchange, the Jewish Agency would agree to the annexation of the Arab part of Palestine by the Hashemite kingdom.

'The King rejected the first condition, since by doing so he would appear to be abandoning the decision made unanimously by the Arabs and the Arab States to send their armies to save Palestine. The King agreed, however, that both the Jordanian and the Iraqi armies would not engage in war against the Jews and would remain on the border designated by the partition plan.

'After an argument which included threats by Golda and a warning by the King, Golda agreed and received the King's promise to keep his word. The meeting ended at 3 a.m. and Al-Zabati took Golda and her companion to the farm near the border, which they reached at 6 a.m. Golda's journey to Amman did not remain a secret since the King himself revealed it, even joking about the rudeness, pride and arrogance of that Jewish woman'.

[22]

In his book about Moshe Dayan, Shabtai Tevet writes (pp. 336-7):
'On 19th March (1949), accompanied by Major Yehoshafat Harkabi, Moshe

met the King in his palace at al-Shuna. According to A. el-Tal, who also participated in the discussion, Moshe Dayan demanded: that the Jewish coastal plain be connected with the Jezreel Valley by Wadi Ara, that the Israeli borders within the triangle include strategic points which would enable the Jews to defend the coastal plain. El-Tal writes that Dayan explained his request for the King's agreement to his demand, 'so that Israel can agree to the principle of the Arab Legion taking over the region, or that the King gives up the idea and permits the problem with the Iraqi army to be solved in the way Israel sees fit'. In other words, this was a clear hint that there would be war if the King did not agree. At the meeting at al-Shuna on 19th March, Moshe obtained King Abdullah's agreement in principle to the transfer of Wadi Ara and the triangle to Israel'.

[23]

Yigael Yadin, who was then the Israeli army's Operations Officer, described another meeting with King Abdullah during the War of Independence in an interview with the journalist, I. Bashan, which appeared in 'Maariv' on 14.5.1967.

'It was after the armistice agreement with the Egyptians had been signed. Moshe Dayan headed our delegation to Rhodes which was holding discussions with the Jordanians and reported that the negotiations had reached deadlock. We received information that the commanders of the Iraqi army, which held the central front, had informed Abdullah that they were going home. We made it clear to Abdullah that if the Iraqis withdrew from the center we had the same right to enter the area as did his armies. Abdullah knew that he could not delay the Iraqi withdrawal and we moved brigades around from one place to another, demonstratively and in broad daylight, so that Abdullah would realize that we were in earnest. Then Abdullah informed us that he wanted to speak to us, without any connection with the negotiations in Rhodes.

'B.G. decided that I would go together with Walter Eitan. Yehoshafat Harkabi joined us. The first meeting was to be held at Abdullah's summer place at Shuni, at the end of March 1949, through the mediation of Abdullah el-Tal, who knew Moshe Dayan. I knew that it would be impossible to consult anyone superior to us during the negotiations, so before the journey I prepared a map of Palestine on which I drew three lines in different colors, representing our demands and the maximum, intermediate and minimum concessions we were prepared to make. We passed through the Mandelbaum Gate dressed as U.N. observers and Abdullah el-Tal collected us in his automobile. Every fifty meters to the Damascus Gate we were stopped by armed guards who asked: 'Min hada' (Who goes there?), and el-Tal would put his head out of the window and say: 'Abdullah Bey'.

'When we reached Jericho we encountered a mass demonstration at the central square. Many people were armed with rifles and revolvers and the mob surrounded the automobile and demanded that we get out and identify ourselves. The driver put his foot on the gas and by some miracle we got out of Jericho alive. Incidentally, when King Abdullah heard what had happened to us he was wild with fury, and ordered that henceforth we should be driven by the men of his personal bodyguard.

'After the customary exchange of polite formalities, Abdullah gave us a gift, a wonderful silver 'shabriyah' (dagger) (now in the Foreign Ministry). Walter Eitan had prepared a gift for the King, a bible in a beautiful Bezalel work, silver binding. When Abdullah opened the bible his face reddened and he asked us angrily: 'Shu hadda?' (What is this?) It seems that on the flyleaf there was a map of Israel in King Solomon's time. 'What's going on here?' the King fumed, 'Mesopotamia, (Aram Naharayim), Egypt', we managed to save the situation with some difficulty by explaining that it was a map of Israel in the time of King 'Suleiman'.

'Abdullah received us in his imposing reception hall. The Prime Minister, Tewfik Abu al-Hodda, sat on his right and the other members of his cabinet on his left. 'How is my friend Shertok? he asked, and asked us to send him his regards. Then he asked, 'And how is Mrs. Meyerson?' Apparently he had been slightly offended because a woman had been sent to conduct political negotiations with him. When we answered, 'Mrs. Meyerson is now the Israeli Ambassador in Moscow', he winked and said: 'Taib, kaluha hunak', (Good, leave her there).

'Then he rose and delivered a bombastic speech. Although he was speaking to us, he intended his words for the members of his cabinet. The main points of the address were: I told you at the beginning that we had no chance of defeating the Israelis, but you would not listen to me. The Arabs are unreliable, and the British cheated us and gave us bad ammunition. The result is that the Israeli representatives sit in the King's palace and dictate conditions to him! I am a Beduin, and we Beduin have a saying which goes; If you are riding a heavily-loaded donkey and you feel that the enemy is approaching, you have two choices: either to be taken prisoner with all the merchandise, or to try to get away, throwing away the bundles one by one. I have asked the Israelis here in order to throw bundles away!

'Then he turned to the Prime Minister, Tewfik abu al-Hodda, and said: 'Now you speak'! Al-Hodda stood up, coughed and said: 'I beg your majesty's pardon, but I do not feel well'! Abdullah made a gesture of scorn with his hand and shouted at him in our presence: 'In that case – atla min hon'! Get out of here. Al-Hodda stood up and went out.

'Then we went to eat a sumptuous meal, served on gold and silver plates. I sat at Abdullah's right and he pointed proudly at everything saying: 'I received that from King George, that is from Roosevelt, and do you see that light fixure up there? Pinhas Ruttenberg gave me that'! We were making polite conversation when the King suddenly said to me: 'Do you know what I enjoy in my spare time? Ancient Arabic poetry'! I remembered my teacher, Professor Benat, who had forced us to learn long, complicated poems of the pre-Islamic community by heart. How I had hated him!

'For some reason, of all those poems one remained fixed in my memory in its entirety, and I began quoting it to Abdullah: The mother mourns her son on the battlefield and says: I fed you at my breast, gave you food, brought you up.... When the King heard that he crowed with joy, embraced me and said: "Upon my soul, that is my favorite poem! Tell me where you know it from"! Of course my standing rose and the atmosphere relaxed.

[24]

In February 1975, when he addressed the students at Bar Ilan University, Moshe Dayan revealed that an agreement had almost been signed with King Abdullah at the time, giving Jordan an outlet to the Mediterranean Sea and annexing the Jewish Quarter of the Old City to Israel. Dayan said: 'I was present when King Abdullah and Reuben Shiloh initialled an agreement in which both sides agreed that the State of Israel would give the Kingdom of

Jordan an outlet to the sea via a strip under Jordanian sovereignty. In return, Jordan would give Israel a passage from the Dead Sea region to the northern part of the Dead Sea and the Jerusalem area. A paragraph of that agreement determined that the Jewish Quarter of the Old City would be part of Israeli Jerusalem. In the final event the agreement was not implemented, as a result of British intervention. King Abdullah told the Israeli representatives, 'The British do not agree to the agreement'. Shortly afterwards King Abdullah was assassinated and a new chapter in the relations between Israel and the kingdom of Jordan began.

Dayan added that Christian-Catholic interests may have been behind the assassination of King Abdullah, who opposed the internationalization of Jerusalem.

[25]

Operation 'Nahshon', as was made clear after the fighting had died down, was mounted at the height of the 'convoy crisis', on the road to Jerusalem, when it was feared that the Jews would lose the transport war. This situation raised doubts as to whether the Jewish State would be able to withstand its assailants. These doubts strengthened the American politicians, who began retreating from their support for the Jewish State, proposing that its establishment be postponed temporarily and that Palestine be placed under the interim rule of a 'Council of Trustees', etc.

Yisrael Galili wrote about this in 'The Haganah Book', Vol. 2, (pp. 126-7), (Hebrew) and some excerpts follow:

'Operation Nahson formed a turning point in the war. It constituted a change for the good, keeping Jerusalem within Israel and turning the battle in our favor.

'It was obvious that Jerusalem mght fall and that a major effort had to be made to save the city, involving the concentration of large numbers of men and arms. The general fearfulness of those days did not undermine the spirit of the Haganah, for fear led to daring, and that gave rise to 'Nahshon'. It was decided that Yigal Allon, the commander of the Palmach, would command the operation, but he was stuck in the bitter battle for the convoy at the Etzion Bloc. Shimon Avidan was therefore appointed commander of the operation.

Food distribution, in line and by coupons

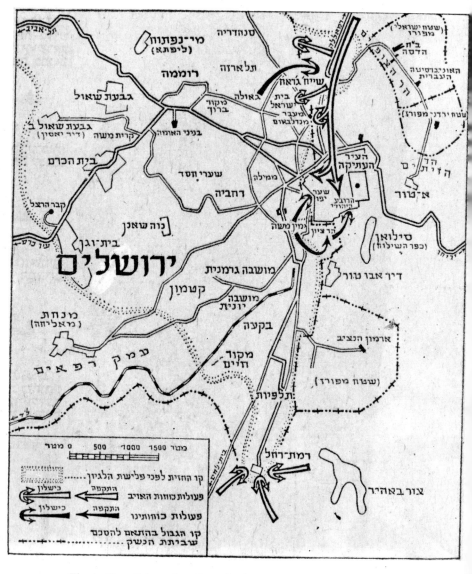

The battles of Jerusalem from the invasion until the first ceasefire
(15.5.1948—11.6.1948)

Before the battle for the Castel

The fighters' faces after the
Castel is taken over

in Moshe (Mishkaanoth Shaananim) in 1940,
from where our forces set out to take
Mount Zion and the Old City

Before the assau~
to take Katamo~

The attack of the Palmach soldiers taking over Katamon

On the day Ein Kerem was taken. the author in conversation with the nuns

A. Weingarten, official representative of the Jewish Quarter in the Old City — returned from Jordian captivity

The ruins of "Batei Machseh" in the Old City of Jerusalem

The way to Zion Gate   Zion Gate — shell pocked

The old path to the Western Wall. Chief Rabbi Herzog accompanied by rabbis.
In front of him march the 'Kwass'

The Swedish Prince Bernadotte "mediator" (left), and with him colonel
Bronson, Y. Schnorman, liaison officer and Captain Pikovski

Mandelbaum Gate,
temporary border post

On the one side, Jordanian soldiers
and on the other, Israeli
(Zahal) soldier and girl-soldier

OFFICIAL PALESTINE PRESS CARD
بطاقة صحفية رسمية כרטיס־עתונות רשמי

Name of Holder اسم حامل البطاقة
שם בעל הכרטיס

COHEN, J.

Signature of Holder

J. Cohen

THIS IS NOT A FRONTIER PASS.
ليس هذه بطاقة لاجتياز الحدود كرטיس זה אינו כרטיס־גבול

1425

Press card of the
Mandatory Government

שם העתון או הסוכנות
Newspaper or Agency الجريدة او الوكالة

שם בעל הכרטיס
Name of Holder اسم حامل الطائفة

מעמד
Status الوظيفه

חתימת בעל הכרטיס
Signature of Holder توقيع الحامل

תאריך נתינתו
Date of Issue تاريخ الاصدار
18.5.1948

יום תום תקפו
Date of Expiry تاريخ الانتهاء
1.10.1948

THE JEWISH AGENCY FOR PALESTINE

Press card of
the Jewish Agency

הרשויות והשלטונות מתבקשים להניח לנושא
התעודה הזאת את כל העזרה הדרושה לו למלוי
תפקידו/ה
يطلب الى الهيئات والسلطات ان تقدم الى حامل
هذه البطاقة كل مساعدة يحتاج اليها لاداء
وظيفته
LES AUTORITÉS SONT PRIÉES D'ACCORDER
TOUTES LES FACILITÉS AU PORTEUR DE
LA PRÉSENTE CARTE.

תאריך
تاريخ
9.9.48

משרד הפנים - מנהל המחלקה לשידור.
הסברה.
وزارة الداخلية ـ مدير دائرة
الاذاعة، والمعلومات، والصحافة والسينما
DIRECTEUR DE L'OFFICE DE RADIODIFFUSION,
D'INFORMATION, DE PRESSE ET DE CINEMATOGRAPHIE

מנהל לשכת העתונות והמודיעין
مدير مكتب العتاحنة والمطبوعات
DIRECTEUR DE L'OFFICE D'INFORMATION
ET DE PRESSE

חתימת נושא התעודה
توقيع حامل الطائفة
SIGNATURE

Press card of
the Government of Israe
Ministry of the Interior

Meeting of the Ceasefire Committee chaired by the Belgian Consul,
Nievenhaus on the right, David Shaltiel, Commander of the
"Haganah" and his assistants. On his left, Abdullah El-Tal,
Commander of the "Jordanian Legion" and his assistants.
In the rear, reporters among them, the author

THE ISRAELI—JORDANIAN "CEASEFIRE COMMITTEE"

Between sessions, snapshots are taken. Fourth from the right — Shaltiel
and next to him, Abdullah El-Tal. Members of the Ceasefire Committee
(American and Belgian), Jordanian officers. Extreme left — the author

"The Burma Road" the Road of Bravery

THE ROAD BUILDERS — WORKING AND MARCHING

The 20th of Tamuz Parade, 1948
The First "Day of the State" in Jerusalem

Adress by David Ben-Gurion on the renewal of
the Jerusalem—Tel-Aviv railway line

The First President, Professor Chaim Weizman at the Temporary State Assembly

The Chief Rabbis Herzog and Uziel, Heads of the State and City Fathers at Herzl's grave — take the oath: "If I forget thee Oh Jerusalem — let my right hand forget her cunning"

"And I will restore Thy judges as at the first". The Supreme Court renews its activities in Jerusalem. The judges left to right: Dunkelblum, Assaf, Zmora (President), Olshan and Heshin

The western Wall on its liberation in the Six Day War (1967)

Commander in Chief Yitzchak Rabin, giving a speech at a liaison officers' conference in the Dan Hotel in Tel-Aviv. On his right — Yosef Schnurman (September 1966)

Sir Alan Cuningham,
The British High Commissioner
to Palestine and
Abdullah, King of Jordan

HAND IN HAND

Weapons confiscated from Arab
ands in the Old City of Jerusalem
displayed for journalists — 1940

Professor Chaim Weizman
press conference in the Ede
Hotel in Jerusalem announc
the British Partition Plan
for Palestine — July, 1940

The day after the United Nations Assembly decision on the partition
of Palestine — masses of Jerusalemites gathered in the forecourt of the
national institutions, 29th November, 1947

Arab rioters burning down the Jewish commercial centre

THE "FIRST MATCH" THAT SPARKED OFF THE 1948 WAR

The British High Commissioner (centre), on his right, the Police Commander, and on his left, the Army Commander inspecting the burnt down Jewish commercial centre

The ruins of the Jewish commercial centre

THE BEGINNINGS OF CHAOS?

The streets of Jerusalem "padded" with barbed wire

The 'Generali' building which was
in the British security zone

And shambles in St. Paul's Street

Shambles and desolation at the Jaffa Gate

Blocks along the pavements

Search for defence weapons on
a young Jewish boy and girl

Armed Arabs block the entrance
into Ha-Shalshelet Street

Explosion in the building of the daily newspaper "Palestine Post"

Ruins of the buildings in Ben Yehuda Street after the explosion
of the booby trapped car

The destruction in the Keren Hayesod building in the forecourt
of the national institutions

The streets of Jerusalem exposed to sniper fire

ידיעות **ירושלים**

יום שלישי
כ"ה
ניסן תש"ח
4 מאי
1948 גליון כג
המחיר 10 מיל

נוסח ע' מתואם בשביל קוראי "דבר", "הארץ", "הבקר", "המשקיף", "הצפה"

הצעה חדשה:

ירושלים תחת דגל הצלב האדום הבינלאומי

לשם כך נחוצה הסכמת היהודים והערבים ושביתת נשק לתשעים יום

הורעשו בתותחים

נ"ת יעקב בעוטרות, צפונה לירושלים, הורעשו אתמול ע"י הצבא הערבי בפני מותחל מן אויב שחוצב בסביבות נבי סמואל.

התקיפה נמשכה כמחצית השעה.

עוד לשעה אתני נשע ומתחומים
צען בריטי ערך מיחיבין בירי
הנמצאת בעיר העתיקה ובירי
שת. מוסרת הודעה ממשלתית.

נכון צבא של 150,000

ערב בינלאומי כדי לכפות
עלינו משטר תנאמנות

זני בנאשוגטון. הצעת אמתליק
רק כיצא אולי היה אחת
הנאמנות. בער ידוע ...

נציג אמריקה - הסדר זמני

הנציג האמריקני מר ...

ועדה השתמשה במועצת הבטחון

מער ט"ס א ... תנאמנות ...

הרבה נשק ותחמושת - שלל ל"הגנה" בכפר סלמה

... "הגנה" בקטמון

ריכי בירושלים ... הצבא הערבי ...

בחזית תל-אביב

שלל רב של נשק ותחמושת נפל לידי ה"הגנה" בקפ ...

ועדת שביתת הנשק למו"מ עם עבד-אללה

... בלונדון

התנקשות בפאראן נהרג אחד

דוברי הממשלה הבריטית:

פינוי הצבא הבריטי לא יושהה אלא יוחש

ראל אין בו משום מיפנה לגבי מדיניות היציאה הבריטית מה...ארץ.

פינוי הצבא יוחש.

ניצול צבאי של מקומות קדושים על ידי ערבים

ההגנה מוסרת את חיפה לשלטון אזרחי עברי

התקונות הצבאית סביבנו

לונדון, 3 (רויטר).

הברית לא פסקה

The last of the British leaving the country by the port of Haifa

Jewish Jerusalem under shellfire

שלטון צבא ההגנה לישראל בירושלים

מנשר מס. 1

בעתון רשמי מיוחד שפורסם אתמול מופיע מנשר
שלהלן:

ה ו א י ל ושטחה של ירושלים הכולל את
מרביתה של העיר, חלק מסביבותיה ומבואו־
תיה המערביים, הנו בחזקתו של צבא־הגנה ל־
ישראל הסר למשמעתי:

ו ה ו א י ל וחובה על צבא־הגנה לישראל
לקיים בשטח המוחזק את שלום הציבור ואת
הבטחון ולשקוד על תקנת החוק והמשפט:

ל כ ן אני, דוד בן־גוריון, שר הבטחון, מכ־
ריז בזה בשם הפיקוד העליון של צבא־הגנה
לישראל, לאמור:

פירוש	1. המונח "השטח המוחזק" פירושו השטח הכולל את מרביתה. של ירושלים העיר, חלק מסביבו־תיה ומבואותיה המערביים והדרכים המחברות את ירושלים עם השפלה, הכל כנתון בתחומי וזקו האדום המסומן במפת ארץ ישראל החתומה על ידי ונהושאת את תאריך היום, יום כ"ו ב־תמוז תש"ח (2 באבגוסט 1948), או כל מפה אחרת שתבוא במקומה אשר תהא חתומה על ידי ותהא מסומנת כנ"ל.
המשפט	2. משפט מדינת ישראל חל על השטח המוחזק.
הסדר הצבורי והבטחון	3. תושבי השטח המוחזק נתבעים בזה לקיים שלום הציבור ומערכתכ לכלתו, ולסיע בידי צבא־הגנה לישראל ככל שיידרשו.
	כל מי אשר יפר כל הוראה מהוראותי, יועמד לדין בפני בית משפט צבאי שיוקם על דעתי או בפני בית משפט אזרחי, הכל כפי שהמקרה יחייב.
פרסום המנשר	4. המנשר הזה יפורסם ברבים בכל הדרכים שא־ראן כעילות ביותר.
תוקף המנשר	5. המנשר הזה ייחשב בר תוקף לכל דבר החל מחצות ליל שבת, ו' באייר תש"ח (15 במאי 1948). ברם לגבי אותם הלקים מהשטח המוח־זק שהוחזקתם עברה לידי צבא־הגנה לישראל לאחר כך, יהא המנשר בר תוקף רק החל מאו־תו הזמן.

ד ו ד ב ן ־ ג ו ר י ו ן
שר הבטחון

ניתן היום, כ"ו בתמוז תש"ח (2 באבגוסט 1948).

במנשר מס' 2 שניתן באותו תאריך נאמר:

בתוקף הטלת שלטון צבא־הגנה לישראל בשטח
המוחזק של ירושלים, אני, דוד בן־גוריון, שר הב־
טחון, ממנה בזה בשם הפיקוד העליון של צבא־הגנה
לישראל את ד"ר דוב (ברנרד) יוסף להיות מושל
צבאי בשטח המוחזק של ירושלים.

ד ו ד ־ ב ן ־ ג ו ר י ו ן
שר הבטחון

Called to enlist

Enlistment parade

Shelled Jerusalem — sandbags
in the windows of the buildings

Shaar Ha-Gaiy (Baab El Waad) where
the Arabs blocked the way to Jerusale

Armoured Arab Legion car
out of action near the
Notre Dame Church

The convoy getting organized to go out to Mount Scopus
escorted by the United Nations

Water distribution in the streets of Jerusalem

Mother and child — in a shelter

The streets of Jullian and Mamilla under shell fire

A heavily shelled building in the Ethiopean Alley

hat name shall be given to the renewed Jewish State? Some suggested "The State of Yehuda"

Long awaited food convoy just arrived from Tel-Aviv

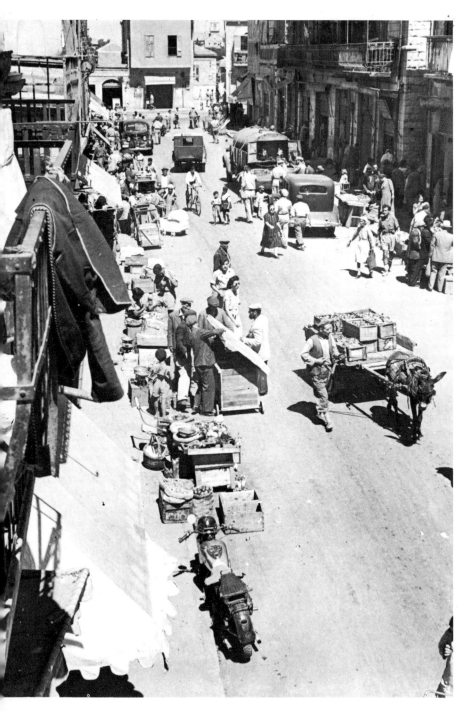

The day after the arrival of the convoy — bying and selling

'That night the forces began advancing towards Naan, the central base and the headquarters of Operation Nahshon. The operation did not ignore the presence of the British army and the possibility that it might intervene.

"While they were standing and deliberating one with the other, Nahshon the son of Aminadav jumped down into the sea first", and so the operation was given the code-name Nahshon.

'The Haganah's bold, Nahshon-like jump saved Jerusalem, and led our forces throughout the country on to victory'.

[26]

Dr. Yitzhak Raphael, a member of the 'Jerusalem Committee' during the siege, published reminiscences in the Independence Day issue of 'Hatzofeh' in 1973. Dr. Raphael's task at the time was to deal with information, fuel and transport. Amongst other things, he wrote:

'There was very little benzine in the city, the fuel stations had closed down during the second week of the siege and the stocks of public reserves ware also depleted. All attempts to place what benzine there was in the city in private hands or in hiding places produced very little results. The sole real reserve, which eased the situation, was the benzine in the tanks of 'Hamekasher'. The company had stock-piled considerable reserves in advance, and had also made sure that it had suitable containers. On the day I was appointed to be responsible for this fuel, the Hamekasher company possessed about 4,000 gallons of benzine. Henceforth the company could not use its fuel for its own purposes unless it had our permission and the keys to the tanks were handed over to me. There were nevertheless good relations between us and the heads of the company, particularly with Mr. Lichtman, and we worked in a spirit of mutual understanding and cooperation.

'The advisory committee recommended that transport in the city be limited to two essential lines only, that a transport license be issued to 'Tnuvah', that two cabs be operated to transport doctors, pregnant women, etc. and that a small number of private automobiles be permitted to function for essential purposes. I approved the committee's recommendations and my instructions were implemented without any difficulties.

'From day to day we worked on additional cuts, whatever we saved from one source or another gave us an extra day or two. At the beginning of June the situation was apalling. There were only three tons of solar fuel, six tons of benzine and 37 cans of kerosene in the entire city. I was waiting for a miracle, but nothing happened.

'The Jerusalem Committee decided not to touch 2,000 of the 4,000 gallons of fuel in the Hamekasher tanks. This amount was set aside for a special need, in case the situation worsened and as a result of the heavy shelling people would be unable to leave their homes and we would have to bring the water to them. This was a wise decision, as it transpired.

'Like the allocation of weekly rations of food, water was also strictly rationed according to family size.

'When sniping and shelling increased, endangering the lives of people who ventured out to get water, we decided that water would be sent round in containers. The vehicle would stop every few meters and the inhabitants would come out to get their ration. The population of Jerusalem displayed admirable discipline. Without panicking or showing fear, and without pushing in front of anyone, they stood in line quietly to receive water.

'One Friday morning one of my assistants, Mr. Adir, suddenly informed me that a stock of ten jerrycans of kerosene had been found in the garden of the American consulate. I told him to send five immediately to the Hadassah hospital, two to the Shaarei Tzedek hospital, two to the Bikur Holim hospital and to bring one to my office together with twenty empty bottles, that evening, the eve of the holy Sabbath. Adir was somewhat surprised by the last point, but did what I had asked him.

'About two hours before the Sabbath began we made a list of ten families, mainly those who had lost a son in battle or old couples who had no one to look after them, we poured the precious liquid into the bottles, and I went out together with Mr. Adir and Mr. Weiss to the houses and presented them with some kerosene for the Sabbath.

'Anyone who has not seen the joyul excitement and tears in the eyes of those precious and honorable people, has never seen happiness'.

[27]

There was good reason to fear that the proclamation of the State would be deferred.

On 3.1.1975 (when he was our ambassador to the U.N.), Yosef Tekoah, now President of Ben-Gurion University of the Negev, said to a 'Maariv' reporter: 'We proclaimed Israel's independence in May 1948, on the basis of the resolution passed by the General Assembly on 29th November 1947 which contradicted the opinion of the U.N. Some people claim still today that Israel was created by the U.N. and that it should therefore adhere to the U.N.'s resolutions. That is simply not true!

'On the day the establishment of Israel was proclaimed the General Assembly sat and discussed setting up a Council of Trustees for all Palestine. The U.N. had, therefore, abandoned the idea of establishing Israel, and the Great Powers, including the U.S.A. and the U.S.S.R., supported the idea of trusteeship. Israel was established only because its leaders were prepared to ignore the difficult international situation and take a step alone, challenging the world and confronting the U.N. with a *fait accompli*. The moment that was done the President of the U.S.A., Truman, recognized the new State and the U.S.S.R. followed suit. But Israel was born in total isolation'.

[28]

Details of the U.S.A.'s intentions to alter its policy and delay the implementation of partition and the establishment of the Jewish state in 1948, about two months before the British left Palestine and the Mandate came to an end, can be read in M. Sykes' book, 'From Balfour to Bevin'. Amongst other things he wrote (pp. 333-338):

"On 19th 1948 the U.S. delegation to the U.N. astonished the world by making a declaration which seemed to be diametrically opposed to American policy as it had been known till then. Ambassador Austin announced that his Government wanted to stop the activities which had been undertaken in order to achieve the partitioning of Palestine, and that the plenum would be asked to discuss establishing a U.N. 'trusteeship' in Palestine, 'without harming the nature of the final political arrangement'. The Jewish Agency and the National Council condemned the U.S.A.'S action.

The President of the U.S., Truman, was angered by what had happened at the U.N. He asked his aides: 'How could this happen? I assured Chaim Weizmann that we were in favor of partition and that we would adhere to it. He must think I'm just a liar'.

'On 23rd April, before setting off to spend Passover with friends, Dr. Weizmann received an urgent summons to go to the apartment of Justice Samuel Rosenman, one of Truman's friends. He went there immediately. The judge had been instructed to tell Dr. Weizmann about a meeting he had had with the President. The President had said to Justice Rosenman simply: "Dr. Weizmann is on my conscience". He described what had happened on 19th March, and explained that he had not been given sufficent information about the briefing which the U.S. delegation in the U.N. had received. He said that his objective was now to restore the U.S. stand in the U.N. to what it had been before 19th March. If the establishment of a Jewish State were proclaimed he would recognize it immediately. He made only one condition: he was prepared to have contact with only one representative of the Jews, Dr. Weizmann. This was kept secret by Dr. Weizmann and his associates and was revealed only in 1962, ten years after Weizmann's death'.

[29]

Moshe Sharett, who was Foreign Minister at the time, writes in detail in his book, 'At the Gate of the Nations', of the change which occurred in the U.S.A.'s attitude to partition and its attempt to defer the proclamation of the establishment of the Jewish State. In common with many others, he obviously did not know of Truman's secret promise to Weizmann to recognize the Jewish State once it was established. He also mentions an explicit U.S. warning against proclaiming the establishment of the State.

[30]

In an article which appeared in 'Haaretz' on 6.5.1973, S. Tevet writes about M. Shertok's attitude to the American 'advice' to defer proclaiming the State of Israel:
'Jewish leaders in the U.S.A. spread rumors that Sharett had agreed to a ceasefire. According to this rumor, which blackened Sharett's reputation for a long time after the establishment of the State of Israel, he had opposed declaring independence on 14th May. Today we have Ben-Gurion's direct report of the discussion between him and Sharett after the latter's return from Lake Success. He claimed that Sharett was not really happy with an absolute

rejection of the American Administration's demand to refrain from proclaiming independence on 15th May, and therefore did not express his personal opinion the next day at the session of the People's Administration. He nevertheless proposed that on 15th May a Provisional Government be announced, namely, that no mention be made of independence or the State of Israel. This was the source of the cable sent by Moshe Medzini, the Haaretz correspondent at the U.N., which appeared in the paper on 12th May, saying that 'A Jewish Government, not a Jewish State, will be proclaimed in Tel-Aviv'.

[31]

In an interview with a correspondent of Davar (6.5.1973), Yisrael Galili described the discussions held by the leaders of the Jewish population as to whether or not to accept the 'advice' given by the American Administration to the 'People's Administration', a few days before the end of the Mandate:

'On 12th May 1948, two or three days before the Mandate ended, the Provisional Government, which was still called the People's Administration, met and discussed the military and political situation. It later transpired that that meeting was to decide whether to proclaim the establishment of the State of Israel or not.

'Yigael Yadin and myself were invited to attend and were asked about the danger, the size of our forces and our ability to withstand attack. Moshe Shertok came to the meeting from the U.S.A. and Golda Meyerson gave a report of her meeting with King Abdullah.

'The People's Administration usually held its meetings in the hall of the J.N.F. building in Tel-Aviv. When I entered, Golda Meyerson came over to me and said she had heard that the British High Commissioner was leaving Jerusalem for Haifa the next day, so that the official departure ceremony could be held there. My reaction on hearing this was: 'Let's say goodby, and not *au revoir*'.

'Moshe Shertok brought with him a disturbing report of the attitude of the American Administration, though I learned its full contents only after the meeting. The Americans had proposed imposing a ceasefire for three months, involving the extension of the British Mandate for another ten days, the restriction of Jewish immigration and various other abominations. The

Americans were afraid of international complications following the proclamation of the State. The U.S. President had offered to place his private plane at the disposal of a mission which would include Jewish and Arab delegates, representatives of the nations and the U.N., and would go to Palestine to arrange a ceasefire for three months. In those circumstances the proposed ceasefire endangered the main principle, the proclamation of the establishment on the Jewish State an worked towards undermining the implementation of the U.N. resolution to establish the State of Israel. Every postponement of the decisive step increased the danger that there would be a change for the worse in the political arena and that the principal parties in the U.N. would lead to the annulment of the resolution of 29th November. The Americans warned our representatives against becoming drunk with victory, reminding them that when the armies of the Arab States invaded us we would find ourselves in trouble and would not be able to complain to them. The embargo on the purchase of arms was in force, the French submitted a proposal which combined the ceasefire with the Council of Trustees and only the Soviets remained faithful to the resolution of 29th November. M. Sharett defined their position as 'a clearly Zionist stand'. The timetable included in the U.N. resolution had been upset by the U.N.'s impotence and the harrassment by the British.

'The ceasefire proposal also involved legal and operative complications, complex problems of supervision and, most inportant, the deferment of the decision to establish the State. The general consensus was that we would not agree to prolong the British Mandate by a single minute'.

[32]

How did the People's Administration decide to refrain from postponing the proclamation of the State, despite the U.S.A.'s attitude? In his article in Haaretz, S. Tevet wrote:

'After an intermission the People's Administration resumed its deliberations, discussing the American intiative and the High Commissioner's proposal for a ceasefire in Jerusalem, to be supervised by the Consular Committee. In the course of the discussion the two proposals got mixed up, and things which were said about Jerusalem referred to the entire country, and vice versa.

'Mordechai Bentov (one of the Mapam representatives, Y.C.) maintained that the concrete question was the ceasefire in Jerusalem, though it was clear that this would lead to a general ceasefire. If the People's Administration were to embark on negotiations about a ceasefire in Jerusalem it would be impossible to proclaim the State during this process, since the American initiative expressly forbade this. We were trapped, but we knew that if we retreated it would do us no good. We did not know what would happen once the State had been proclaimed. Ben-Gurion was confident in his heart, but this had no concrete basis as we were facing regular armies about whose abilities we knew nothing.

'When the decision was made, only six representatives were in favor of rejecting the ceasefire proposal and proclaiming the State, as had been planned. They were: D. Ben-Gurion, M. Sharett, A. Zisling, M. Bentov, B. Shitrit and F. Bernstein. Four spoke in favor of accepting the ceasefire, they were D. Remez, E. Kaplan, P. Rosen and M. Shapira. The decision was made by a hair's breadth'.

[33]

The last days of Neveh Yaakov and Atarot were described in the Haganah Bulletin for 1974, edited by Yaakov Orlonski, by the lawyer, Zvi Tal, encouraged by the Jerusalem scholar, Dov Nathan Brinker, one of the founders of Neveh Yaakov and the publisher of 'The Jerusalem Calendar'. On 9.4.1948 he wrote:

'A sergeant of the British Flying Division came to our village and announced that a convoy of the Arab Legion was about to pass by the village and that if a single shot was fired the Legion would wipe the village off the face of the earth. Then he left. Soon afterwards the Legion apeared, coming round the bend from Atarot. Their armored vehicles took up positions and began shelling us, taking us by surprise. That was our first encounter with cannon shells, and they depressed the spirits of our men greatly. As we had no anti-tank weapons the armored vehicles came within a few dozen meters of us. Gangs joined in the assault, attacking with mortars and machine-guns. The electricity was cut off, the telephone lines between the positions were disconnected and each position functioned independently. The enemy broke through and conquered

the tower at the entrance to the village as well as the first house. All that time
the radio sent out calls for help. The replies we received encouraged us. We
knew they would not desert us. With God's help we repelled the enemy,
causing them serious losses. One of our number was killed and several
wounded'.

On 15.5.1948 he wrote:

'Yesterday, Friday night, the men of Atarot took the airfield after the British
had left it. The Arabs attacked immediately. Then we received the order to
leave Atarot and concentrate our forces in Neveh Yaakov. Together we are
about one hundred and fifty people, and with the supplement of their weapons
there are chances that we might hold out. On Saturday night we set out to
occupy the hills on the way to Atarot, to ensure that the road was clear. The
men of Atarot marched silently, bypassing the Arab villages. We left the lights
on in Atarot, so that the enemy would not realize we had left.

'We have heard of the fall of the Etzion Bloc, and the news fills us with dread
and sorrow. If the Bloc could not hold out, how can we? We knew about the
enemy's forces concentrated in the area, and the strength of his armored corps
and cannon. In the morning the enemy started shelling the empty village of
Atarot. Only at 11 did they realize that the place had been abandoned. With
pain we watched Atarot go up in smoke, as a result of the fire set by the enemy.
All our property and the toil of years has been lost'.

On 17.5.1948 he wrote:

'Yesterday, Sunday morning, the great attack on Neveh Yaakov began. It was
the last battle. This morning they began shelling us from Bir Naballah. They
fired systematically at one house after the other, destroying them all. After the
initial shelling, heavy tanks and armored vehicles appeared. We tried to repel
them with our Italian rifles, and managed to stop them each time they tried to
advance. Our machine-gunner was blown up by a shell. The doctors were kept
busy. At two in the afternoon the defenders were exhausted. From town they
informed us: 'Hold on, your chances are good'.That was the reply we received
to our request to send an armored column to our aid. The commander
understood that the column was on its way. Encouraged by the news, we
fought and even launched a counter-attack. Our few bullets caused many
deaths among the enemy forces, but towards evening the shelling stopped and
the Arabs began storming us from every side. We were tired and hungry and

did not believe we could stop them. Five of our number were dead and forty wounded. The enemy drew back and took up positions around the village. We had no chance of holding out for even a few hours against such large numbers of enemy tanks and armored vehicles, while we had no anti-tank weapons. The commanders decided that we should leave the village.

'We destroyed what we could, took some of the arms and ammunition and all our wounded. At 1 a.m. we prepared to leave. Our hearts were heavy. Another Jewish settlement was being abandoned'.

*

A more detailed description of the stand made by the inhabitants of Atarot and Neveh Yaakov and the evacuation was written by Mr. F. Goldwasser, one of the inhabitants and defenders of Neveh Yaakov, and is to be found in 'The Book of the Haganah', Vol. 2 (pp. 181-188) (Hebrew).

[34]

Abdullah el-Tal published a book about this war, entitled 'Memories'. A Hebrew translation was published in 1960, by the Ministry of Defense. The preface was written by the head of the Intelligence Section of the General Staff, Major-General Haim Herzog, and stated that el-Tal 'went down in history' as the commander of the Arab Legion who entered Jerusalem in May 1948 and left it as a political exile in October 1949. El-Tal writes of King Abdullah as if he betrayed the Arab cause, and also claims that the British hindered the Arab Legion in its war against the Jews. Major-General Herzog rightly warns the reader not to believe everything el-Tal writes, although many facts — particularly those about the Arab Legion — are usually accurate.

El-Tal died in 1973 in Amman, where he had returned thirteen years previously, after several years of exile in Cairo.

In his book (pp. 173 and 174) el-Tal complains that his suggestions for attacking the Jews in Jerusalem were ignored, quoting a letter he sent to Headquarters in Amman as proof:

'Most Secret.

'Commander of the Fourth Brigade.

'As a result of studying the situation and analysing the general position in

Jerusalem, I regard it my duty to send you this report, so that you can do what is necessary. There are more than fifty thousand Arabs in the Old City of Jerusalem, living their normal lives. This does not mean, however, that they are prepared to endure shelling by the enemy's cannon, or even by mortars. The Jews will undoubtedly do this when the ceasefire ends, since they brought mortars and sufficient ammunition, and probably heavy cannon too, to Jerusalem. Militarily speaking we are not afraid of an increase in the strength of the Jews. Shelling does not affect the morale of brave soldiers, but the problem we may have to face is that of the civilians, for we have not yet forgotten the disaster of Jaffa.

'Consequently, in order to save the situation, I propose that we switch from defense to attack. Since the ceasefire has put an end to all hope of conquering New Jerusalem by siege, the attack will not be effective unless we follow this plan:

'1. The control of Shaar Hagai will be handed over to the Iraqi or Egyptian army.

'2. All the battalions now in Shaar Hagai will join those in Jerusalem, forming an efficient force that can launch an attack on one or even two fronts.

'3. The forces camped at Ein Karem and Bethlehem will join in the great attack as soon as it begins.

'4. The attacks will be implemented in two stages. At the first stage the objective will be Allenby Square and Zion Square. At the second stage it will be the rest of Jaffa Road, where Jewish resistance will grow weaker. In this way we will strike at the Jews of Jerusalem before they terrify the peaceful inhabitants and try to attack us.

21.6.1948   Kaid Abdullah el-Tal,
                                             Commander,   the   Sixth
                                             Batallion'.

[35]

Why did the Arabs flee? M. Sharett answers this question in his book, 'At the Gate of the Nations', (pp. 328-330):

'What caused this mass flight? The Arab representatives drew a picture of how "the Jews descend like a pack of wolves on innocent, defenceless Arabs and how the Arab nations enter Palestine with all haste in order to save their oppressed brethren". This story was a pack of lies.

'The flight of the Arabs occurred soon after the first disturbances in December and January when Palestine was still under the British Mandate. The authorities did nothing to stop the process, on the contrary, there were signs that they welcomed it.

'The following account by a British eye-witness, which appeared in the London weekly, 'The Economist', a journal which can hardly be considered to favor Zionism, sheds some light on the Arabs' motives for leaving:

'"Shortly after the Jewish authorities had called on all the Arabs to remain in Haifa, taking it upon themselves to ensure their safety, various elements persuaded the Arabs that it was safer to run away. The crucial point in all this was the announcement broadcast on the radio by the Arab Higher Council, telling all the Arabs to leave and declaring that once the British left Palestine the united armies of the Arab States would invade the country and throw the Jews into the sea. It was hinted quite clearly that Arabs who remained in Haifa and accepted the protection of the Jews would be considered traitors".'

[36]

A foreign journalist, John Roy Carlson, who spent most of the War of Independence on the Arab side with the Egyptian and Jordanian commanderes on the Jerusalem front, writes in his book, 'From Cairo to Damascus', about the flight of the Arabs from Palestine in general, and from Jerusalem in particular, and about the creation of the 'refugee problem' (p. 164):

'The flight psychosis which seized the Arabs, leading to the mass flight of Moslems and Christians, is a phenomenon which is difficult to explain. It was mass hysteria caused by poor morale and fear of vengeance for the murders and plundering done by the Arabs since 1920. The Arab leaders, and especially those associated with the Mufti, encouraged the Arabs to leave, promising them that within thirty days not a single Jew would remain alive in Palestine. The Arab leaders said that once the Jews of Palestine had been thrown into the sea, the Arabs could return to their homes and even pillage the considerable Jewish property. They also hinted that anyone who refused to leave was pro-Zionist and would be punished.

'By contrast I know of many cases in which Jewish leaders begged Arabs, particularly the Christians, to remain, even promising to guarantee their safety'.

[37]

During the months of siege in Jerusalem, newspapers and bulletins appeared and were snatched up eagerly by the population. Below are a few lines about these newspapers, so that their memory should not be lost for ever.

'Hayom'

On Sunday, 18th January 1948 a Jerusalem morning daily began appearing, this was 'Hayom', (Today), edited by Yitzhak Greenbaum. The publisher was A. Peled, Ronald Press Ltd., Agrippas Street. After the 96th issue it was transferred to the Lipschitz Press, on the day the thirty-five boys fell on their way to help the besieged Etzion Bloc.

An announcement which appeared in its first issue said, amongst other things: 'The first issue of our Hebrew paper, which we hope will become the paper of Jerusalem, appears today. This will redeem the honor of our capital, which does not have a single Hebrew daily'.

The publishers, journalists and even the vendors of 'Hayom' complained of the hostile attitude of the Tel-Aviv newspapers. The newspaper vendors alleged that the agents of the Tel-Aviv newspapers had threatened that if they did not stop distributing 'the Jerusalem paper' they would not receive the Tel-Aviv paper for distribution. In the twenty-first issue of 'Hayom' (10.2.1948) we read of a 'ban' imposed by the Tel-Aviv papers on anyone selling 'Hayom' in Jerusalem.

In an editorial which appeared in the hundredth issue of 'Hayom', (13. May 1948) on the eve of the proclamation of the State of Israel, we read:

'Ever since our daily press based itself in Tel-Aviv, no daily paper which tried to eatablish itself in Jerusalem has managed to sell so many copies. It is a good omen for our newspaper, especially if we recall that during the first months it had to overcome the 'ban' imposed by the Tel-Aviv papers. They wanted to kill the paper at the very outset, fearing that it would become popular and harm their monopoly. They preferred that the Jewish readership of Jerusalem should learn to read English, rather than that a new Hebrew paper which would compete with them should be established. They were well aware of the fact that the connection between Jerusalem and the coastal plain could be cut off and that the residents of Jerusalem who read only Hebrew would be left without a daily paper at all in difficult times, when it is particularly hard to manage without a paper. That did not concern them'.

'Hayom' stopped appearing at the end of 1949.

'Hayoman', The organ of Agudath Yisrael

On Wednesday, 12th February 1948, the first issue of 'Hayoman', the daily paper of the Agudath Yisrael movement in Palestine appeared. Its offices were in Babad Building, Jerusalem, and it was printed at the Sfara Press. Uriel Tzimmer was the person responsible for it.

On the day the British blew up a block of houses on Ben-Yehuda Street (22.2.48) in Jerusalem, at 6 a.m., a special edition of 'Hayoman' appeared, containing the first information about the explosion and the victims.

As Passover 1948 approached, the directorate of the paper met to discuss whether and how to publish the paper on the intermediate days of the festival, when one does not work. It was decided to publish it, and the following explanation appeared at the top of the front page:

'Because of the great interest displayed by the public in everything happening in the country and abroad at the present time, a permit has been given by our rabbi, may he live long and happily, and the senior president of the rabbinical court, may he live long and happily, for 'Hayoman' to appear, in altered format, during the intermediate days'.

The 'altered format' was that a quarter of the front page remained empty, bearing the words 'Because of the sanctity of the intermediate days'. This, incidentally, is the practise adopted by the newspapers of the 'Aguda' still today.

In 'Hayoman' we also read of the service held on 15th June 1948 in memory of Yitzhak Ben-David, the chairman of the Jerusalem Journalists' Association who was killed by the shrapnel of a shell on his way home from work.

On 21st June 1948 the paper published a detailed list of the 400 inhabitants of

Jerusalem who had been killed as a result of the cruel and murderous bombardment during the period between 15th May and 20th June, only 35 days.

'Hamevaser', an evening paper

During the last days of the appearance of 'Hayoman', Agudath Yisrael published an evening paper, 'Hamevaser' (the first issue appeared on 17th February 1948), 'The Central Organ of the Agudath Yisrael Organizations'. The publisher and editor was Menahem Porush, 'with the participation of a group of reporters from Agudath Yisrael circls'. On 13th May 1949, a few days before the first anniversary of the fall of the Jewish Quarter in the Old City, we read in this paper a special call by Rabbis Israel Zeev Minzberg and Ben-Zion Hazan, who had raised the flag of surrender on behalf of the Jews of the Old City, to the Jewish population of the State of Israel and Jerusalem: 'To remember and recall ancient Jerusalem every year, and to recite a memorial prayer for it on every anniversary of its fall, the 19th of Iyar'.

This paper appeared for about twenty months, until 24th August 1950, when the daily organ of Agudath Yisrael, 'Hamodiyah', which is still published today, began appearing.

From 'Hadashot Tzohorayim', to 'Davar Yerushalayim'.

The Jerusalem Workers' Council sought ways of publishing a daily paper of its own. A few days after the joint paper, 'Yedioth Yerushalayim' stopped appearing, it began publishing a bulletin entitled 'Hadashoth Tzohorayim', (Afternoon News) edited by I. Klinov. The bulletin contained between two and four pages (eight pages on Fridays and on the eve of festivals) and appeared in tabloid format. The first issue was published on 28.5.1948.

In one of the issues (24th June 1948) we read:

'People want real ministers. Official letters to Kaplan (Eliezer Kaplan, the first Minister of Finance, Y.C.) must address the minister as 'Sir'. 'Comrade' is no longer an acceptable form of address. Henceforth Israel has ministers, so the nation has decided. In this connection, it should be noted that the Tel-Aviv press is usually united in full support of our Government'.

While 'Hadashoth Tzohorayim', which died after a few days, was still appearing, preparations were being made to publish another afternoon paper, 'Davar Yerushalayim'. (Jerusalem News). Mr. Dov Rabin, one of the army's education officers, (and later the secretary of the World Society for the Study of the Bible) was asked to edit the paper.

The first issue was published on 13.7.1948, and it continued appearing for four months, in 111 issues.

A battery-operated radio was obtained, so that many news items could be gathered. The first person to promise to contribute (and to keep his promise) was Yitzhak Ben-Zvi, later the second President of Israel. He sat and wrote articles and items in his hut in Rehavia, often by candle-light. The paper was edited also by candle-light in the cellar of the Lipschitz Press, the windows of which had been blocked by sandbags. Regular contributors included Y. Shochman, Jean Daniel and others. A. Lutzki wrote about the Arabs and Professor D. Ashbel about the sites which had been conquered. The paper appeared in a two-page format, with four pages on Fridays and the eve of festivals.

The exodus from Jerusalem was criticized in this paper. ('Of all the members of the Jewish Agency, only two are left in Jerusalem'. 'Of all the members of the Executive of the National Council, only two remain in Jerusalem').

The newspaper naturally supported the appointment of Dov Joseph as Military Governor of Jerusalem. One of the issues contained an article by Dr. I. Kaestner (who was murdered a few years later because of a trial relating to the period of the holocaust and the rescue of Hungarian Jews) about the Mufti's plans to destroy Tel-Aviv and Jerusalem.

In another issue an article appeared under the headline: 'Father! How Long Can One Live Without a Tomato?' (The piece described the problem of supplies, the lack of fruit, vegetables, eggs, etc.).

In the same edition there were articles about how to prepare 'humus', the problems of allocating water, burning garbage, the dismantling of barricades from the time of the Mandate, and preparations for 'Agnon Week', (Agnon was then celebrating his fiftieth birthday).

'Haheruth', (The Etzel organ)

On Tuesday, 2nd June 1948, a daily newspaper called 'Haheruth', (Freedom) 'The Paper of Fighting Jerusalem', began appearing in Jerusalem. Its offices and directorate were at 9 Hasollel Street. After the sixth issue it was printed at the Azriel Press, and the offices and directorate moved to 16, King David Street. A. Dror was in charge. It appeared until 1.10.1948, when a notice was printed that henceforth a daily entitled 'Heruth' would be published in Tel-Aviv, by the Heruth Movement (founded by Etzel). The paper on which it was printed was booty taken from the enemy. As there was no electricity, the presses were worked by hand.

On 22.6.1948 a special edition of 'Haheruth' was published, in which the inhabitants of Jerusalem were informed of 'battles in the streets of Tel-Aviv' over the ship, 'Zeev Jabotinsky' ('Altalena'). Two days beforehand, on 20th June, the paper had published the information that Rabbis Hazan and Mintzberg, the men who had raised the flag marking the surrender of the Jewish residents of the Old City, had been allowed by Abdullah el-Tal, the commander of the Arab Legion, to enter the Jewish Quarter in the Old City and remove scrolls of the law from the synagogues. This had not in fact happened.

Another item (July 1948) stated that several foreign correspondents, most of them British, were in Rhodes and wanted to come to Jerusalem, but absolutely refused to accept entry visas from the Israeli authorities, claiming that they did not recognize Israeli rule in Jerusalem. The Government, naturally, rejected their application.

Mr. Aviezer Goldstein (Golan) described the founding of the newspaper, 'Haheruth', which appeared for about four months:

'Just before Passover 1948 Mordehai Kaufman (Raanan), the Etzel commander in the Jerusalem region, (today the manager of the 'Israel' Press) proposed publishing a one-time newspaper for the Etzel soldiers, who were then being massed in two camps in Jerusalem.

In the offices of 'Hamashkif' Golan found an old block with the name of the newspaper, 'Massuot'. And so the newspaper put out by the Etzel had at its masthead the name, 'Massuot'. Mr. Golan was severely reprimanded as it transpired that 'Massuot' had once been a paper published by Lehi.

The Salomon Press possessed a priniting press dating from 1882 (made in

Austria) which was worked by hand but had been later converted to electricity. As there was no electricity, the owner of the press agreed that Golan could work it by hand provided he found men to do it, as all his employees were serving in the army. With the help of Etzel headquarters ten printers were found in the ranks of the organization. 'Haheruth' was printed for about a week at the hand press, and then moved to the Azriel Press.

'Kol Hamagen Halvri' (The Voice of the Jewish Defender)

The Haganah broadcasts were stencilled and sent to various news agencies, foreign and local correspondents, individuals associated with public bodies and heads of institutions. This material, which was prepared by Abraham Hurst, sold like hot cakes, because the information it contained was reliable. Many people tried to get hold of and read this daily bulletin, which was published by the 'Jerusalem Information Office', particularly as few of them could receive the Haganah radio broadcasts.

In fact, this bulletin began appearing a long time before the siege, during the first days of Arab terrorism, when the broadcasts of 'Jerusalem Radio' were unreliable.

The bulletin of 10.12.1947 contained the statement that the Haganah had rejected charges made against it that it had 'not done enough' to save the property of Jerusalem merchants whose stores in the Commercial Center had been looted and burned by Arab rioters. The following passage appeared in 'Kol Hamagen Halvri' in this connection:

'In reply to many questions, there is no intention of returning to the position of self-restraint adopted during the disturbances of 1936—39'. A list of incidents in which members of the Haganah had shot and killed armed assailants was given. A long, detailed account of how the British police had used physical violence to stop Haganah forces from coming to the rescue, and how they had nevertheless managed to prevent loss of life and heavier damage to property, was given.

For many months a daily bulletin appeared entitled, 'To Colleagues in the Bases', containing 'dry' but useful information about what was happening in and around Jerusalem, attacks on transport in Arab neighborhoods and on the road to Tel-Aviv, preparations by the Arabs in Sheikh Jarrah (near Shimon

Hatzadik), the Old City, Tzur Baher (near Talpiot) and other areas to attack Jews. The bulletin sometimes contained items from foreign sources (Palcor, etc.) about the political campaign in the capitals of the world.

One of the bulletins contained the blessing sent by Chief Rabbi Herzog to the members of the Haganah: 'You are making history. The Lord has helped you and you are strong and growing stronger for our people and the cities of our God. The six million martyrs who were killed by wild beasts in human form hoped and believed that their redeemer lives and that their brethren in Zion, the house of our life, would arise and revive the hope of Israel so that Israel would once again be the light of our holy law. I say to you what the priest and the prophet of war said to Israel when the army went out to battle: 'Fear not, hasten not, neither be ye dismayed. Put your trust in the rock of Israel, and its' redeemer.

At the end of the bulletin there was an announcement: 'The men at the Etzion Bloc will send regards to their families on the eve of Passover, at 3 p.m. on the 44 wavelength approximately'.

Later on 'To colleagues in the Bases' featured an extensive section of regards sent by soldiers to their families in the Old and the New Cities as well as to other towns and villages in Israel. It also contained details of battle in various parts of the country. Only some of the bulletins carry serial numbers (I found numbers up to 150 in 'The Archives of Religious Zionism', Jerusalem, the Rabbi Kook Institute).

'Kol Yerushalayim'. (The Voice of Jerusalem)

The Jerusalem Committee devoted one of its major departments to information. It was headed by Yitzhak Werfel (later Raphael), who was also responsible for fuel and transport. His aide in the sphere of information was his secretary, Asher Hirschberg. A large handbill, headed 'Pay No Attention to Unfounded Rumors', stated that an information bulletin entitled 'Kol Yerushalayim' would also be published. The announcement was set up and printed by hand at the 'HaIvri' Press. The bulletin was stencilled and distributed in limited numbers twice a week. 'Kol Yerushalayim' usually contained a short article written by the editor, reliable information about what was happening in the city and its institutions, and news from the rest of the

country and the various fronts. Children pasted up the bulletin on the walls of
houses, synagogues and public places. It was also sent to senior officials and
public figures.
Information about the distribution of food rations formed the most 'interesting'
and detailed items in 'Kol Yerushalayim', alongside items about rations and
permits to leave the city. Storekeepers were warned to make sure their stores
were open between 8 a.m. and 4 p.m. without a break for lunch, for the
distribution of food. In one of its issues, 'Kol Yerushalayim' published the
following caution to the population:
'Don't lock your doors! The experience of the past few days has proved that
enemy shells are unable to penetrate our stone walls and reinforced concrete
ceilings. On lower storeys one is almost completely safe from harm. The
population is asked not to lock their front doors at all, because someone may
want to come in from the street and seek shelter during a bombardment'.
Another bulletin bore the following notice: 'Do not walk about the streets for
no purpose. Remain calm and collected during a bombardment'. In another
one, under the headline, 'And Our Camp is Holy', we read an appeal not to
loot abandoned houses, including those of Jewish families which had been
obliged to leave their homes temporarily.

The weekly, 'Iton Hamagen'. (The Defender's Paper)

This paper was also widely-read because of the reliability of its information
and factual descriptions. It was published by the Jerusalem branch of the
Haganah's information office, and was printed at the Ronald cooperative
press, then moved to the Brigade press in Jerusalem after the 11th issue. After
its 24th issue (24.9.1948) it was published by the Israeli army's Education
Service, attached to the Jerusalem Region Headquarters, at the regional press.
Approximately fifty issues were published, the last one on 12.4.1949.
Its regular contributors included Eliezer Argov, Shalom Ben Horin, Benjamin
Yaffe, Daniel Sher, L. Dani. Yona Cohen and others.
In addition to providing a variety of material for the population of Jerusalem at
the front and the 'rear', Iton Hamagen' declared war on those who sought to
exploit the difficulties of the moment by engaging in looting. The commander
of the Jerusalem Brigade affirmed that there had been cases of robbery and

pillage in Jerusalem neighborhoods taken from the enemy. Orders had been issued to the military governors and all officers to use every means in their power to prevent looting. 'Anyone found with stolen property is liable to be shot immediately', was the sentence with which this announcement ended.

On 18.5.1948 'Iton Hamagen' reported that 'because of the electricity cut the broadcasts of 'Kol Hamagen HaIvri' could not be received by the population, and that therefore 'Yedioth Hamagen' would appear at noon, containing items of information for the public'.

A few days later, when forces of the Haganah, Etzel and Lehi were making valiant attempts to break through the wall of the Old City and come to the aid of the inhabitants of the Jewish Quarter, the following broadsheet was published:

'To the Jews of Jerusalem. The heart of every Jew in Jerusalem is with the forces fighting on either side of the wall, but sympathy alone is not enough. Anyone capable of bearing arms should present himself immediately. Anyone able to serve in the People's Guard should do so forthwith. And to all inhabitants of Jerusalem, your supreme duty is to keep calm! Do not panic or become indifferent. With firm spirits we will face what is to come'.

The weekly, 'HaOlam' (The World)

This was the main journal of the World Zionist Organization, and appeared in Jerusalem every week (printed at the Ahva Press and edited by Moshe Kleinman. The acting editor was Moshe Cohen).

This weekly devoted considerable space to discussing the problems which would arise once Jerusalem was under international rule. Y. Ben-Zvi published an article on the appropriate name for the 'State of Jerusalem', proposing that it be called, 'the Jerusalem region'.

About half of each issue was dedicated to accounts of the events of the previous week throughout the country, and in Jerusalem in particular.

'Hed Modiin'. (Information)

The religious division of the Haganah in Jerusalem, 'Modiin', issued a bulletin of its own, 'Hed Modiin'. It appeared from April to July 1948 and contained articles about the geography of the country and sites which had been conquered or had served as battlefields. Each such article appeared under the heading: 'Know what you are defending, and for what your comrades fought and fell!'

'Yediot Keren Hayesod'. (Keren Hayesod News)

This bulletin also provided information to the public, and in March 1948 published items about the battles in Israel and the efforts to build the country. One issue headed, 'After the Tragedy in the Keren Hayesod Building', was devoted to the work of the building laborers in Jerusalem, who were rebuilding the ruined houses in Ben Yehuda Street and the destroyed wing of the National Institutions building, where, 'the sound of the hammers blends with the sound of firing'. There were also descriptions of the lines for rations, and the fact that 'for ten days Jerusalem was completely cut off from Tel-Aviv and the rest of the country'.

'Neroth Shabbath'. (Sabbath Caudes)

The main object of this weekly was to bring the Sabbath to the attention of its readers, though it also featured articles about the siege and the heroism of fighters and defenders. It was published under the auspices of the Rabbi Kook Institute, its editor was Rabbi Mordekhai Cohen and the acting editor was Yitzhak Werfel.

The issue of Passover 1948 contained Yaakov Ramon's poem, 'My Jerusalem is Bleeding'. The weekly had a regular section entitled, 'Jerusalem, the Geographical Capital; Sabbath, the Temporal Capital', featuring legends and stories as well as descriptions of life in Jerusalem, centering on the theme of the Sabbath.

In one of the descriptions of the siege we read about the ration of 900 grams of bread allocated to three persons in Jerusalem, to last from Friday to Sunday midday, about women who went out to gather wood for cooking, etc.

Rabbi Y.L. Hacohen Maimon, whose pen-name was 'Israel's Minister of Religion', wrote an article entitled, 'Towards the State of Israel', which constituted the address he had given to the U.N. Investigatory Commission on

Partition. The paper also included Yosef Patai's poems on the State of Israel, such as 'To the Ministers of the Revival of Israel', etc.

Below is a characteristic editorial published during the siege. Others like it appeared in many of the newspapers published in Jerusalem at that time: 'This issue appears after a brief interval. Anyone who knows what Jerusalem has gone through during the siege will understand the reason for this delay in publishing 'Neroth' (candles). But they have not been extinguished. We continue, and will go on doing so, with God's help. We are armed with greater faith that our aims will be achieved, with the establishment of the State of Israel in the land of Israel. For out of Zion shall go forth the Law, and the word of the Lord from Jerusalem. And we ask all our readers and writers to continue'!

Jerusalem editions of Tel-Aviv newspapers.

Both 'Yedioth Aharonoth' and 'Yedioth Maariv' produced special local Jerusalem editions. The paper would come from Tel-Aviv at night, printed on one page only with articles (reports, notices, etc.). In Jerusalem local material would be printed on the other, empty page. On several occasions, because of their haste, the printers would print the second, Jerusalem, page upside down to the first one.

When the road to Tel-Aviv was cut off and the papers did not arrive, the Jerusalem representatives of these papers brought out Jerusalem editions. Sometimes, when events and conquests justified or obligated this, they brought out two or even three 'special editions' on the same day.

On 13.4.1948, as well as on several other days, Yedioth Aharonoth appeared in a one-page edition in Jerusalem, its second page remaining blank. The same happened with the issue of 2.5.1948, when Katamon was conquered by the Haganah. In the second edition it was reported that there was to be 'a ceasefire of 48 hours and that Jerusalem is to be declared an open city'.

These special newspapers appeared in double spacing, because of problems with the electricity supply, etc.

The struggle with the censorship.

In addition to all the difficulties and problems of Jerusalem journalists during the siege and even during the 'honeymoon' period of the young State, there was the obstacle of the double censorship. Jerusalem reporters had to submit every item of news and every article to the censor in Jerusalem, before sending it to their papers in Tel-Aviv. In Tel-Aviv, too, all copy had to be shown to the censors. This sometimes led to ridiculous situations, when the Jerusalem censor allowed something through but the one in Tel-Aviv did not, and vice versa. When things had gone too far, a delegation of Jerusalem newsmen presented itself before Lieutenant-Colonel Isser Bari, the Head of Intelligence and the Military Censor, who came from Tel-Aviv together with Mr. Dror, the censor there. There were a number of valid complaints about duplications of censorship, the abundance of contradictions between instructions, the absence of any way of verifying whether an item was correct or not, etc. There was no one from the army in Jerusalem who could guide or direct the journalists, and there was no help in obtaining information. Worse than that, the journalists said, offical army announcements were given in English, because they were intended primarily for foreign correspondents. The censor permitted no addition to or interpretation of army notices. Even when the reporters witnessed events or incidents – after all, the 'front' was right under their noses – the censor did not allow anything to be added, no matter how trustworthy. The journalists also complained that there were no tours of the Jerusalem front for local reporters. I. Shochman (Davar) said bitterly: 'The censorship treats us Jerusalem reporters as if we were enemies of the State'. One of the claims made was that the censorship excised the term, Jerusalem 'corridor', insisting that 'region' be used instead. Another complaint to which the journalists attached particular importance was that if an article were submitted in their own name, as the fruits of their own efforts and at their own responsibility, it was rejected, whereas if the source was given as one of the foreign correspondents the same article was accepted.

Bari's reply was that there was no comparison between our censorship and that of the British Mandate, and that any attempt to equate the two was simply offensive. It was possibly to criticize the censor's methods of working, but not to slander him. The censorship was not the right address for all the complaints and it was not capable of publishing detailed reasons for its rejection of items, nor was it obliged to do so. He also defended the double censorship in Jerusalem and Tel-Aviv. He admitted that there were loopholes, accounting for the fact that one censor allowed an item through while the other did not, so that the news appeared in one newspaper and not in another. "We are trying to correct that", he said, "but have not yet succeeded".

A reporter from Hatzofeh read out an item which had been rejected by the Tel-Aviv censor, even though in Jerusalem it had been passed for publication. It read as follows: 'Rabbi Professor Simha Assaf, Rector of the Hebrew University, and Dr. V. Senator informed journalists in Jerusalem of the preparations for expanding the University. The date on which the accademic year will begin will be made public, he said, when the Minister of Defense keeps his promise to release three hundred students. Felix Bergman and S. Halkin have been invited from abroad to lecture. The University authorities have several hundred crates of books which have been sent from Poland, Antwerp and Amsterdam'.

No explanation was given for the rejection of this item. The Tel-Aviv censors complained mainly about journalists who tried to 'slip past' the local censor. The Hatzofeh reporter complained about the excision of articles he had submitted about a visit to an artillery unit, the water situation in the city, the names of victims in Jerusalem, etc. He complained: 'you specifically forbade the publication of the name of Zeev Herzog, who was killed when accompanying the American Consul, but the next day it appeared in 'Haboker'.

The censor replied that this had not been the result of discrimination, but of chance. In another case, where the name of an officer called Ayalon had appeared in an article on the parade in Jerusalem (Independence Day 1949), the reporter had had to write a letter of apology, as the censor had not authorized the publication of the name.

[38]

About nineteen years after the fall of the Old City, Major-General Uzi Narkiss stood facing the wall around the city once again, this time from the east. From the peak of Mount Scopus he sent his soldiers (in the Six Day War) into the Old City, this time through the Lions Gate (St. Stephen's Gate). He admitted to his associates: 'For nineteen years I have felt uneasy because my men had to abandon the Zion Gate and the link with the besieged Jewsh Quarter was cut off'.

[39]

Eliyahu Sela, the commander of the unit which broke into the Old City, on 17th May 1948, the Palmah's 'Portzim' Unit, gave a detailed explanation of the action and the reasons for abandoning the Zion Gate in the tenth issue of 'Lamerhav'. He claimed that the mission given to the 'Portzim', commanded by Uzi Narkiss, Yosef Tabenkin and Eliyahu Sela, was merely to undertake a diversionary action near the Damascus Gate. When the Palmah officers said that they were not familiar with the Damascus Gate, it was decided that the diversionary action should be transferred to the Mount Zion area. It so happened that during the course of the action they took Mount Zion, and this formed an important turning-point. Eliyahu Sela stressed in his article that the capture of Mount Zion had not, in fact, been one of the objectives which the Palmah was supposed to undertake.

[40]

Accusations that the Provisional Government had reached a 'secret agreement' with Abdullah, the King of Transjordan, to divide the city of Jerusalem and 'abandon the Jewish Quarter in the Old City', were made in an article by Mordekhai Raanan, the commander of Etzel in Jerusalem in 1948, in an internal bulletin of the Etzel. He also claimed that all the military actions were made to coordinate with this 'agreement', and that this was why the Jewish Quarter had not remained in our hands after the War of Independence and was not taken afterwards from the Jordanians, and also why the Zion Gate was conquered and then abandoned.

[41]

A different explanation of the military 'failures' in Jerusalem was given by Yigael Yadin, the Operations Officer during the War of Independence (in an interview with R. Bashan, 'Maariv', Independence Day issue, 14.5.1967.
'I would like to go back to the accusations made from time to time: why isn't 'it' in our hands, and why is 'it' in enemy territory. The discussion seems to me now to be academic, even though every failure and setback had its reasons at the time. To return to the subject of the Old City, the question of why it is not

in our hands is constantly being asked. I do not wish to pass judgment. At a
certain stage, before one of the ceasefires, the commander of Jerusalem, Major-
General Shealtiel, wanted to take the Old City by a frontal attack. Because of
considerations of time, place and forces it was clear to us at Operations Headquarters that it would be better to conquer the Old City by an indirect
approach, namely, by first conquering Sheikh Jarrah and Mount Scopus, since
then we would have better chances of taking the Old City'.
In the same interview Yigael Yadin also said:
'I sent Shealtiel, with Ben-Gurion's permission, a cable saying: "If it is possible
within the short time at our disposal to try and attack either the Old City or
Sheikh Jarrah, it is preferable to take Sheikh Jarrah". Shealtiel tried
nevertheless to attack the Old City. His argument was that the preparations for
that operation were already at their height, and that if he altered the plan he
would lose either way'.

[42]

Abdullah el-Tal described the failure of our forces to hold the Zion Gate in his
own way, in his book, 'Memories':
'At the Zion Gate we undertook a diversionary action which no one knows
about till this very day. This is what we did. The small force we sent to guard
the gate on the night between the 17th and 18th May 1948 informed us that the
Jews were massing on Mount Zion in order to break through and augment the
Jews of the Old City or get them out of there. I instructed the commander of
the unit not to fight too stubbornly in the battle, so that the Jews would get as
many of their number as possible inside the walls, but that he should prevent
their exit that night, until I managed to send the main force, commanded by
Rais Muhammad Mussa, to the gate. The Jewish attack began on the night
between 18th and 19th May. Eighty-five soldiers of the Haganah and the Etzel
entered the Jewish Quarter but did not get out, because in the morning I sent
the major force, which I had prepared specially, to the Zion Gate. That day the
trap was sprung.
'The Jews did not stop attacking the main gates for a single night. They
risked their lives and suffered many casualties in order to reach the Jews
trapped in the Old City. The biggest attack was launched on the night of 24th

May 1948, when the best soldiers of the Palmah went into battle against our troops in the Zion Gate area. The attack began at four in the afternoon and was preceded by a bombardment of mortars and a mine-thrower (the 'Davidka'). As night fell their men began approaching the Zion Gate. Our soldiers, who were at the ready that night, held their breath and waited until the Jews came up close so that they would be sure to hit them. All at once a hail of hand grenades descended on the Jews, who were approaching the wall with a large mine which they intended to explode. The mine blew up in their midst, blowing them to bits. The Palmah soldiers were terrified and began retreating in panic after our machine-guns had mown down 60 of them.

'The battle ended at ten that night. We had not known that that attack had been serious, and had been mounted by the Palmah. By chance our radio operator at Ramallah intercepted a cable sent by the Jews of Jerusalem to Tel-Aviv, informing them that the attack by the Palmah had failed and that the unit involved had lost 60 men'.

[43]

The attack by the 'Portzim' was also described by Rachel Yannait Ben-Zvi, in her diary of the siege, which she dedicated to 'Our boys in the Palmah'. In the chapter published in the 'Jerusalem Calendar' for 1949, edited by D.N. Brinker, she wrote:

'This is the third night that I am riveted to the window facing the Jewish Quarter, which is under attack by the Arab Legion.

'I run down to the cellar, where they are picking up news. I recall the voice we heard last night, full of sorrow, despair and hope at one and the same time, begging for help from his brethren:

— We can't hold out any longer.

— The ammunition is finished. The enemy is approaching. They are coming up towards us from Habad street, which we have evacuated.

We are transfixed to the radio. We send them a message:

— This is Daylight, this is Daylight. We are making our way to you! Hold on!

'The Palmah has already begun its attack. A terrible battle breaks out. It continues. the long hours crawl by, then suddenly we hear the news: they have broken through the Zion Gate, the Palmah is inside. But the Palmah only breaks through and conquers. The Palmah does not have time to stand and guard. They appeared like redeemers for a while, and when they left they took with them the spirit of redemption from the Jewish Quarter in the Old City'.

[44]

What was it like to be inside the Jewish Quarter, waiting for reinforcements to break through, when the gate was opened for a few hours and then recaptured by the enemy? A description appeared in 'The Story of the Old City', by Adina (published by Marachot, 1949).

'On the evening of 17th May, after the fighting had died down, our comrades began taking up fresh positions in the limited area left to us... They were very tired by now, and could hold on only because they hoped that reinforcements would be arriving soon... Two days afterwards the Legion entered the battle, beginining with a cannon bombardment. Exhaustion set in, and with it depression. There were cases of shock and nervous collapse, people had stopped believing in the reinforcements, deciding that the city had abandoned them. I believed that the reinforcements would arrive, maintaining that it was inconceivable that the head-quarters in the New City would decide to desert the Old City and us all.

'At dawn next day the first men of the Palmah force broke through... After five months of siege an aperture had been opened to the world outside the wall by our own army, our own strength, not the British. The end to our suffering had come.

'Some of the soldiers and reinforcements entered the Jewish Quarter and scattered within it. Some reached the hospital, where we welcomed them joyfully, asking them questions about what was happpening outside the wall. We were no longer alone, no longer cut off. We were connected with the outside world.

'The flashes and explosions continued outside. I had never heard anything like it. They broke through with the help of the 'Davidka', and the noise was tremendous. I thought then that the entire Old City had been conquered and that our forces were already standing beside the gates of the Mosque of Omar. And then, before we could turn round, the men of the Palmah had vanished. Suddenly we were besieged again. When dawn broke we realized that our joy had been unfounded. The reinforcements consisted of 80 men, most of them from the Home Guard, new recruits, and a few from the Civil Defense (aged 40 or more)'.

[45]

Yesterday Lehi headquarters invited local and foreign correspondents to an urgent meeting. The commander was introduced to us as 'Mr. Shapira'. All that we were told about him was that he had been an officer in the Polish army. At the end of the meeting Mr. Shapira asked the British journalists not to describe him, so that the British would not have heart attacks.

The meeting, he said, was intended to give an answer to 'distorted information' published by the Haganah about the battle in Jerusalem in general, and in the Old City in particular. He said that at a meeting of commanders of the Haganah, Etzel and Lehi on Friday night coordinated action had been discussed. He maintained that only the Lehi representatives had demanded the liberation of the Old City at the earliest possible moment and by a lightning attack. The other organizations, he said, had spoken of maintaining existing positions at this stage. Lehi had paid no attention to this, Mr. Shapira continued, and their men had advanced in a two-pronged attack, on the Jaffa and Damascus Gates. The Arab gangs had concentrated all their forces against Lehi because there were no attacks elsewhere. A bitter battle had developed and the Lehi commander had asked the Haganah commander to instruct his soldiers to enter the fray, considering the circumstances. We requested that his forces attack the Commercial Center, which was still empty, widen the front and thus harass the Arabs attacking us. Two hours later we received the following reply from Haganah headquarters: "We will help you provided you withdraw to the Afek Bank region, in accordance with the Haganah plan which designates the forward position there".

'We suffered losses, but continued to fight. When there was absolutely no hope that the others would join the battle, we retreated to Barclay's Bank, and all hope of saving the Jewish Quarter from the siege was lost'.

[46]

The attempt to break through into the Old City, the reasons for it, and the diversionary action which was initially a successful military action but turned into a failure which aroused negative reactions and personal quarrels are described by the commander of the action, Uzi Narkiss, in 'Comrades' Bulletin', 1974 (published by the organization of members of the Haganah in Jerusalem, edited by Yaakov Orlovski), under the heading, 'The Battles for Jerusalem — a Personal View'.

After describing the battle for the Castel by the Palmah, led by Yosef Tabenkin, Narkiss gives an account of the last attempt to establish contact with the inhabitants of the Jewish Quarter of the Old City. He notes that the action on Mount Zion, of which he was the commander, 'was intended to serve only as a diversionary action for the breakthrough attempt by the Haganah, Etzel and Lehi at the other gates to the Old City'.

Narkiss' description of the action reads as follows:

'I well remember the assault on the Zion Gate, in a final attempt to link up with the Jewish Quarter in the Old City. The commander of the 'Portzim' Batallion, Yosef Tabenkin, had to go to the coastal plain that day, and as his second-in-command I was ordered to take charge of the action on Mount Zion, which was intended to serve only as a diversionary attack for the breakthrough attempt by the Haganah, Etzel and Lehi at the other gates to the Old City.

'Later on I was summoned to David Shealtiel, the district commander, to coordinate the plan of action. There, in the presence of Yitzhak Rabin, the commander of the Harel Brigade to which the Portzim Batallion belonged, it was decided that the battalion would undertake a diversionary action in the south, opposite Mount Zion, and would be replaced by Jerusalem Haganah forces if it managed to conquer the mount. I reminded the district commander that only about one hundred and twenty soldiers fit for battle would reach town of the batallion which had come to Jerusalem numbering one thousand men. I requested, therefore, that after the breakthrough the Palmah would be replaced by the Haganah, which was better at holding territory. Shealtiel agreed.

'My plans and those of the Jerusalem regional command were very simple. The reason for this was that we had none of the information which is needed in order to make detailed and complex plans, such as maps, intelligence information and auxiliary equipment. We did not have much in the way of weapons, a team of two-inch mortars, a three-inch mortar, a few machine-guns and a 'two-pounder' which we had taken from the British and for which we had very little ammunition. There was also the famous 'Davidka' which made a tremendous and terrifying noise but did not do very much actual damage with its shells.

'The commander of Yemin Moshe described what he had been through, but did not tell us anything new about the enemy and his activities. The Jerusalem regional command of the Haganah did not know anything either. We had a tourist map of the Old City, published by the Mandate Government, which included Mount Zion and the Valley of Hinnom at its margins, but did not show the Sultan's Pool.

'The Palmah force which arrived took cover in the synagogue of Yemin Moshe. I summoned the officers for the briefing. Under the cover provided by all the weapons in our possession, the force would leave Yemin Moshe, cross the bridge over the Sultan's Pool between us and Mount Zion and climb the mount. The platoon which broke through first would conquer the big building and the other two would pass it, climb the narrow slope in a flanking movement and capture the buildings on the top. There was no information about what resistance was to be expected or about an enemy ambush, and so the briefing was very short and straightforward. We opened fire shortly before midnight.

'It is interesting to note that when the residents of the Jewish Quarter sent anguished cries for help over the radio, similar cries were being sent by the Arabs. Glubb Pasha, the British commander of the Legion, quotes them in his book, 'A Soldier with the Arabs:' 'Help! Help! The Jews have reached the Jaffa Gate! They have captured Sheikh Jarrah! They are climbing over the city walls. Help!' The nerves of the Arabs were not very strong either.

'I contacted the beleaguered inhahabitants of the Jewish Quarter, told them that there would be an action that night and asked them to keep calm. Meanwhile I sent machine-guns up to the church on Mount Zion, in order to help the Haganah forces to complete the conquest of Abu Tor. The Haganah forces which were supposed to replace us did not show up, and the 'Portzim' Company spread out on the mount to defend it.

'The planning of the breakthrough for that night was also very simple, and followed our usual plan of action. We had no information, and no contact with brigade intelligence, regional command or the enemy. One platoon was to provide covering fire, while the other would burst through the gate, once it had been blasted open, and reach the Jewish Quarter.

'I contacted Shealtiel and informed him that we would break through, despite the state the men were in. I suggested that they prepare a convoy of supplies, ammunition and first aid equipment to be transferred to the people in the Jewish Quarter. The order echoed and resounded through the dark hollow of the Valley of Hinnom, and the forces set out without a review, with hardly a single word. We were little more than a reinforced company, exhausted and decimated by defending the road to the besieged capital for almost six weeks. The Davidka shell shrieked and exploded with a frightful din. The first building was taken. Two platoons passed the first one and began clearing the buildings on the mount. The fourth platoon came up at dawn and dug in at the top. We had captured Mount Zion. In the morning we learned that our diversionary action had been the only one to succeed. The forces of the Etzioni brigade which had attacked the Jaffa Gate, had not succeeded in breaking through, and Etzel and Lehi, which had attacked the New and Damascus Gates, had also been repelled. The people besieged in the Jewish Quarter were desperate. Their radio, codename 'Tzabar', sent despairing appeals for help, which were heard clearly in my headquarters.

'At this point David Shealtiel contacted me, explained the situation of the people in the Jewish Quarter and asked if we could break through at the Zion Gate. I replied that we would try, and asked him to provide forces to replace us after the breakthrough. He agreed and asked us if we had flags. I asked him why, and he answered that according to the tradition of the French Foreign Legion, in which he had served, we had to raise the flag on top of the Dormition or David's Tower if we conquered them. We did not have any flags.

'I reminded him that the forces on Mount Zion had not yet been replaced, and he replied that the reinforcements would arrive soon. After the conversation I gave a report on the situation to Yitzhak Rabin, the commander of the Harel Brigade.

'Shealtiel's reinforcements reached Yemin Moshe in the afternoon of 18th May. They comprised eighty members of the Home Guard, under the command of Mordekhai Gazit, whom I knew from the Castel. They had been equipped with steel helmets which were too big for them, apparently obtained from the British, and each of them had a rifle and bullets. They had been brought together by the Jerusalem command, but had never constituted an organic fighting unit. Some of them had been told they would be home within a few hours. Gazit doubted their ability to fight and claimed that they would be unable to fulfill their mission. I told him of the plan to break through the Zion Gate and proposed that his men hold the point after it had been broken open. Since the force in front of me amounted to barely half a company, I hoped that Shealtiel would send additional men, as promised, to hold the mount, and also that they would be in better shape and capable of holding the break-through point. I arranged with Gazit that meanwhile he and his men would go up the mount, and at night we would see what would happen.

'While we were getting organized to break through we had to call on the volunteers to do the job, since no organic platoon was capable of doing it. One platoon was unable to continue, and those of its men who were still alive and unhurt were split up amongst the others. The soldiers, who moved like sleep-walkers, were totally exhausted, and swallowed quantities of novydrin pills. Gazit's reinforcements replaced a few of the men holding Mount Zion, and some of these volunteered to come to our aid. All this time the exchange of messages calling for help and giving encouragement between the people in the Jewish Quarter and myself continued.

'David Elazar (Dado) was given command of the platoon which was to break through once the volunteers had been organized. When the platoon began advancing, the others opened covering fire on the gate and the wall. The explosives thundered and the force stormed forward into the open gate, reaching the defenders of the Jewish Quarter within a few minutes.

'The moment that the siege was broken, deserves the pen of a greater writer than myself. In rapid succession I experienced the joy of victory, of having brought redemption to the besieged inhabitants of the Jewish Quarter, the gloomy knowledge that my forces were incapable of holding onto their achievement and the gnawing fear that the Haganah's regional command would not keep its commitment to send reinforcements so that we could reap the fruits of our victory. The mission had been completed, what an illusion!

'The Jews of the Jewish Quarter were ecstatic and did not know how to express their love for the soldiers of the Palmah, among whom Benny Marshak, who was everywhere, was the most prominent, as usual. The men of the Palmah were also confused, because the great moment of the breakthrough was already being diminished by the humiliation of the question: what happens next?

'As I waited for the reinforcements I was sure that the convoy of supplies would arrive, but all we got was a few first aid items, so the soldiers gave their ammunition to the defenders of the Jewish Quarter. I informed Shealtiel that our men were inside and that I was waiting for a force to take over the breakthrough point and hold on to the corridor we had opened to the Old City. Very little remained of the Portzim Battalion, I said, and it was unable to fulfill that mission.

'When no appropriate response was forthcoming, I contacted Gazit and asked him to occupy the corridor. Gazit again explained that his men were incapable of doing this because of their exhaustion and inexperience.

'The skies began to redden in the distance, the Mountains of Moab turned blue and the silhouettes of the towers began to emerge from the background. We received a report of activity in the Armenian Quarter, facing the Zion Gate, and I feared that this was the beginning of a counter-attack (and in fact Abdullah el-Tal, the commander of the Legion, notes in his memoirs that that morning he sent two platoons of Legionnaires to take the Zion Gate). The commanders in the field stressed over and over again that the Palmah was unable to hold both the corridor and Mount Zion, where only a few defenders were left, and which could be lost if the Legion launched a counterattack. Gazit was convinced that his men could not fill the breach, and no other forces arrived.

'Having no alternative, I decided that the reduced Palmah force would withdraw from the city and concentrate on Mount Zion. I suggested to Mordekhai Gazit that if he could not hold on to the break through point and the corridor, he should get his men into the Jewish Quarter to help the inhabitants until we broke through into the city again. Gazit maintained that his men were not able to do that either, but in the end he agreed.

'Glubb Pasha's soldiers closed Zion Gate and a few days later the Jewish Quarter fell and its inhabitants, together with Mordekhai Gazit — who had been wounded meanwhile — were taken prisoner. As the men of the Portzim Brigade were returning to their base in Kiryat Anavim a truck overturned and forty soldiers were wounded. The attempt to save the Old City left Mount Zion, which was conquered in a diversionary action, in Israel's hands. The national significance and tactical importance of the mount are not enough to compensate for the inadequate planning and execution of the action by the regional command of the Haganah.

'In my opinion, the inadequacies were due to the fact that the entire action was based on planning for one stage only, without giving any forethought to exploiting any local success and making it the focal point of the entire operation. There was not, nor is there till this day, sufficient clarity regarding what were the functions of the various forces. Etzel and Lehi, which attacked the Damascus and New Gates, claim that their task was to be a diversionary action only, while the Etzioni Brigade at the Jaffa Gate was supposed to break into the city. As far as I remember, I was told that day of three tactically unconnected attacks by the Etzel, the Lehi and the Haganah, while the Palmah was suposed to provide a diversionary action in the south. The fact that there was no clear decision as to what was to happen should one of the attacks succeed, or as regards their objectives and ways of utilizing them, indicates the way in which the entire operation was conducted. The coordination between the various forces was very general, and considerations of a different nature altogether occupied a major role in the planning. The Palmah was not concerned with what was happening at the Jaffa Gate, and vice versa. If the regional command had been ready to send appropriate reinforcememnts to Mount Zion in order to utilize the point where the breakthrough had been made, the fate of Jerusalem for two decades might have been different.

'To David Shealtiel's credit it should be said that the difficult conditions of those times placed an extremely heavy burden on the shoulders of the commander of the city. On the morning I asked him for reinforcements to hold the breakthrough point into the Old City, the Arab Legion attacked Sheikh Jarrah, and he had to decide where to send the meager reserves at his disposal.

'In retrospect, it seems to me today that if we had not left the breakthrough point and had held the gate, despite our small numbers and our exhaustion, the Jewish Quarter might have remained in our hands, but we might have lost Mount Zion in a counter-attack by the Legion. I personally regretted my decision to leave, but I doubt whether we could have done anything else.

'As a result of the Mount Zion action David Shealtiel and I quarrelled bitterly and had no contact with one another for many years. but on 8th June 1967 Shealtiel appeared together with a host of other guests at Binyanei Haooma in Jerusalem to congratulate me on the liberation of the Old City. He crossed the war room in the hall which served as the headquarters of the Central Command, and seemed to hesitate as he approached me, as elegant as ever.

Nevertheless he came up to me, embraced me and moved almost to tears kissed me and said: 'Uzi, today everything that has passed between us is over. I have forgotten everything. You have my blessing'.

[47]

The journalist, Walter Lacqueur, wrote the following complaint concerning the treatment of foreign correspondents:
'The foreign correspondents, who were concentrated in Jerusalem for many years, are moving to Tel-Aviv in ever-increasing numbers. They maintain that it is true that in Jerusalem they can find the best material for 'stories' and that the Christian world is far more interested in Jerusalem than in Tel-Aviv or Haifa, but it is impossible to send a cable from Jerusalem to London in less than 14 hours, namely, twelve hours longer than any London or New York editor is prepared to accept.
'The foreign correspondents also claim that Jerusalem will not be very important to the Jews, and will become another Safed. Foreign tourists will be sent there to inspect the antiquities, but all the institutions and undertakings connected with the present will be situated within the borders of the State of Israel'.
The weekly, 'HaOlam', also carried an article on this subject (June 1948).
'Large numbers of foreign correspondents came to Israel in mid-May. In the absence of any Government decision to define authority, the main burden of organizing relations with the press has fallen on the Foreign Minister. The exigencies of the military situation have inevitably led to the restriction of the correspondents' freedom. In this sphere the Foreign Ministry has been forced to concede with regret that it has failed to ensure that events in Israel receive the coverage they deserve. Considerable efforts are being made to set things right and to fill the gaps in this sphere'.
There were nevertheless some foreign correspondents who chose to remain in Jerusalem, and transfer news and articles to their papers and agencies in various ways, describing what they had seen and heard in besieged Jerusalem. Their articles aroused considerable interest in the world press.

[48]

In his book, 'Cairo to Damascus', the journalist, Roy Carlson, writes about the 'brilliant' life of a reporter up against the censorship (p. 198):

'The American journalists nearly went mad with frustration. Their wonderfully dramatic stories about the defense of Jerusalem, the breakthrough into the Old City, the successes of the Jews on the various fronts, life under siege and the dreadful shelling, were all piled up on the censor's desk. The press officers of the Haganah were stony-hearted and devoid of any sense of public relations. The three photographers, Tom Pringle and Jim Fitzsimmons from the Associated Press and Robert Cox from Paramount, suffered most of all. Jim and Tom took hundreds of photographs, developed the films, packed up the negatives, gave the photographs appropriate captions and... nothing. The negatives found their way to the censor's desk, next to the frozen manuscripts'.

[49]

The following description of the surrender of the Jewish Quarter is given by Carlson, in his book, 'Cairo to Damascus', (pp. 225-240).

'On the night before the surrender of the Jewish Quarter, the Arab Legion intensified its fire at the narrow area where the Jews were concentrated. Flames could be seen shooting up from many houses. In the morning the Arabs were informed that the Red Cross had proposed an 'honorable surrender' to the Jews. Abudllah el-Tal said that he would wait until 1.30 p.m. and if they had not surrendered by then the shelling would be renewed with even greater intensity. After a few hours the Arabs saw the white flag borne aloft by the Jewish delegation.

'Alongside Rabbi Ben-Zion Hazan, a tall man who held his head high and walked as if he did not know what fear was, trotted Yisrael Zeev Minzberg, a small man who looked fearfully from one side to another.

'The negotiations were very brief. Captain Mohammed Bey explained the conditions for surrender, which were to be either accepted as they stood or rejected. The two old men retraced their steps. The Arabs waited for two or three hours, then began to fear that the Haganah would try to break through again.

'Just as they were about to start firing again someone shouted: "They're coming, They're coming!' Rabbi Hazan, the Mukhtar, Weingarten, and the commander of the Haganah, his arm bandaged, came accompanied by an armed Arab officer. The head of the Ceasefire Committee, Pablo Azcarate, was also there. In a dry voice el-Tal read out the conditions of surrender: A. The Jews will give up their arms. B. All the healthy males will be taken prisoner. C. The old people, women, children and wounded will be allowed to cross into the New City, on the basis of a special arrangement with the Red Cross. D. The Arab Legion will take responsiblitiy for the lives of the prisoners. E. The Arab Legion will take the Jewish Quarter.

'I followed the soldiers. Every now and again we had to jump or run, as we were in danger of receiving a burning shower as we passed burning buildings. An Arab officer offered me a scroll of the law which was in excellent condition, but I was afraid to take it in case the mob thought I was Jewish. My benefactor then threw the scroll of the law to the side and someone trod on it. I saw a column of young Jewish boys surrounded by Legionnaires. I went over to a group of old people as they walked with bent backs murmuring verses from the bible. probably from Lamentations.

'Next day I toured the burnt, destroyed Jewish Quarter in the company of an English-speaking Legionnaire. Groups of looters had descended on the Misgav Ladah hospital, carrying their booty, whatever they could lay their hands on, on their heads, in sacks, on the backs of donkeys and in hand-carts. Legionnaires were everywhere, but did nothing to stop the pillage. The once-splendid synagogue, the 'Hurva' had been ripped apart. A tablet bearing the ten commandments hung crookedly on a wall, and parts of scrolls of the law lay about the ruins. The legionnaire accompanying me said: Here is the Jewish atom bomb", and pointed to the 'Davidka', which had cast fear into the hearts of the Arabs'.

[50]

About two weeks after the last Jew had left the Jewish Quarter of the Old City (27.6.1948) I heard about the heroism of our soldiers inside the walls of the Old City, outnumbered ten to one, from Tzippora, a girl from Tel-Aviv who had served in the Jewish Quarter as a medic. Hanoh Tempelhof, who was wounded there, filled in some of the details. This is what Tzippora told me:

"How did I get into the Old City? Do you remember the convoys which were sent there in such a degrading way? The British, in their infinite kindness, would accompany the transfer of food supplies to the Old City 'with the agreement of the Arabs'. In the one but last convoy 'teachers and counsellors' were to be sent in large numbers, but because of a dispute the British decided to delay it. After a lot of persuasion, they agreed to transfer the food, though all the people were sent back.

'The last convoy was delayed because two rifles had been stolen from the local police. As a result no food was sent into the Jewish Quarter for about a week. Finally the convoy was allowed through, and with it seven men teachers and five women teachers. The men were covered with blankets, "so as not to annoy the Arabs".

'We bribed the British officer so that we could bring in a Louis machine-gun. The officer whispered his thanks and walked away. On our first Sabbath there the Weingarten family gave a party in our honor. We toured the defense positions, and found the morale A1. We enjoyed our visit to the 'Defenders' Club', which was adorned with appropriate slogans at the entrance and pictures on the walls. Inside it was a reading room with a rich library of books collected and donated by the children of the New City. There was also a reasonably-priced snack-bar, providing a warm, friendly corner for relaxation. The establishment and organization of the Club had been the work of Abraham, the commander of the Old City, who had been expelled by the British. The young men and women enjoyed learning the new songs and dances which we taught them.

'Lessons were held in the Sephardi Talmud Torah, as the girls' school was near the Armenian Quarter and came within the enemy's line of fire. The pupils displayed admirable dedication and willingness, which was the thing that kept them going in the dark days which followed. Arab snipers aimed their fire there from over the wall, above Mount Zion, and pupils were wounded sitting at their desks. Consequently, we sat them around the walls, leaving the center empty.

'Old people and children went out to build fortifications under a hail of Arab bullets. Everybody joined in the work; Boys and girls, women and old people lifted sacks, filled them with earth, and carried them up or down to the positions. We moved from one vantage point to another through holes in the walls of the houses. The Lobinski Position faced the iron gate in the Street of the Jews, on the border with the Moslem Quarter, on the second floor and in the cellar. This position had been used by the British, and we found all kinds of graffiti they had left. One of them read: "Beware of Jewish girls, they'll get information out of your mouth and you into trouble". On the right was the Rabinovitz position, with an enemy position nearby. About thirty Etzel soldiers were in the Nissan Beck synagogue, and there were positions in all the other alleys and courtyards too.

'On 16th May the Arabs began their attacks. After making long preparations and receiving modern, heavy weapons from the British, the Arab Legion launched itself against us. It seemed that they had expected to conquer the Old City, or at least to defeat its Jewish inhabitants, within two or three days, but they were wrong. The attacks were bitter, difficult and persistent, using every kind of modern weapon, from rifles to mortars and cannon. From the attacks it was obvious that 'experts' had directed them. The British obviously knew our positions from 'the old days', and that made it easier for the Arabs to aim their fire so as to destroy our holy places and murder innocent souls.

'On 17th May the Arabs tried to advance and conquer the Nissan Beck synagogue, and the Etzel killed a great many Arabs there. The next day Rabbi Yitzhak Orenstein and his wife were killed. The Arabs returned in greater numbers and laid explosives which broke open a wall in the synagogue. The Etzel soldiers ran out of ammunition and threw bottles and stones in order to ward off the enemy.

'On that day, 17th May the first urgent message for help was sent from the Jewish Quarter to headquarters in the New City. At noon we heard that the enemy had burst through and destroyed the courtyard of Batei Warshaw. The third storey of the building was on fire and people ran immediately to save the second storey. At the same time the enemy launched other attacks. Mordekhai Pinkas shouted: 'Dig in in the Street of the Jews', and the spirit of Massada enveloped us all. We knew we were fighting a desperate battle, we had felt the enemy's strength and his numerical and military superiority, but nevertheless we stood firm and girded our loins for what was to come. The boys ran to the Street of the Jews, the girls went to the end of Habad Street, to the positions in the courtyard and one of them gave the order to fortify the positions.

'From headquarters in the New City we received the order over the radio:

'Hold on. Reinforcements will come'. That day the Arabs, led by the British, used a new device. They tied a bundle of explosives together and threw them towards our houses, thus blowing up several buildings and destroying the positions in the courtyard in Habad Street.

'On 17th May several of the local inhabitants asked the Haganah commander to surrender, but he refused, claming that the commander of the city had promised to send reinforcements and urging us to hold on. The inhabitants and the defenders made jokes about that statement, saying ironically to one another: 'The reinforcements are in the Zion cinema', 'The reinforcements are in Jaffa Road', and so on. But they fought on heroically, hoping and praying that the reinforcements would come quickly, before it was too late.

'On the morning of Wednesday 19th May Palmah soldiers broke through the Zion Gate, repelled large enemy forces from Mount Zion and took control of it, linking up with the defenders inside the walls. You can easily imagine the joy of the besieged inhabitants when the soldiers reached them.

'Our soldiers could have saved the situation then but they did not know how to use the few precious hours. The reinforcements were not fighting men, and not a single additional Bren machine-gun was brought in. All we were given was eighty rifles with ammunition. Neither the badly wounded nor women and old people were evacuated. Eighty men of the 'Auxiliary Company', aged over thirty and forty years old were brought in Most of them were family men who feared for the fate of their wives and children, maintaining that they had been cheated and had been brought in under false pretences. Some of them had never been in battle before and had not even been trained to use arms.

'During the first half of that day the Arabs were in a state of panic and confusion and we had a unique opportunity to attack and conquer the whole of the Old City. But the Palmah had already left; once they had fought and broken through their task was over. They had done their job and left. At 4 a.m. our forces held the Zion Gate. At noon A.....r and T.....r came, bringing chickens from Yemin Moshe, they were so sure that the connection with the Jewish Quarter would be maintained. It was a rather foolish exaggeration because at 1 p.m. the enemy recaptured the Zion Gate, and again we were cut off.

'Again we experienced dark and difficult days of siege, only now we had additional people, who were wounded and inexperienced. Only a few of them were useful as reinforcements, and they deserve to be remembered and to have the story of their heroism and devotion told.

'The enemy attacked the Jewish Quarter in waves. Every house became a fort, and every alleyway the front. Abraham was sent to direct the military action and organize the life of the beleaguered inhabitants. He was devoted and exact, agile and diligent, distinguished by his beard his height, and his deeds. He soon won the full confidence of the fighting and defending public, as well as of all the inhabitants of the Jewish Quarter from all ethnic communities. The Jewish Quarter was divided into blocks, alleyways and passages were used to maintain contact between them and the distribution of food was organized to prevent hoarding and so that no one would go hungry. Idleness was stopped, with all the irritability it caused and everybody was employed in some activity or other, whether in fortifications, woodwork or the study of the Torah.

'The Arabs received large reinforcements of Legionnaires, equipped with cannon, mortars and modern weapons. The Jewish Quarter renewed its calls for help.

'Every day we broadcast twice: "The Arabs are advancing. Many houses are on fire. We will surrender if you don't send help quickly". From the New City we received the following answer: "We have been hearing that from you for a week now. Don't panic. Hold on and help will come". For two days and nights the Jewish Quarter endured the heavy shelling and concentrated attacks of the Legionnaires. The number of dead and wounded rose and the doctors could do nothing to help those who were badly wounded. Many people died of their wounds simply because there was no way of operating on them immediately, and in some cases their dressings were not changed when they should have been. On every side we heard the cries of brave young men who now lay helpless, going out like candles. There was no water. There was plenty of food, but it was in Misgav Ladah hospital, where we could not reach it. The enemy shelled the hospital too, while badly wounded men were still being brought in from the positions. Those who were lightly wounded continued fighting. We were waiting for one of our planes and on Wednesday night one flew over and dropped something that fell near what had once been a Matza factory which the British had blown up to make things easier for the Arabs, and the package fell into enemy hands. On Thursday a plane flew over, did not drop anything and left. The enemy was already in Hamidan Street, from where they continued firing with three-inch mortars and throwing explosives and incendiary material to which they had tied string. They set fire to every Jewish house and street they conquered, storming into the synagogues in a frenzy of vengeance. They destroyed everything that was sacred, looting and pillaging on every side. One position after the other was captured, one house after the other was set on fire, the flames ascending heavenward. The besieged Jews watched in anguish, but continued to wait for help from outside. The rabbis and dignitaries of the Old City appealed to the Haganah commander to surrender in order to salvage what could be saved. We had fought a heroic war in which many had fallen, and those who were left were hungry and tired after fighting an enemy which was better equipped and superior in numbers. The young commander replied: "We will die, but we will never surrender. It is better to die than to live in servitude. As long as we have weapons we will carry on fighting, until our comrades from outside come to our aid". But aid did not come. Additional attempts to break through failed, coming up against large enemy forces. Again the rabbis asked the defenders: "You are braver than lions, yet you must not be the cause of your own deaths. The Torah commands you to preserve your lives, because they are sacred to the nation". The inhabitants assembled in the four synagogues, the Istambul, Rabbi Yochanan ben Zakkai, and the others.

On that bitter Friday (28th May 1948) the enemy took our positions in the Street of the Jews, next to the Sephardi Talmud Torah (Hahakura) and in Hamidan Street, and mounted a heavy attack from those three directions. Our forces were inferior in weapons and numbers and the Legion entered from the side of Hamidan Street, where the religious students of 'Yavneh' lived, near Misgav Ladah. Suddenly flames burst out of the old hospital, Misgav Ladah, which housed the ancient and extensive library of Rabbi Hazki Medini, the owner of Sedei Hemed. Grim items of information came thick and fast. The young radio operators announced:

— The Arabs are in Misgav!
— The Arabs are in Turgeman!
— The Arabs are in Midan!
— The Arabs are at Hakura!

Again an urgent call for help was sent by the people in the Jewish Quarter, who saw their houses going up in flames and their comrades being killed. 'We are

surrendering. We can't hold on any longer'. The reply was: 'No. Don't give up.
We have no order for you to surrender. Try to hold on. Out'. We knew,
however, that we could not guarantee the safety of the Jewish Quarter and its
population any longer. We could no longer stop the residents from doing what
was desirable and necessary and we began destroying the weapons. The
commander shouted: 'Don't ruin the arms. We may still need them to fight
with'. The transmitter was destroyed and the rifles, Thompsons, Stens and
Mausers, were laid in piles. We had acquired many of our weapons just a few
days previously, when we had launched a counter-attack and the enemy had
suffered many casualties, leaving us quantities of arms. We did not have
enough bullets, however, and there were no shells for the mortars. We also had
arms we had purchased from the Arabs during the siege — even then they
would do anything for money — and some we had brought in under the noses
of the British, who had been glad to take the bribe we offered. Now that our
situation had worsened and our ammunition had run out we laid down our
arms'.

The heroic struggle and stubborn stand of the defenders of the Old City, which
lasted for six months, came to an end at noon on 28th May 1948, after the
defenders' ammunition had run out and their last bullet had been fired. The
Arabs and their British officers could hardly believe their eyes when they saw
that there were just thirty-nine unhurt fighters, and all the rest — about two
hundred — were wounded. Even the enemy could not help marvelling at their
stubborn spirit.

[51]

A few days before the last British soldier left Palestine and the State of Israel
was proclaimed, considerable publicity was given to King Abdullah's
announcement that the Arab Higher Council, headed by the Jerusalem Mufti,
Haj Amin al Husseini, had no right to represent or speak on behalf of the
Palestinian Arabs. The king maintained that he had been asked to defend the
Palestinian Arabs and that henceforth his kingdom represented them at the
U.N. and elsewhere.

At a later date, in an interview with foreign correspondents, King Abdullah
explained his army's involvement in the war in Palestine. He said that his task

was to ensure that the partition resolution was implemented and that he had the assurance of Ernest Bevin, Britain's Foreign Secretary, that the area designated as an Arab state by the U.N. would be annexed to Jordan.

Christopher Sykes also writes on this point in his book, 'From Balfour to Bevin', (pp. 319 and 306).

Abdullah el-Tal describes the attempt to establish a 'Palestinian Government', in his book, 'Memories', pp. 260-262, 272-274.

[52]

In an interview in 'Davar' of 6th May 1973, I. Galili, Minister without Portfolio, said that a separate Arab state was no longer on the agenda. Amongst other things, he said:

'The other side means the Arab states. Since 15th May they have become the dominant factor. The Palestinian Arabs were weak and divided, their leaders had fled and deserted them and the Palestinian state was never considered. It did not take long before the Palestinian Arabs were no longer an independent military or political element which had to be included in our considerations. The representatives of the Arab countries treated the Palestinian Arabs as inferiors, as of no importance. They understood neither their feelings and aspirations, nor the military and political potential which could have been developed among them. The commanders of the invading armies treated them insultingly, not bothering to mold them into a military force. The leaders of the Palestinian Arabs, who had rejected the proposal to establish their own state in part of Palestine, were supported vociferously by the Arab states. The invasion by the Arab armies was intended to destroy the Jewish State, not to establish a Palestinian one. The question of an independent Arab State in part of Western Israel no longer occupies our thoughts, Arab aggression and the invasion by the Arab armies removed the subject from the agenda.

'If we examine the official documents prepared prior to the establishment of the State and official statements made at that time, such as Ben-Gurion's declaration as chairman of the Agency Executive or chairman of the People's Administration, we find virtually no serious and detailed reference to the network of relations between us and the independent Arab State which was supposed to be established in part of Palestine. The Arabs took the subject off the agenda. The Arab leaders and rulers declared their political and military opposition to the establishment of the State of Israel because they rejected any compromise solution through partition. The rulers of the Arab States prevented the creation of any serious representative body for the Palestinian Arabs, and no representative organization which could negotiate with us while accepting Israel's existence was ever established.

'The interesting fact is that when a government was established in Gaza and the Mufti, Haj Amin al Husseini, the leader of the Palestinian Arabs, came to Gaza, all his demands for adequate representation of the Palestinian Arabs were rejected, and he was expelled ignominiously. If the Arabs had managed to win any territory in Palestine it is almost certain that it would have been carved up among the Arab countries, without establishing a Palestinian Arab State. King Abdullah did not recognize the government set up in Gaza. He annexed the West Bank, with British support, to the dissatisfaction of the Arab rulers and at the invitation of the leaders of the West Bank. The 'government' in Gaza survived miserably and meaninglessly, until it was disbanded by the Arab League in September 1952. The Egyptians did not allow it to rule even in Gaza. Had the Palestinian Arabs had representatives who were willing to negotiate with us, everything would have been different'.

[53]

In his book, 'To Jerusalem', Bernadotte wrote of his conversation with King Abdullah about the conditions for the ceasefire. Abdullah said to him: 'Your intentions are honest, you are like a brother to me, but I cannot allow a single drop of water or one pound of food to be brought into Jerusalem during the ceasefire'. Nevertheless, Bernadotte persuaded him not to starve Arabs and Jews. (pp. 55-56). In his discussions with the representatives of the State of Israel Bernadotte announced that he would not allow fighting men to enter the country, that only a limited amount of supplies would be permitted into Jerusalem and that he would ensure that neither side gained any military advantage from the ceasefire. (ibid. p. 60).

On 12th June, the second day of the ceasefire, Bernadotte tried to find hungry and thirsty people in Jewish Jerusalem, but did not observe any. He saw, so he wrote in his book, Jews walking about the streets, enjoying the sunshine. (p. 80)

On p. 99 he wrote: 'My experiences of the last month have strengthened my opinion that the resolution passed by the U.N. Assembly on 29th November 1947 was an unfortunate one. One did not have to be a prophet to foresee that this resolution would lead to serious conflicts and would not last long. The artificial borders allotted to the State of Israel, and the united opposition of the Arab world against the partition of Palestine and the creation of a separate Jewish State, would obviously lead to war. The creation of a united state in Palestine, with special rights for the Jews, would have been preferable'.

The 'mediator', Bernadotte, also wrote in his book that the Negev and Jerusalem should be given to the Arabs, and that the Arab part of Palestine should be united with Transjordan. He did in fact submit proposals along these lines, but they were rejected.

The Egyptian Prime Minister, Nukrashi Pasha, told Bernadotte that the Arabs would never agree to the establishment of a Jewish State. Bernadotte replied: 'Personally I am not at all happy about the U.N. decision, but meanwhile the Jewish State has become a reality'.

[54]

Abdullah el-Tal wrote the following about the ceasefire in his book, 'Memories' (p. 104):

'The members of the political committee of the Arab League made the most serious mistake in the history of the wars in the Arab Middle East by agreeing to lift the siege on the city of Jerusalem, thus saving one hundred thousand Jews who were about to surrender or die of hunger and thirst... They agreed without thinking about what would happen only ten days after that unhappy day... They agreed before they realized that Jerusalem is everything in Palestine, and anyone who has conquered it has won the battle... They agreed before hearing what the Arab commander of this great city had to say (the Arab commander was the author, Abdullah el-Tal – Y.C.)... They agreed before thinking about the intentions of the British, who had decided to save Zionism by saving its heart, Jerusalem. They agreed before forming a correct opinion about the conditions of the ceasefire, and without demanding that there should be at least some supervision of the life-line to Jerusalem and Arab control over the supplies brought into the city. They agreed. Had they not done so the entire battle for Palestine would have gone differently. I consider all the Arab States responsible for the decision which was made in Amman on that black day.

[55]

Only a year later were details of the serious shortage of food given. At a speech made to 'The Journalists' Newspaper', Daniel Oster, the mayor, admitted that the first ceasefire had saved Jewish Jerusalem from starvation. He said that on the eve of the feast of Pentecost (Shavuot) 1948 the last few sacks of flour were collected and there was only a very small amount of solar oil. This meager quantity was given to the bakers, who baked bread for the festival. There was not enough flour and the matzot (unleavened bread) which were found in the storehouses and which were distributed the day after the festival, saved the situation.

The Minister of the Interior at the time, Yitzhak Grinbaum, recounted that near Pentecost he sent an urgent cable from Jerusalem to David Ben-Gurion, informing him of the dearth of food in Jerusalem. This cable provided an additional incentive for the Government to agree to the ceasefire.

Rabbi Berlin described the situation in Jerusalem during the period before the ceasefire to Tel-Aviv reporters in the following words:

'On Pentecost 1948 the Jews of Jerusalem celebrated the three Foot Festivals: they celebrated the giving of the Law, they ate matzot and they sat in tabernacles (shelters)'.

[56]

Why did the rabbis refuse to permit bread to be baked on the Sabbath in besieged Jerusalem? Dr. Zerah Warhaftig told me.

'It was in June 1948, during the worst of the siege, when there was a terrible shortage of food in general, and of bread in particular. The rations were extremely small. Dr. Bernard Joseph, the head of the Jerusalem Committee, came and told me how serious the situation was. The city was on the verge of starvation, he said, and he feared there would be demonstrations. There was still a certain amount of flour, and we had to make haste and bake enough bread to give out to the people. It was Friday and we had to ask the rabbis for a special permit to bake bread on the Sabbath. I hurried to the house of Chief Rabbi Herzog and described the situation to him, while he listened with great anxiety and concern. At his request I hunted for and found an automobile, toured the streets of Jerusalem under a hail of shells and, at considerable risk, brought Chief Rabbi Uziel and Rabbi Zvi Pesach Frank, the President of the Rabbinical Court of Jerusalem, to his house. Dr. Joseph joined us and described the full gravity of the situation to the rabbis, claiming that it was necessary to bake bread for two days and nights in succession, starting that day. Only three bakeries were working and bread had to be prepared for Sunday morning, to save the inhabitants of the city from starvation.

'We listened, giving his words our fullest attention. The rabbis began discussing the ins and outs of the Law, seeking precedents, quoting interpretations of the law and trying to find a formula for a permit, ways of working on the Sabbath with some 'change' and all that it involved.

'While the discussion was going on Dr. Joseph was called to the phone. A few minutes later he was called to another urgent phone call. One conversation followed the other, Dr. Joseph spoke loudly and angrily, and his words could be heard through the wooden partition. We realized that a representative of the workers at the bakeries was at the other end and that they insisited on receiving extra payment for working at night. Dr. Joseph replied in the negative. "No. On no account will you get so much extra. If you don't want to, don't work at night". So saying, he slammed the receiver down.

'The rabbis were astounded, fell silent and began thinking. After a few minutes Rabbi Herzog said to Dr. Joseph: "We cannot issue a permit to bake bread on the Sabbath if night work is cancelled because of a wage dispute".

'Dr. Joseph listened impassively, stood up, took his leave of us and left'.

Z. Warhaftig was Minister of Religion for many years. In 1948 he was a member of the Provisional State Council. On behalf of the National Council he dealt with the Legal Department of the future State, with giving legal aid to 'La Asirenu' (for our Prisoners), was active in founding 'Yad Vashem' and was one of the first members of the National-Religious Party.

[57]

About two years after the War of Independence Yaakov Orland wrote a play called 'This City', whose main theme was the siege of Jerusalem and the

Neturei Karta's demonstration and call to surrender. At the end of the first performance Yitzhak Ben-Zvi expressed his disapproval of this kind of calumny. The writer of this book also spoke against the intentions and content of the play and the distortion of the truth which in involved. The play and its theme were also 'tried', and were soon removed from the stage.

G. Stern, one of the staff of the Mapam paper, 'Al Hamishmar', also published an article condemning the libel in the play and emphasizing the fact that Radio Ramallah had spread those rumors in order to sow dissent among the Jewish inhabitants.

[58]

In his book, 'Memòries', under the heading, 'The Jordanian Government Wants to sell the Western Wall to the Jews', Abdullah el-Tal wrote (p. 178): 'On the morning of Saturday, 19th June 1948 I recieved a phone call from Amman from Sheikh Ahmad al Shunkeiti, the Minister of Education and the President of the Religious Court. He wanted me to agree to the proposal put forward by Lash, the commander of the division, giving the Jews permission to visit the Western Wall once a day. He added that the Government and the king had agreed and that in return the Jews would pay fifty thousand pounds to an Arab charity. I replied that in the past the Jews had offered the Moslem Supreme Council one million pounds to buy the Western Wall or to change the 'status quo' regarding their holy wall.

'That evening I received an official letter informing me that at a meeting of the representatives of the Ceasefire Committee it had been decided that a daily visit of not more than fifty people would be permitted to the Western Wall, where they would remain for not more than one hour, and two hours on Fridays, accompanied by an observer from the Ceasefire Committee. The visitors would not be allowed to carry arms of any kind. My reaction to Lash's proposals was to file away his letter and ignore its contents completely. On the phone I replied that I agreed to the Jews' request provided they permitted us to visit our holy places in Jaffa, Acre and Haifa. After that Lash did not mention the subject of the Western Wall again'.

[59]

The letter of appointment which Ben-Gurion gave to Shealtiel contained instructions to 'raise the Jewish flag atop David's Tower'. That was on 6th February 1948. Shealtiel, the new district commander of Jerusalem, was told to link up the Jewish 'islands', namely, the Jewish neighborhoods which were surrounded by Arab neighborhoods; to gain time; to unite the fighting forces (Haganah, Etzel and Lehi) and, once the British left, to take over the buildings and areas which they had held.

Abraham Arest, one of the commanders of the Haganah, wrote in Maariv on the eve of Independence Day 1966 about Shealtiel's arrival in Jerusalem and his actions as the commander of besieged Jerusalem.

'One day at the beginning of 1948 Shealtiel came to me with a note from Berl Katznelson which read: 'David Shealtiel, one of our best men, is moving to Jerusalem. Work must be found for him. I'm sure you'll do your best. B.K.'.

'I knew him from that day on as a colleague on the Haganah's district command (when he came to Jerusalem at the beginning of 1948) and as an officer at district headquarters during the war for Jerusalem.

'Naturally, he was criticized by those whom he had always opposed, Etzel and Lehi. He was also censured by the population of Jerusalem, which was concerned with public relations. Shealtiel, however, always said that he had been sent to Jerusalem to conduct a war, not politics, and that is just what he did.

'It is a fact that most of New Jerusalem, all of Jewish Jerusalem, was conquered. It is a fact that this was done, after the conquests of the Palmah, by the armored corps and Home Guard of the Etzioni Brigade, commanded by David Shealtiel. This was stated publicly and commended by the commanders of the Palmah, who stressed the comradely spirit of the Haganah.

'Anyone who knows in what conditions and with what means these conquests were made knows how great was the achievement of Shealtiel and his staff in the defense of Jerusalem. Jewish Jerusalem survived because of the spirit and endurance of its inhabitants, the Palmah and the men of the armored corps and the Home Guard, led by Shealtiel.

'During the war in Jerusalem there were bitter battles for Ramat Rachel and the site passed from one side to the other. When it was necessary to conquer it for the third time, after it had been taken by the enemy and won back twice —

once by the Haganah and once by Etzel — Ziama Aharonowitz, (Zalman
Aranne) whose luck had brought him to Jerusalem during the siege, asked me
to go with him to the commander of the Harel Brigade of the Palmah (Yitzhak
Rabin) and persuade him to send his men for the third time to take Ramat
Rachel from the enemy. Ziama addressed the commander of the Harel Brigade
as a civilian, saying: 'I was always an opponent of your late mother, Rosa
Cohen, but when I was right she always accepted my opinion, and when she
was right I accepted hers'.

'The commander of the Harel Brigade, Yitzhak Rabin, said that there was no
need to 'persuade' him, as he would in any case send the Palmah to win Ramat
Rachel from the enemy. But David Shealtiel would have to send men to hold
the point after it had been conquered, as there was no logic in boys being killed
to win a point if those whose job it was to hold it did not do what they were
supposed to.

'And so the Palmah conquered Ramat Rachel and David Shealtiel sent men to
hold the spot, as he had done previously with Katamon, which had been won
by the Palmah and later held by the soldiers of the other brigades of the
Haganah.

'Shealtiel's unfriendly relations with the various public institutions of Jerusalem
were caused by the fact that ever since the major institutions had left Jerusalem
there was no public authority (despite the various positive activities undertaken
by the Jewish Communal Council). This changed when Dr. Dov Yosef (then
Bernard Joseph) was appointed chairman of the Jerusalem Committee and
then Military Governor of the city, and cooperated in spheres which were
essential for the war, such as supplies, water, fuel, etc. Both Dov Yosef and
Shealtiel knew that in those spheres there was no difference between the army
and the public, and that everything was for the war, for independence and for
Jerusalem'.

That is what Arest, who was familiar with all the details, wrote. At every
opportunity Sheaitiel was showered with questions about the Old City of
Jerusalem, about the heroism of its defenders, who received no aid or military
backing from the fighting forces in New Jerusalem, about the failure to retain it
in 1948, etc. The questions annoyed him very much.

In those days rumors spread like wildfire, and the Jerusalem reporters heard
that there had been 'a secret meeting between Mrs. Golda Meir and Emir

Abdullah', and that Abdullah had promised that his soldiers would 'sit quietly', conquering 'only the Old City', while the Jews would 'accept' the annexation of the Arab State by the kingdom of Jordan. It was impossible at the time to have this story confirmed or denied. It was also claimed by some that Shealtiel rather than anyone else had been appointed commander of Jerusalem because he had agreed to act within the framework of this 'secret agreement' with Abdullah.

In his book, 'The Faithful City', (p. 194) Dr. Dov Yosef stated that one of Shealtiel's basic mistakes was that he had not informed the civilian authorities of the gravity of the military developments and the critical situation of the people in the Old City.

[60]

The appointment of a Military Governor for Jerusalem and the personality of the man served as a bone of contention for the inhabitants of Jerusalem.

First of all, the title 'Military Commander of the Occupied Territory of Jerusalem' seemed to indicate the Government of Israel's agreement that Jerusalem was only 'occupied territory', held by the Jewish State but not part of it. Secondly, the individual appointed to this position did everything he could to concentrate all the tasks and authority in his hands, leading to a damaging and regrettable power struggle. While there were some spheres with which a number of authorities wished to deal, there were other important ones which affected the daily lives of the population and with which not a single authority was involved, each one trying to push the responsibility for the various blunders on to the others (according to a report prepared by Mr. H. Margalit, a member of the Committee for the Rehabilitation of Jerusalem, published in Haaretz, 11.1.1949). The heads of several public institutions in the city continued with their activities, behaving as if they 'knew not (Dov) Joseph'. The Military Governor of Jerusalem, Dov Joseph, regarded his task as 'the first step in forging the indissoluble bond between the eternal city and the State of Israel', regarding his appointment as 'the most efficient way of ruling Jerusalem by the Government of Israel and in its name'.

In Davar Yerushalayim, the bulletin of the workers of Jerusalem, an article appeared under the heading, 'Jews Reject the Jewish Governor', attacking the opponents of Dov Joseph, who had remained in Jerusalem throughout the siege and particularly Lehi, which had called Yosef a 'traitor' in its leaflets. Etzel had got the inhabitants of Jerusalem to sign a petition calling for a referendum on the inclusion of Jerusalem within the State of Israel. The Government made every effort to put a stop to this referendum, and army vehicles drove around, calling on the inhabitants not to participate in it. Y. Ben-Zvi wrote an article in Davar Yerushalayim on the appointment of the Military Governor and his Council, saying, amongst other things: 'We do not know and no one knows to this day what authority has been given to the military authorities of Jerusalem, if the Minister of the Interior (Greenbaum) and the ten members of the Provisional Government have been unable to get to Tel-Aviv for several weeks, whether by land or by air, and have not been able to participate in the Provisional Government. And what about the workers and the merchants, the men of science and the man in the street? Both sides, Jerusalem and the State, suffered from this state of affairs, but whereas the Government has found a solution for the ten missing members from Jerusalem, Jerusalem has not found substitutes for the ten responsible leaders, the members of the National Institutions, the working men and men of industry, the technicians and laborers, who left the city without a word of farewell for those who remained behind'.

The Military Commander, Dov Yosef, assembled his Council seven times. Some people regarded the 'Governor's Council' as the 'parliament of Jeruslem'. Considerable time and many discussions were devoted to the composition of this 'Council'. In the final event, instead of an active Council of thirteen members, it comprised twenty-seven people. Nevertheless, complaints were voiced by various organizations that there had been 'discrimanation'.

The 'Governor's Council' comprised representatives of all the parties as well as two observers from Agudath Yisrael. They gradually realized the importance of the institution of the Military Governor, both internally and externally, although members of the Council were disappointed by being limited to a purely advisory capacity. The Military Governor would present a problem, listen to the discussion and the various suggestions, but act as he saw fit. The members of the Council complained that the Governor would repeat to them things he had said to the reporters at his bi-weekly meeting with them. The committees which assisted the Governor were also appointed by Dov Joseph as he wished. He nevertheless regarded the Council as the 'parliament of Jerusalem', symbolizing unity and cooperation.

[61]

In February 1949, six months after the appointment had been made, the position of Military Governor of Jerusalem was annulled, At the meeting in which he took leave of his post, Dov Yosef said:

'It has been six months since our Government appointed me the Military Governor of Jerusalem. The declaration of the Military Governor in the occupied territory of Jerusalem was the first step towards forging the indissoluble bond between the eternal city and the State of Israel.

'A lot has happened since 2nd August last year. The situation has changed radically. From a state of perpetual danger, daily shelling and firing, civilians being wounded and killed, we have reached a stable military situation, with peace and quiet, even though this is a state of ceasefire. It is clear that our enemies have grown tired of war and apparently desire peace.

'From a situation of a lack of food, water and fuel, we have reached a state of affairs where we have enough for all our needs. The usual services have been established in the city, and we have electricity, telephones, lighting and municipal services. All the restrictions on transport and on the city's connections with the rest of the country have been removed and the limitations on the various areas of life have been lifted. A new road, 'Heroism Road', guarantees our continual link with the coastal plain. A well-organized municipal government has been established, serving the public constantly and devotedly in a effort to supply all its needs. Economic life has returned more or less to normal, and the problems which still remain derive primarily from the state of war. On the one hand, because of the mobilization, trained workers are missing, while on the other, many of the firms and enterprises which moved outside Jerusalem because of the siege have not yet returned. Many Government clerks who used to spend their money in Jerusalem have been transferred to Tel-Aviv and this has had an adverse effect on commerce. The Dead Sea Works have stopped making their usual contribution to the life of the city, and some of the farms around the city have been weakened or have disappeared. The solution of these problems requires the serious and concerned involvement of our Government. Government offices should be moved to Jerusalem, industry should be strengthened immediately and the sources of income in the city should be enlarged. The day is not far off when Jerusalem will once again be the capital of our State'.

[62]

In his book on Moshe Dayan (pp. 302-304), Shabtai Tevet wrote about Major-General Moshe Dayan's appointment as commander of the Jerusalem Brigade, and everything connected with it: (parts of the quoted passage have been omitted)

'The discussion of his appointment began because neither Ben-Gurion nor the General Staff were satisfid with the commander of Jerusalem, Major-General David Shealtiel, and agreed that he had to be replaced by a bold and active commander. On 24th June 1948 Yigael Yadin suggested that Eliyahu Ben Hur (then Cohen) replace Shealtiel. Ben-Gurion proposed his own candidate, Moshe Dayan, though the opposition to him was widespread. Major-General Shealtiel, who was asked to give his opinion about his successor, also opposed Moshe. Galili defined the appointment as 'strange'. Hillel Pepperman, the brigade operations officer, welcomed Moshe Dayan's appointment instead of Shealtiel, whom he considered to be 'the worst possible man to put in Jerusalem', and whose operations were 'operative folly'.

[63]

It was said of the new commander, Dayan, that he tended to ignore the U.N., preferring to find a direct route to the Arab commanders. When the Arabs attacked our positions our people would submit complaints to the U.N. observers, as had been their practise, but the new regional commander despised these 'complaints' and the 'reactions' of the U.N. observers.
Dayan demonstrated this approach of his every day, expressing his opinion that the U.N. observers were totally superfluous.

[64]

The head of Bernadotte's staff, Colonel Lindstrom, who was with the Count when he was murdered, wrote about Bernadotte's murder in an appendix to the latter's book, 'To Jerusalem', (p. 199):

'As we approached Jerusalem the radio operator entered holding a cable containing a warning not to land at Kalandia and an announcement that all planes would be shot down. We agreed that this was false too, decided to ignore it and landed at the airfield without any mishap'.

(A description of the journey back from the training farm follows) 'We drove quickly through the neutral zone as the snipers were very active there, and I breathed a sigh of relief when we passed unharmed through the Jewish lines near the road-block in the Greek Colony. The barrier was up, but when the guard saw us he lowered it half-way, then raised it again and finally lowered it completely, obliging us to stop. The Jewish liaison officer shouted something in Hebrew to the guard, who raised the barrier and let us pass. After the murder we suspected that the strange activities with the barrier might have signalled to the murderers that we were on our way, and perhaps even in which automobile Bernadotte was travelling. At any rate, it is almost certain that the murderers knew which car he was in and even in what place he was sitting.

'Immediately after passing through the barrier, we met several trucks full of Jewish soldiers and an armored vehicle in which Dr. Joseph was travelling. We continued through the Katamon quarter towards a building called 'Biberman House', went through another road barrier without being stopped by the guards, and then our three cars were overtaken by a large auxiliary automobile full of Jewish soldiers. When we got to the top of the slope we were stopped by a jeep which was blocing the road. This was bigger than the ones used by the Jewish army, and we thought that it might be one of those stolen from the U.N. observers at the Y.M.C.A. and painted brown. The driver seemed to be trying to turn it round nervously and clumsily, and finally stopped in the middle of the road. The four men inside it wore the khaki uniforms of the Jewish army, with shorts and peaked caps. Three of them jumped out and walked towards our automobile, two on the right and one on the left, while the driver remained in the jeep. The people in the first automobile thought that this was another check and Captain Hillaman shouted something in Hebrew to the two men on the right. Later he said that he had told them to let the automobiles through as everything was alright.

'While this was going on the third man ran past the first two vehicles and reached ours. He looked at us through the window, which was open on my side. He was smooth-shaven, thin and very dark, looked well-trained and about thirty years old. We also thought that he wanted to examine our documents and while we were still getting them out he suddenly poked his sub-machine-gun through the window and fired a round of bullets at Bernadotte and Saraut. It was almost five o'clock, according to Jewish time. Ater firing a few more shots at our radiator he ran backwards to the jeep. Colonel Bagley jumped out, tried to wrestle with him and was badly burned in his face by the spark of a bullet.

'The next day we learned that Bernadotte had been hit six times, one of them in his heart, and had been killed almost immediately. Colonel Saraut had seventeen bullet-wounds.

'On 20th September the murderers sent a letter to the French news agency, expressing their regret at the fact that Saraut had been killed because of a 'fatal error'. They wrote: "Although in our opinion all the U.N. observers belong to foreign forces of conquest which have no right to be in our country, the French Colonel was killed because of a fatal error. Our men thought that the officer sitting next to Count Bernadotte was the anti-Semitic British agent, General Landstrome".

[65]

Abdullah el-Tal praised Bernadotte's support for the Arabs. In his book he wrote (p. 169):

'My orders from Amman were to welcome Bernadotte in the name of the Government when he reached the airfield at Kalandia (Atarot) on 12.6.1948. I headed the reception line and was the first to greet the international mediator. Bernadotte accepted aref-el-Aref's invitation to visit Ramallah. The object of the invitation was to enable Bernadotte to see the suffering of the refugees with his own eyes. After visiting Ramallah and drinking a cup of tea there he went to Jerusalem, where I talked to him for an hour in my headquarters. During our discussion I described the details of the military situation in Jerusalem, the fact that the city was cut off on all sides by the Arab forces and that had it not been for the ceasefire it would have fallen into our hands. I took him on a tour of the main military positions, where he could see the high morale of our soldiers for himself. My meeting with Bernadotte that day had a crucial influence on his decision to solve the problem of Jerusalem by handing it over to the Arabs'.

[66]

Another layer in the fortification of Jerusalem, an important step and an encouraging and exciting event, was the reopening of the railway line between Jerusalem and the coast on 8.8.1949. The Israel Railway Company renewed its services after reaching an agreement with the Jordanians to give them the village of Beth-Iksa near the Jerusalem-Tel-Aviv highway (near 'Mitzpeh', the tomb of the Prophet Samuel), in return for the use of the railway track which passed through Jordanian territory, including the area of the village of Batir, (Beitar) where there is a fortress from the period of the destruction of the second Temple.

We used to say that it was impossible to miss that train, which had functioned during Mandatory times. It travelled so slowly that one could alight and descend while it was in motion.

The whistle blew proudly, the train chugged along gaily and wherever the train passed, whether the settlement was new or old, people waved, their eyes damp with tears at the sight of the Israeli train making its way from Tel-Aviv to the wounded capital.

Amongst the guests invited on the inaugural journey were the Minister of Finance, Eliezer Kaplan, the Minister of Transport, David Remez, the Tel-Aviv station-master, Berkovitz (to whom Kaplan whispered: 'Do you know how much this is costing the treasury?'), the Lydda station-master, Wleichmann, the Jerusalem station-master, Gordon, and others.

At eight o'clock precisely the train gave a long, clear whistle and began to move. It included pasenger cars and freight cars carrying food and building materials, a car for the guests and a restaurant car as well as twenty-four tons of books for the University Library, for 'if there is no learning there is no bread'.

Merchants, storekeepers, laborers, artisans, clerks and mere passers-by left their affairs and came, for this was no everyday affair. After years of bloodshed, when the clatter of the wheels and the shriek of the whistle had been silent, we had reached the stage of 'bon voyage'.

We reached Lydda Station, the main station during the Mandate period, the junction for lines going to Damascus, Aleppo and Turkey in the north, and Alexandria and Cairo in the south. At Lydda an Arab official from the Mandate period, Cassis, came on board, and the reporters engaged him in conversation. For thirty years he had been in Haifa, had been transferred to Lydda last year, and was loyal to Israel. He told us about Nasr, a relative of his, who had been Aharon Aharonson's cart-driver in Zikhron-Yaakov. His other relatives, he said, had fled to Lebanon. His daughter, Yula, a handsome girl of seventeen, presented a bouquet to the Minister of Transport. She was learning Hebrew diligently, and was teaching the children of the Arabs who had remained in Lydda. Naturally, speeches were obligatory, and the Minister of Transport was asked to address the throng. As was his custom, Mr. Remez spoke briefly and movingly, saying one sentence which remained engraved on our hearts: 'The railway of Israel, the people of peace, is going to Jerusalem, the capital of the State of Israel and the city of peace'.

The train stopped at Har-Tuv Station. Before us lay what was left of the 'Samson' cement factory and the village of Har-Tuv, which had been occupied by the Arabs until the Israeli army had arrived.

The train made its way through the Jerusalem Hills. We recalled the children's song: 'Between rocks and hills, the train flies'. as the train passed high crags. We passed near Batir and saw soldiers of the Arab Legion posted on the hilltops. Below, on a dirt track near the railway, were jeeps carrying Israeli soldiers. We had a pleasant surprise when Arab villagers from Batir waved to us in greeting, and we waved back to them happily. The same happened as we passed the Arab village of Beth Tzefafa, which lay half in Jordanian territory and half in ours, when Arabs greeted us from both sides of the barbed wire fence which divided the village.

We went through Mekor Haim and Baka. Women from the oriental communities ululated and crowed, as is their fashion, and people stood at both sides of the track, waving their hands or handkerchiefs. At the Jerusalem Railway Station we had a pleasant surprise, the Prime Minister, Ben-Gurion, was waiting for us and the station was covered by a sea of flags. The Minister of the Interior, Immigration and Health, Moshe Shapira, joined the V.I.P.S. in their special car. The Jewish Agency Executive interrupted its weekly meeting and its members also came to the station. The crowd included the mayor, Daniel Oster, and the heads of the other institutions. Army and police companies formed a guard of honor and the police band played lively tunes. The mayor declared that in the not too distant future all the Ministers and their senior officials would move their homes and offices to the capital. The Prime

Minister, Ben-Gurion, spoke excitedly and at length, saying, amongst other things, that Jerusalem had always been a focal point of our battle for independence, that the heroism of the inhabitants of Jerusalem had also reached admirable peaks and that the Arabs had begun their war against the State of Istael by burning the Commercial Center in Jerusalem. They had continued by killing people all along the road from the coastal plain to Jerusalem in an attempt to sever the eternal city of the Jewish nation from the center of the rest of the country. They had blown up the pumping station at Latrun in order to bring Jerusalem to its knees for lack of water. They had brazenly desecrated the sacred places of the holy city, wantonly destroying magnificent synagogues in both the New and the Old cities. The Chrisitan world had seen, heard and remained silent, only the Jews had risen up to aid their besieged brethren in Jerusalem. Jerusalem would once more be the capital of the State, builded magnificently, the city of justice, the faithful city.

As usual at national occasions such as this, we concluded by singing 'Hatikva' (the national anthem) enthusiasticaly.

[67]

One evening (27.9.1966) we met together with some of the men who had been Israeli liaison officers during the period of the establishment of the State and had dealt with representatives of the U.N. Egypt, Jordan, Syria and Lebanon. At the time those involved in the fighting had envied the liaison officers, claiming that they had a good time, drinking with the men of the U.N. In actual fact however they worked very hard, and when the soldiers rested and the shooting died down, wherever there was a brief respite at the military front, the liaison officers went into action on the political front.

At the initiative of Mr. Yosef Shani (then Shnurman), the Israeli liaison officers assembled in the Dan Hotel, Tel-Aviv, in September 1966. They knew the place well from the time it had been a small building called the Kaethe-Dan Café, were they would have a drink with the U.N. officers and talk about restraining the fighting.

In a brief opening speech, Yosef Shani mentioned the names of those who were no longer with us, including Asher Levitzki, Colin Gillon (Galkman), Rafi Salomon, Yona (John) Adler, and others. The first speaker, Baruch Komarov, related how the liaison unit which he headed had received its name, 'Baruch Baruch':

'At first we were a small group whose function was not very clear. We were told that U.N. observers were about to come to the country to separate the warring parties, though no one knew quite how they would do this. I was summoned to Haganah headquarters and told to form a unit of liaison officers to deal with the observers. It should be remembered that we were still a clandestine organization and no one was to know what was going on. We did not know how and in which capacity Yaakov Dori would appear before the U.N. observers. Would they be told he was 'Chief of Staff'? The head of operations was Yigael Yadin, and I was appointed chief liaison officer, together with Walter Eitan, Reuben Shilon (Zaslani) and Yigael Yadin. Once, at one of the first parties at which foreigners (from the U.N.) were present, Moshe Sharet forgot my underground name and addressed me by my name, Baruch. From that time it was decided that the unit was to be called 'Baruch, Baruch', and that is also how I signed our documents to the U.N. In Jerusalem there was a special liaison unit between the Haganah institutions and the members of the U.N. Conciliation Commission. That unit was also attached to us. Our unit grew when headquarters for the observers were set up in Haifa. There was no shortage of work as there were frequent infringements of local ceasefire agreements, complaints and counter-complaints were submitted, and so it went on.

'People 'outside' said that we were 'having fun', but we worked day and night. We had to be ready to go out at all times to accompany U.N. observers wherever necessary, including to danger spots, and to do our duty. So that we would not be taken by surprise and so that our men could make whatever preparations were necessary, we asked the U.N. to inform us of their visits at least two hours in advance. It was important for us at that time to obtain favorable reports from the U.N. observers.

'About a year later a meeting was held, at which the Chief of Staff during the war, Yaakov Dori, stressed the important role we had played and expressed his appreciation for our unit, which was about to be disbanded. Once the Armistice Agreement had been signed at Rhodes there was no further need for our unit. We submitted a memorandum to the Chief of Staff, giving details of our activities, and sent a copy to the Foreign Ministry. It was decided that our men would be attached to the armistice committees working with Egypt, Syria, Jordan and Lebanon. None of us was a politician, but our work made politicians of us and some of us did in fact go politics; once a trickster always a trickster'.

Lieutanant-General Mordekhai Makleff said:

'A lot of water has flowed under the bridge since we participated in negotiating the Armistice Agreements in Rhodes with Syria and Lebanon. The negotiations began with the British in Haifa on Passover 1948, when the liaison officer was Harry Beilin. The British informed us that they were going to leave the city, and that night we took rapid action and conquered it. Salomon, the lawyer, phoned me and said: "The British want a ceasefire". Mr. Gott Levin, the head of the community, was called to Stockwell's headquarters. I went along and sat at the side. The British officer shouted: "I want quiet. Immediately. Do you understand"? "No". I replied. "We wont agree to a ceasefire". He grew angry and then said: "We will meet at four this afternoon at the Municipality". At four the British commander, Stockwell, came to the Municipality with two tanks. The last shot was fired at approximately that time. Some of the Arab dignitaries of the town were already there, and one of them said to me: "I know you, your grandfather and mine were born here. What's going to happen"? I remained silent. They were talking about a ceasefire. Stockwell said: "It's what the little chap sitting there (pointing at me) says that matters". I said: "No". The Arabs went off for consultations and never returned.

"We agreed with the British that we would receive the remaining arms there, that our men would replace theirs at the check-points, and that we would make sure that they could leave in safety. And that's what happened. The next day the soldiers of the Haganah and the British troops stood together at the check points. Stockwell asked us to guarantee that our men would not shoot his, and that they could remove the weapons from the Tirah camp and take them to the harbor. I told him: "We will transfer your arms train from Tirah camp to the port". After hesitating he agreed, the Haganah issued permits to the British and they operated the train under our supervision.

'I participated in the signing of the agreement with Lebanon at Rhodes. They tried to find a uniform for me and after some efforts found one that Eliyahu Sasson had once worn, though it was a trifle large on me. Shabtai Rosen was also there. It was clear to us that the discussion at Rhodes would be about 14 villages on the Lebanese border, or as it was known then, the international border. The Lebanese Chief of Staff, Salem, was there, and he and Eliyahu Sasson reminisced together about the period of Mardam Bey's rule.

'I said to them: "How long are we going to sit here? Let's finish or go our separate ways". Sasson said to me in amazement: "How can you speak like that to them"? But there were no problems with the Lebanese during the rest of the negotiations. We asked them straight out: "Wen will we sign a peace treaty?" And they replied: "We're ready, but you must remember that Lebanon will always be the second Arab state to do so".

'My nephew was a prisoner-of-war in Lebanon and was made commander of the prisoners there. On occasions the Arabs would hit him, but when they found out that he was related to the man who was conducting negotiations with them they stopped.

'In the agreement we made with Lebanon we gave up an important card in agreeing, on Government instructions, to withdraw from fourteen Lebanese villages.

'The negotiations with the Syrians were more difficult and took longer, and while they were being held (for about one hundred days), there were three successive heads of State in Syria: Husni Zaim, Hinavi and Shishakli. At the beginning of the negotiations the Syrian commander refused to shake our hands, and for a whole day people tried to presuade him to give us his hand. Riley and Henri Vijier convinced him in the end and he shook our hands. We sat round the negotiating table and the Syrian representative demanded that we give the Syrians Haifa, no more, no less. I said: "We want Damascus". This argument went on for three days, until we finally agreed to give up Damascus and in return the Syrians would give up Haifa. The U.N. representative asked us angrily: "Why have we wasted three days on this"? The Syrian commander, Salan, smiled and said: "What's wrong, can't one want anything?"

'Then the discussion about the Hula began The Syrians wanted the border to go along the water-line, but we did not agree to that. On the fifty-first night of the negotiations the Syrian commander said to me: "In fact, you and we have the strongest armies in the Middle East". I replied: "Right, but against whom"? Somewhat nonplussed, he answered: "I hadn't thought about that". The Syrians began arguing about which war-ships would be permitted to either side. I said to him: "The half-tracks". He asked: "the half-What"? We agreed finally that the border would run between the mouth of the Jordan and Ein-Gev, and continued the discussion about the line from Tzemah to Al-Hama. They claimed that the area was Wakf property and could not be in Jewish hands. The Syrian representative said: "We have been sitting here for one hundred days and haven't received anything".

'The Syrians were in fortified positions on our territory, but retreated after the negotiations. The agreement was a good one as far as we were concerned. On one occasion, when there was some problem about the diversion of the river water, I went to the border and met Shishakli at the Syrian Customs point. People from the U.N. were there. Shishakli turned up in an armored automobile, we went into a room and sat at the table. He took out a revolver and laid it beside him, and I asked him: "Why are you sitting there with a revolver"? He answered: "It's not you that I'm afraid of, I don't trust the men who accompanied me". During the negotiations he tried to remain firm. When we had concluded he said to me: "Can you come to Damascus"? "Only leading a paratroop or armored brigade", I replied. Shishakli was accompanied by Nasr, the commander of the Syrian Air Force and one of the Syrians' best commanders. He told me explicitly that he was hoping to see the day when we would sign a peace treaty. He was an Alawi and has been murdered since. After those difficult and exhausting negotiations we had to go to Ein Gev and explain to the members of the kibbutz that we had not abandoned them or forgotten 'the other side of Lake Tiberias'.

When it was Lieutenant-General Rabin's turn, he said that he would speak not as today's Chief of Staff but as someone who had participated in the ceasefire negotiations with Egypt at Rhodes. Yosef Shnurman was then under the command of Haim Herzog, who was responsible for liaison with the British. We received an order to capture Sheikh Jarrah in Jerusalem, and had taken it. The Arabs had left, though there was still a British position in the house where the Mufti lived. We were in Nashashibi's house. The Palmah's fifth batallion, led by Zivi Shafriri (killed in the Sinai Campaign), attacked the British position and conquered it. In the morning the British came and told Vivian (Haim) Herzog that our military actions in Sheikh Jarrah had endangered their route of withdrawal from Jerusalem to Haifa, and insisted that we leave the neighborhood, giving us an ultimatum which would end at six that evening.

After consulting Ben-Gurion and Yitzhak Sadeh, we decided not to abandon our positions in Sheikh Jarrah, as by doing so we would leave ourselves open to any number of British ultimatums forcing us to leave other areas too. At 5 p.m. the Black Watch got ready, drawing up tanks and cannon. We thought that this was just to frighten us, but it soon transpired that they were in earnest. At six they opened heavy artillery fire and began advancing. We returned their fire, killing a British soldier. Several of our men were wounded and we decided to retreat; part of our force went to Mount Scopus and part to nearby Jewish neighborhoods. We left our only Fiat cannon there as well as a large quantity of arms. Yosef Shnurman was asked to negotiate with the British as I looked like a boy then. I told Shnurman, who was the Jewish Agency's liaison officer with British headquarters: "I'll go with you as your driver or companion". We went to the British commander and after lengthy negotiations he placed three tanks at our disposal. That was the first time I had ever been in a tank. It helped us to get up to Mount Scopus and evacuate our men from there without wasting manpower and we also salvaged the better part of our arms. We stopped at Nashashibi's house, but when we went in we could not find the weapons we had left there.

'In June 1965', Rabin continued, 'eighteen years afterwards, I visited London in my capacity as Chief of Staff. There I met the same commander, General Jones, who was responsible for the production, insurance, purchase and sale of arms. We talked of barious matters, and in the course of our conversation we realized that he had been the commander of the Black Watch in Jerusalem when I had commanded the Jewish defense company, and that we had fought one another at Sheikh Jarrah. He remembered everything and said: "We promised Shnurman we wouldn't give Sheikh Jarrah to the Arabs, and we kept our word". And they had in fact handed Sheikh Jarrah over to us.

'I joined the negotiations with the Egyptians at Rhodes. Uniforms were hurriedly made for us from U.S. Army surplus. Eliyahu Sasson was given the uniform of an American Lieutenant-Colonel, and his uniform was altered to fit me. General Riley commented at the time: "Your uniforms are very similar to those of the American army".

'The Egyptian delegation included Saif a-Din, the head of the mission (who has since died) and Mahmud Riadh, who was then an Intelligence Officer (and later became Foreign Minister). The head of the mission was an extremely well-mannered men. He once made a comment which annoyed Yigael Yadin, who angrily threw a pencil towards him. Saif a-Din remarked: "I thought that I was dealing with gentlemen". The talks were adjourned for several hours because of that.

'A few months ago', Rabin continued, 'I met Ralf Bunche for lunch in Jerusalem. He said to me: "Do you remember Yigael Yadin's pencil? It almost cost us the agreement with the Egyptians".'

Moshe Yuval told us the following story: 'The subject of liaison officers was new to both the U.N. and to us then, and the men did not know what they were supposed to do. Some of the U.N. people thought that the Jewish Agency was a commercial undertaking. In effect, Abba Eban, David Horowitz and others fulfilled the tasks of liaison officers with the U.N. Some Americans told the British: Give the Jews a state and you can be sure it won't last long. Why is that? they were asked. No state can survive without income tax, they replied, and which Jew will agree to pay taxes?

'We faced the thorny problem of how to ease the transition from being the 'Jewish Agency delegation' to being the 'Israeli delegation'. Permits stamped 'The State of Israel' reached our representatives at the U.N. from Israel, but we did not know how we would be referred to in the U.N. the day after the State had been proclaimed. The problem was solved effortlessly, however. Gromyko, the Soviet representative who was then chairman of the Security Council, simply invited 'the representatives of the State of Israel' to the conference table of the Assembly'.

Haim Herzog, who was the first liaison officer to the U.N.'s Implementation Committee, said: 'The members of the U.N. Implementation Committee arrived in February 1948. Only Israel was prepared to cooperate with them, as the Arabs opposed them, and the Chief Secretary to the British Government, Gurney, was also hostile. The chairman of the Committee was Pablo de Azcarate, and we also met the Committee's Norwegian military expert. Its members were simply ignored, and were not supplied with anything, though because they had pretty secretaries they managed to get some supplies from the British police. A meeting was arranged with the delegation over lunch, but on the day of the meeting the buildings of the National Institutions in Jerusalem were blown up. Shiloh was badly wounded in the cheek, and came to the meal, which was held in his house, heavily bandaged. Sasson escaped by a miracle, and was completely covered in dust. Afterwards, when we left Shiloh's house, together with the chairman of the Committee, we saw that the Institution

buildings were already being repaired. Azcarate said to his colleagues: "Don't
worry, a nation like this will survive".

'We accompanied them to the coastal plain, together with British guards, as the
Arabs suspected that Azcarate was Jewish. We returned from our tour of
Jerusalem on the day the doctors and professors were killed in the Hadassah
convoy. The U.N. Committee prepared its report, and it was a favorable one.
'On our return from Rhodes', Herzog continued, 'we were sure that within six
months we would sign a peace treaty with the Arabs. We even started thinking
about which of us would be ambassador in Damascus, Cairo, Beirut and
Amman. In one of these discussions we asked Reuven Shiloh where he would
like to be Israeli ambassador. He replied: "I'm prepared to go to Cairo, but
only as the second ambassador". "Why"? we asked. "Because the first one will
undoubtedly be assassinated".

An old sea-dog, the first captain of the Israeli navy, told a fairly simple tale:
'When I was released from prison in Venice', he said, 'I was appointed to a
committee on behalf of the navy. Our task was to aid, namely, to disguise, our
activities from the U.N. officers posted at Haifa port and along the sea coast to
prevent us importing arms. On one occasion a ship reached Haifa carrying
tanks and other weapons, and I told the stevedores to unload the cargo only
after midnight. For some reason, however, they decided to get on with the job
and began unloading late that evening. The U.N. people came out of a movie
house and saw lights on at the port and a convoy of tanks racing up
Independence (Atzmaut) Road. They hurried to the gate of the port and
attempted to enter. Our men at the gate phoned me, saying: "Two observers
want to come into the port and there is no one from our side accompanying
them. What shall we do"? I said: "Arrest the two observers. Stop the
unloading immediately. Put out the lights". I hurried over and found the
observers seething with anger. I spoke to them soothingly, saying: "Were you
really arrested? It's impossible. There must have been a mistake". They simply
didn't know who was talking to them. I apologized, we toured every corner of
the port and found that 'everything was in order'. The observers looked around
in silence, probably realizing that they had missed something important'.
Gershon Gera told a similar story:
'We were informed that one of our batallions was on its way to the Negev with
Yitzhak Rabin, and we were afraid that the observers would see the batallion
and ruin the plan. "What shall we do"? I asked. "Take them to a bar in Rishon

Letzion", I was told, "and give them plenty to drink". They readily accepted
my invitation to go to Rishon Letzion for an hour and have a drink, and we
drank them under the table.

'How did I become a liaison officer?' Gershon Gera continued. 'It was like this.
Once Baruch Baruch and Michael Hanegbi saw me arguing with one of the
observers, an American major, who wanted to know what was in our convoy,
sardines or petroleum. Petroleum was a 'military commodity' which could not
be transported without a special permit. Our men heard me saying to him:
"You can't tell me what we're carrying here. If Captain Gera tells you it's
sardines, that's it. You're just an observer and your job is to observe and make
a report to your superiors. That's all".

'In another case things fortunately turned out for the best. When the Egyptians
were trapped in the Faluja Pocket in the south, approximately where Kiryat
Gat is today, they submitted endless complaints about the behavior of the
Israeli soldiers, which was, "hard", "rude", "cruel" and so on.

'A complaint was made that an Israeli soldier had raped an Arab woman, and
U.N. headquarters sent the Swedish officer, Stevenson, to investigate. He was
accompanied by the commander of the Egyptian force, Muhammad Taha Bey,
known as 'the Black Tiger', and myself.

'An Arab woman of about sixty was brought before us, insisting that she had
been raped by an Israeli soldier. I went over to the woman, pointed at one of
the U.N. officers and asked her: "Look carefully at that man. Is he the one
who attacked you"? The women looked at him and said: "No". I pointed at
someone else standing nearby. She looked at him and said. "No". After a while
I brought in the Swedish officer, who was a handsome fellow, and I said to the
old woman: "Look carefully. Is this the soldier who assaulted you"? The
woman inspected the good-looking officer from head to toe and said: "Yes,
he's the one". She went over to him and spat in his face. Stevenson, taken
aback and confused, wiped the spit from his face without realizing what had
happened. I explained to him that the old woman accused him of being the
soldier who had 'raped' her.

'He took the Egyptian complaint and ripped it up'.

[68]

The Mandelbaum Gate was mentioned many times during the War of

Independence in Jerusalem and was visited by soldiers, statesmen, tourists and important guests. What was this place and what was the origin of its name? Reb Simha Mandelbaum of Poland, one of the first manufacturers in Jerusalem, owned a clothing factory and wanted to help the development of the city. In 1925 he bought land in an isolated spot not far from Batei Ungarin on one side and Nahlat Shimon on the other, and built a three-storey house there. He died about a year later, in 1930, after which his wife, Esther, a woman of valor, ran her husband's business.

During the war of defense against the Arab gangs (1947) and the War of Independence (1948), the house was a defense point for the Jewish forces from which they defended the neighborhoods in northeastern Jerusalem. The Arabs directed heavy fire against it and it was a target for their attacks. Its occupants had to move away, and the last people to live there were Reb Simha's sons, Baruch and Yehiel Mandelbaum. The defenders referred to the house as 'shaked' (almond; mandel-baum — almond tree).

The building passed from one side to the other several times during the fighting. The Arabs blew it up, killing a number of defenders (including Zvi Tamari), and nothing was left of the imposing building but one wall.

The name, 'Mandelbaum House' and later, 'Mandelbaum Gate', gradually became famous. The area around it was no-man's-land, where people from both sides met and crossed the border. Any adult, child or donkey who had crossed the border in error was brought to the Mandelbaum Gate, where Arab and Jewish officers served side by side.

It was at this point that the bi-weekly convoy, which went via Sheikh Jarrah to the Israeli exclave on Mount Scopus every other Wednesday, was checked. In accordance with an Israeli-Jordanian agreement, food and fuel was taken up in. two or three armored vehicles and 'policemen', who were really soldiers, were replaced. The check was very thorough, lest arms or extra food be 'smuggled' in, and was made by U.N. personnel in the presence of Jordanian officers. Now and again it was the focal point of tension when, on one pretext or another, the Arabs announced that "the convoy would not be allowed through", and Israel replied that "the convoy will go through, come what may".

Prisoners were exchanged at the Mandelbaum Gate, which symbolized the bisected, separated nature of Jerusalem. When Jerusalem was liberated in the Six Day War (1967), the Jews of the city burst through with shouts of joy and tears in their eyes, saying: "We have gone through the Mandelbaum Gate"!